THE FUTURE OF THE PRISON SYSTEM

The Future of the Prison System

ROY D. KING

University College of North Wales, Bangor

ROD MORGAN

University of Bath

with

J. P. MARTIN

University of Southampton

J. E. THOMAS

University of Nottingham

Gower

Published by

Gower Publishing Company Limited,
Westmead, Farnborough, Hants, England

British Library Cataloguing in Publication Data

King, Roy David
    The future of the prison system
    1. Prisons — England
    I. Title   II. Morgan, Rodney
    365'.942   HV9647
    ISBN 0 566 00348 1

ISBN 0 566 00348 1

Printed in Great Britain by
Biddles Ltd., Guildford, Surrey

Contents

Preface

This book arose out of our dissatisfaction with the deliberations of the May Committee of Inquiry into the United Kingdom Prison Services, which reported in October 1979, and our belief that some more systematic view of the prospects for the future of the prison system was required.

The Inquiry was announced on 2 November 1978 when the escalating industrial actions of prison officers began seriously to disrupt the work of the courts and the prison governors warned that the prison system was in imminent danger of collapse. Industrial relations in the prison service had been deteriorating for some time, and matters had come to a head ostensibly over what were known as 'continuous duty credits'. But the prison system had been passing through the most troubled decade of its history. The prison population had continued to rise and many prisoners were housed in appallingly squalid conditions; a National Prisoners' Movement (PROP) had grown up in an attempt to protect the rights of prisoners; and the powers of the Home Office were being challenged in courts at home and in Europe; serious disturbances and riots had occurred in maximum security prisons which had led to reprisals against prisoners; and prison staff generally had lost any confidence they might have had both in the way their tasks were defined and in the nature and quality of central management. Most informed commentators felt that a wide-ranging independent review of the prison service was long overdue.

On 17 November the Home Secretary announced the terms of reference for the Inquiry. In an ill-considered attempt to kill two birds with one stone the Home Secretary set the industrial relations issues in a broad context. While the terms of reference left some important matters outside the Committee's remit, there was enough within it to give the appearance of a comprehensive review. Indeed in other circumstances something might well have been achieved. Two factors seriously undermined any hopes of success, however. The first was that from the outset the Minister had stressed the urgency of the Inquiry: prison officers had suspended their actions temporarily but would not wait for ever and the Home Secretary wanted a report by the end of March 1979. The second was that the Committee seemed lacking in the kind of expertise that would be required. It comprised: a mayoress, a personnel director, a senior trade unionist, a company managing director, a member of a prison board of visitors, a former director of NACRO, an Irish mayor, and a Scottish sheriff and a retired chief constable, presided over by a member of the judiciary. Few could claim special knowledge of the prison system. The Committee had no staff, other than a small Home Office supplied secretariat, and no resources to speak of. It did not seem likely to be in a good position to evaluate the evidence it received.

With only four months at its disposal, the May Committee invited written evidence by Christmas 1978. Like many others we strove to meet this preposterously short deadline. It seemed obvious that the main concern would have to be with industrial relations and we had no serious expectation that the Committee would, or could, do justice to the underlying problems in such a short time. Though we had little or nothing to say about continuous duty credits or any of the other staff grievances, we were anxious that broader issues should not go by default. Our fear was simply this. That since the terms of reference appeared to go far beyond industrial disputes then, if this opportunity was missed, it might take another decade of even more serious troubles before the prisons were looked at again. Accordingly we prepared two fairly substantial documents for the May Committee, one by the Christmas deadline, the other a few weeks later.

The May Committee soon decided that the Home Secretary's timetable was unrealistic, and that it would be inappropriate to make an interim report on prison officers' pay and related issues. On 21 February 1979 Merlyn Rees announced that the Committee's findings would not be available until the summer of 1979. We took the opportunity of this delay to edit our evidence, which was then published by the Universities of Bath and Southampton in April 1979. We hoped that others might be encouraged to join the debate. Meanwhile the Committee, with our permission, invited the Home Office to comment on our evidence. At our request we were subsequently afforded an opportunity to reply to the Home Office, both in writing and in oral evidence which we gave to the Committee in May 1979.

Whatever the merits of the May Committee Report — on the immediate matters of industrial relations, for example, and on its modest proposals for reforming the organisation structure — in our view it failed, as we had feared it would, on the larger problems. We reach this judgement not because our own alternative strategies for the future of the system were rejected, but because *all* alternative strategies were rejected. Although the Committee expresses satisfaction that their Report 'does proper justice' to what they were required to investigate we cannot share that view. The fact is that on virtually every issue of importance the May Committee recommendations represent the re-affirmation of existing Home Office assumptions and policies. It is important that neither the Government nor the public should be left to believe that the Committee did do justice to its wider task. We were therefore extremely grateful to our publisher, John Irwin, for his suggestion that we should up-date our analysis of the future of the prison system in the light of Mr Justice May's Inquiry.

In preparing the present volume we have reviewed most of the written evidence that was submitted to the May Committee; and we would like to thank all those organisations and individuals whose unpublished evidence was made available to us. Our own views on the future of the prison system have not changed much in this process, and many of the ideas expressed in the first four chapters were already contained in our original evidence. We have, however, substantially re-worked them for this volume to take account of the evidence of the Home Office and others, as well as the verdict expressed by the May Committee. We have not had the space to go into quite the same detail about some of our proposals in this volume as we did earlier. Details can be discussed if there is any willingness on the part of the authorities to listen. For the present it seems more appropriate to get agreement about general principles and the setting of standards.

We are no more expert now than we were before on continuous duty credits and the like, and this book gives virtually no attention to such matters. This is not to say that we regard these as unimportant. But, unlike the other issues discussed here, pay and conditions are matters for negotiation between the Home Office and the POA, and they will have to be resolved in that way whatever the framework for the prison system as a whole. We should also make it plain that we have not tried to provide a comprehensive coverage — there is nothing for example on Scotland or Northern Ireland — because it seemed better to concentrate on those aspects of the prison system we know best. For this reason we have been very glad to commission chapter 5 on Prison Management from Dr J.E. Thomas and chapter 6 on Maintaining Standards from Professor J.P. Martin. Although we had written something about these matters in our evidence, we claimed no special expertise on them and had no time to develop it for this volume. Accordingly we turned to those of our colleagues who did have that expertise and whom, we felt, were likely to share our general perspective. We are most grateful to them for their contributions; and with Professor Martin we would like to thank Joan Higgins, Graham Zellick and Professor Francis Jacobs for their valuable comments on chapter 6.

The rest of this book has been very much a collaborative exercise. Purely as a result of an enforced division of labour to meet our publisher's deadline, Roy King wrote the Introduction and chapters 1 and 3, and Rod Morgan wrote chapters 2, 4 and the Conclusion. We hold ourselves jointly responsible for their contents although we were glad to have John Martin's comments on chapter 1.

We are, as ever, greatly indebted to our wives and children: Janet, Simon and Matthew King; Karin, Magnus, Toby and Benjamin Morgan.

Thanks are also due to Alison Heywood who typed the final draft.

We hope that this book will make some contribution towards the making of a smaller, more humane and more justifiable prison system — but at the time of writing it is hard to be optimistic.

Roy D. King, Bangor
Rod Morgan, Bath

March 1980

Introduction

This book is about the future of the prison system. It has been written in the light of the findings of the *Committee of Inquiry into the United Kingdom Prison Services* under the Chairmanship of Mr Justice May which reported in October 1979. Although this is obviously not the place to embark on a detailed history of the prison system it may be helpful to some readers if we say a little about the development of the service and to provide a brief account of the events which led to the establishment of the May Committee. The initiated will probably prefer to go straight to chapter 1.

Some historical background

It is in the nature of prison administration that its history is punctuated by scandals. In the eighteenth century gaols were administered by local justices. They were numerous, most of them were small, and as John Howard's account of *The State of the Prisons* (1777) testified, they were corruptly run and riddled with disease. By an Act of 1823, however, local justices were required to reform their prisons and provide quarterly reports to the Home Secretary. In 1835 an independent inspectorate was set up, albeit with powers that were largely limited to the shaming effects of criticisms in their published reports.

Central government at that time was responsible for some convicted felons, who would formerly have been transported or executed, and these were housed in the notorious prison ships or 'hulks'. In 1821 the first national penitentiary was established at Millbank and this became the nucleus of a system of convict prisons administered by a new Directorate formed in 1850. The first Chairman was Colonel Jebb, the architect of Pentonville, who had earlier been Surveyor General of prisons and advisor to the Home Office and local authorities on prison construction. There followed a period of intense prison building activity and a more or less determined attempt was made to impose a uniformity of design and regime on the Pentonville model. These efforts were greatly strengthened in 1865 when the Secretary of State acquired powers to withhold monies from recalcitrant local authorities.

In 1877 a new Act effectively established a single prison system, with central control of convict and local prisons vested in a Prison Commission, assisted by the Inspectorate and a departmental staff. The first Chairman was du Cane, who had been Jebb's successor as Surveyor General. Many small and redundant prisons were immediately closed in a process of rationalisation that continued into the twentieth century. In the prisons that remained du Cane operated a regime of silence, separation and penal labour that survived for nearly twenty years. But a series of newspaper and magazine articles about the brutalising consequences of this policy gave rise to such misgivings that a Departmental Committee under Mr Herbert Gladstone was set up to investigate prison conditions. The Gladstone Committee went considerably beyond their terms of reference and argued for a more individualised regime that would be more likely to serve reformative or rehabilitative ends.

The principles laid down by the Gladstone Committee in 1895 have served as guidelines for the prison system ever since, though developments were slow, patchy and sometimes contradictory. Du Cane was replaced by Ruggles-Brise who, as well as founding the Borstal system, implemented many of the recommendations of the Gladstone Report. Yet the era of Ruggles-Brise ended with an indictment of the prison regime comparable to that which concluded the era of du Cane. The experiences of imprisoned conscientious objectors and suffragettes led the Labour Research Department to set up an unofficial enquiry in 1919 — much to the consternation of the authorities. The report was published by Hobhouse and Brockway under the title *English Prisons Today* in 1922. Ruggles-Brise retired whilst this latest attack on the prison system was in the press and he was succeeded by Waller. At about the same time Alexander Paterson, formerly a director of the Borstal Association, was appointed a Commissioner. Though never the Chairman he became the most celebrated and influential of prison administrators. His paternalistic yet inspirational approach was able to withstand the backlash following the so-called Dartmoor 'mutiny' of 1932, when the staff regained control of the prison only with the use of carbines and the help of the police. Under successive Chairmen from Waller to Fox, Paterson was associated with many liberal developments. It was Paterson who coined, or borrowed, the famous aphorisms: 'It is impossible to train men for freedom in a condition of captivity' (Prison Commission, 1932, p.12) and 'Men come to prison *as* a punishment not *for* punishment' (Ruck, 1951, p.23). These aphorisms have sustained, though often confused, the prison service to this day.

Paterson died in 1947. It was left to Fox, Chairman of the Commission from 1942 until 1961, to incorporate the concept of 'the training and treatment of convicted prisoners' into the Prison Rules of

2

1949; and to develop an organisational structure for the prison system within which training might be carried out on a more systematic basis. But Fox faced problems that had been largely unknown since the time of the Gladstone Report. At the end of the Second World War, after long years of stability which in turn had followed upon years of decline, the prison population began to rise. The local prisons, which received prisoners from the courts, began to fill to overflowing as prisoners awaited places in the training establishments. Fox's answer was twofold: a demand for more research that would help to defeat recidivism and a demand for more prisons. The former was answered, in some degree, by the establishment of the Home Office Research Unit and an Institute of Criminology at Cambridge. The latter by the building programme put forward in the 1959 White Paper, *Penal Practice in a Changing Society* of which Fox was the leading draftsman. The White Paper also looked forward to a 'fundamental re-examination of penal methods, based on studies of the causes of crime' that could become 'a landmark in penal history and illumine the course ahead for a generation' (Home Office, 1959, para 24).

In 1964 the Government decided that the time was right for that fundamental re-examination and appointed a *Royal Commission on the Penal System*, under the Chairmanship of Lord Amory, with the widest possible terms of reference. Two years later six of its eighteen members resigned, convinced that no set of general principles for the foundation of penal policy could be found. The only Royal Commission in history not to produce a report was therefore dissolved on 24 April 1966, and in its place the Advisory Council on the Penal System was established to deal with such topics as the Minister might refer to it on a piecemeal and pragmatic basis (Morgan, 1979).

By then, however, important developments had taken place in the prison system. In 1963 the Prison Commission was dissolved and merged into the Home Office. Peterson, who had succeeded to the Chairmanship of the Commission two years earlier on the death of Fox, became the head of the new Prison Department.

In the next few years some of the most notorious prisoners in the country succeeded in escaping, thereby exposing the extent to which the Patersonian influence had actually contrived to disregard a basic pre-requisite of any prison system — security. Not surprisingly, perhaps, the pendulum then swung the other way. At the end of 1966 Lord Mountbatten presented his *Report of the Inquiry into Prison Escapes and Security*, and recommended that all high security risk prisoners should be placed in a single new escape-proof prison. Two years later, the Advisory Council, who had been asked to consider *The Regime for Long Term Prisoners in Conditions of Maximum*

Security, overturned Mountbatten's proposal and suggested that high risk prisoners should be dispersed among several maximum security prisons. The suggestion was accepted by the Government and a new era was ushered in.

Despite the prison building programme, the Victorian heritage of local prisons remained overcrowded and in need of redevelopment. Though they were not the dens of vice and pestilence that Howard had found their predecessors to be, they hardly spoke well of 200 years of civilised development.

Between these extremes of overcrowded squalor and oppressive maximum security, the rest of the prison system continued with its attempt to offer treatment and training that would prevent prisoners from coming back into the system. All the results of research showed that they were failing in that endeavour.

A new White Paper, *People in Prison* (Home Office, 1969) tried to reconcile the proven need for security with the disproven effectiveness of prison treatment against the background of a prison population that was reaching ever new heights. But with no great success, for the decade which followed was the most troubled in the entire history of the system. The latest authoritative account of prison policy and practice, *Prisons and the Prisoner* (Home Office, 1977) can only seem a rather glossy public relations exercise in the face of the mounting difficulties.

The events leading to the May Inquiry

The troubles that beset the prison system in the last decade came most immediately from the dramatic actions of prisoners and staff. Although arguably these troubles had much deeper roots, in the continuing failure to bring nineteenth century aspirations into line with twentieth century realities, it is sufficient here to draw attention to the more visible events which led to the establishment of the May Inquiry.

In the three years preceding the May Inquiry the numbers of incidents of what the Home Office calls 'concerted indiscipline' by prisoners averaged about thirty per year (Home Office, 1979, para 88). Roof climbing by prisoners had become one of the most difficult problems the authorities had to face, not only because it placed staff at a physical disadvantage but because it gave prisoners immediate access to the press and television. If prisoners had learned nothing else in their attempts to redress grievances they had learned the value of publicity. The general level of indiscipline had, if anything, declined since the

4

peak year of 1972, but the 1970s were characterised by prisoner disturbances in a way that had not been seen in any earlier decade.

The actions of prisoners were of two kinds, and it is important to distinguish them. On the one hand were broadly based, and largely passive demonstrations designed to draw attention to prison conditions and to the need to protect the rights and civil liberties of prisoners. The Home Office had acknowledged in the title of its 1969 White Paper that there were *people* in prison, not just inmates. Inspired by the development of prisoner unions in North America and Scandinavia, a group of ex-prisoners and academics unveiled the embryo National Prisoners' Movement (PROP) in May 1972. It was dedicated to radical penal reform and to improving the conditions for people in custody. Civil disobedience demonstrations were held, peacefully and often with good humour, in prisons of all types throughout the country. They were either co-ordinated by PROP or were in sympathy with its aims (Fitzgerald, 1977). These quasi-industrial actions culminated in a national prisoners' strike on 4 August 1972 which, even on the most conservative official estimates, involved 5,500 prisoners in twenty-eight establishments (Home Office, 1973, para 147). Although these activities have continued, neither the Home Office nor the Prison Officers' Association has been prepared to acknowledge the existence of the prisoners' union.

On the other hand were a series of spectacular and often violent disturbances and riots, which caused considerable damage to prison property and placed many prisoners and staff in fear of personal injury, either in the course of the incidents or in their aftermath. Though none of these events were on the same scale as those of Attica, New York, in 1971 or Santa Fé, New Mexico, in 1980, the fears of both staff and prisoners were sometimes justified. Without exception the most serious disturbances of this kind occurred in the maximum security dispersal prisons: at Parkhurst on 24 October 1969; Albany on 8 September 1971 and 26-28 August 1972; Gartree on 26 November 1972; Hull between 31 August and 3 September 1976; and Gartree on 5 October 1978. Often these riots and disturbances were accompanied by sympathetic demonstrations at other establishments. The Parkhurst riot was perhaps chiefly notable for the fact that subsequently seven prisoners were convicted in the criminal courts and sentenced to further terms for their part in the violence. The Hull riot will go down in history because it was members of staff who were subsequently tried and convicted for their contributions to the reprisals that occurred afterwards. The riots also produced some internal reviews of policy which generally led to a hardening of attitudes. Following Albany and Gartree in 1972, the Home Office introduced special 'control units' for trouble makers over and above the existing segregation units. They had hardly been used before a public outcry forced their abandonment in 1975 and recently their legality under the Prison Rules was challenged unsuccessfully in the courts. Following Hull in 1976, the Home Office introduced specially trained riot (MUFTI) squads to quell disturbances.

Incidents of industrial actions by staff were far more numerous, however, than protests by prisoners. From 1973 to 1975 branch members of the Prison Officers' Association were in dispute, on average, on seven separate occasions per year. In 1976 the number of industrial actions rose to thirty-four and in 1977 to forty-two. But in the year preceding the setting up of the May Inquiry there were no fewer than one hundred and fourteen separate actions in sixty different establishments (Home Office, Evidence, II, Paper IIE2, para 8). Yet historically industrial actions by prison officers had been virtually non-existent.

Only gradually has the prison service emerged from its militaristic tradition. From the earliest days of the Prison Commission recruits had been drawn largely from the armed services. Industrial attitudes were discounted in favour of loyalty and a sense of duty. The *Prison Officers' Magazine* which first appeared in 1910 was opposed because it was too 'militant'. When prison officers joined police officers in a strike action in 1919 they were dismissed from the service. For the next twenty years the Commission was able to hold the line with a Prison Officers' Representative Board, but in 1939 the right to unionise was conceded and the POA was born. Throughout the days of the Prison Commission, however, prison officers were expected to know their place. Paterson is quoted as saying: 'I don't want to attract to this service young men who are concerned about their pay or their careers' (Watson, 1969, p.70).

After the War, and especially after the end of National Service, the young officers were drawn from a broader spectrum. This was also partly a matter of deliberate policy, because it had long been felt that the military-style prison officer had not been sufficiently receptive to the liberalisation of the prisons. At first the change in recruitment had a barely perceptible effect. But in the last fifteen years or so the numbers of prison officers virtually doubled, and new staff have come more and more to reflect the prevailing attitudes towards industrial relations.

Perhaps not surprisingly it was the advent of the National Prisoners' Movement, with its protests about prison conditions, that first brought matters to the boil for prison staff: for it is a truism that staff share the same conditions as prisoners. The POA opposed PROP from the outset and prison officers repeatedly and publicly dismissed all types of prisoner disturbances as the work of trouble makers and subversives. Staff attitudes began to crystallise around the perceived weakness of the Home Office in relation to the growing number of demonstrations — so much so that staff industrial actions and prisoner disturbances began to intermesh. At least one major disturbance was provoked in Albany, for example, because the POA threatened to work to rule unless a stronger line was taken against subversives (King and Elliott, 1978).

Most of the early industrial actions by the Prison Officers' Association were led by the National Executive. But from 1975 onwards it was, more often than not, the local branches which took the lead, sometimes in defiance of the authority of the NEC. As a result it was becoming at least as tenable to speak of 'subversive staff' as of 'subversive prisoners'. The real escalation of industrial actions occurred in 1976, when restrictions on public expenditure led to the imposition of budgetary control over the hours of overtime. Until then, as the tasks of prison officers had grown, first through the demands of treatment and training and later of security, the POA had been remarkably successful both in getting a huge increase in staff and in maintaining high levels of overtime for their members. With budgetary control, overtime was reduced and take home pay fell significantly for many prison officers. The POA adopted a stance of non—co-operation and local branches began to make a variety of claims for special allowances that would compensate for loss of overtime. These were usually backed by the threat, and often the reality, of industrial action.

Most types of industrial action served at once to disrupt the administration of prisons and to restrict the regimes of prisoners. Depending on the nature of the action, quite profound effects could be achieved in any type of institution. But industrial action was likely to be especially effective in the local prisons and remand centres where the administration is complex and the regime already restricted by the poverty of facilities and the pressure of numbers needing to use them. The POA, however, had adopted a policy that industrial action should not be allowed to disrupt the work of the courts or to interfere with the administration of justice. With few exceptions that policy was respected by local branches until 1978, when the dispute over 'continuous duty credits' — payment for meal breaks taken during duty hours — came to a head. In September and October of that year Ashford branch delayed the production of some prisoners at court and refused the reception of others who had to be held in police cells. Following an unofficial conference at Pentonville in October, widespread industrial action was threatened with effect from 5 November which would include court disruptions regardless of any instructions or advice which might be received from the National Executive.

The question of who runs the prisons had been posed in no uncertain terms. In a letter to *The Times* on 30 October 1978, prison governors complained at the 'deplorable lack of leadership' from the Home Office and warned that the prison system was in imminent danger of total breakdown. On 2 November, the Home Secretary, Merlyn Rees, announced to the House of Commons that he intended to set up 'an Inquiry to consider the causes of the present situation that exists in the prison system'.

The May Committee

Although it was obvious that the Inquiry was established to head off the threatened actions, and would therefore have to address itself, and quickly, to matters of industrial relations, it was no less obvious that there were more deep seated problems facing the prison system. There had been no searching appraisal of them since the work of the Gladstone Committee of 1895. The Royal Commission of 1964-6 which might have illuminated 'the course ahead for a generation' had been disbanded in disarray, and events had moved on dramatically since then. Rupert Cross had concluded his delightful Hamlyn Lectures as long ago as 1971 with the message that 'no matter what the source may be (Advisory Council, Departmental Committee, Inter-departmental Committee or Royal Commission) we want another Gladstone Report' (Cross, 1971, p.190). Perhaps this Inquiry would provide that opportunity? In any event the Press and interested parties from inside and outside the service persuaded the Home Secretary, if indeed he needed persuading, to widen the issues.

On 17 November 1978, Merlyn Rees announced that Mr Justice May had been appointed Chairman of the Committee of Inquiry with the following terms of reference:

To inquire into the state of the prison services in the United Kingdom; and having regard to:

(a) the size and nature of the prison population, and the capacity of the prison services to accommodate it;

(b) the responsibilities of the prison services for the security, control, and treatment of inmates;

(c) the need to recruit and retain a sufficient and suitable staff for the prison services;

(d)   the need to secure the efficient use of manpower and financial resources in the prison services;

To examine and make recommendations upon:

i.   the adequacy, availability, management and use of resources
in the prison services;

ii.   conditions for staff in the prison services and their families;

iii.   the organisation and management of the prison services;

iv.   the structure of the prison services, including complementing
and grading;

v.   the remuneration and conditions of service of prison officers,
governors and other grades working only in the prison
services, including the claim put forward by the Prison
Officers' Association for certain 'continuous duty credit' payments and the date from which any such payments should
be made;

vi.   allowances and other aspects of the conditions of service of
other grades arising from special features of work in the
prison services;

vii.   working arrangements in the prison services, including shift
systems and standby and on call requirements;

viii.   the effectiveness of the industrial relations machinery including departmental Whitley procedures, within the prison
services.

Although some matters of importance were excluded from the May
Committee's terms of reference, the remit was sufficiently wide for a
quite comprehensive review of policy. After all, as Cross had noted, the
original terms of reference of the Gladstone Committee related to
'prison conditions' but this did not prevent them from making 'statements of principle which were to operate as guidelines for seventy years
to come' (Cross, 1971, p.190). There were, however, two problems that
seemed likely to inhibit a comprehensive review. The first was the
shortage of time and the second an apparent lack of relevant expertise.

The Home Secretary wanted a report in four months, by the end of
March 1979, and the Committee began its work on this basis calling for
evidence to be submitted by Christmas 1978. In the event it could not
meet the deadline, and the Home Secretary announced a delay on
21 February 1979. The Committee took ten months over its labours,
delivering a report to the Home Secretary in September, which was
then published in October 1979. Time enough, and more, for intelligent

and fair minded people to adjudicate on an industrial dispute. But hardly time for a Committee with little or no prior knowledge of the prison system to grasp the underlying problems and formulate solutions, however hard they might try.

In this book we attempt to evaluate the work of the May Committee and to judge how far it could be regarded as 'a landmark in penal history' that would provide appropriate guidelines for the future of the prison system. We do so through a consideration of the crucial problems which face, and will continue to face, our prison service. We begin at the beginning by asking what the prison system is for.

1   Prison rule one: rhetoric or reality?

The May Committee discovered at a very early stage in its deliberations that it could not do justice to its terms of reference without breaching them, by 'first considering, and reaching conclusions upon, the purpose of imprisonment' (May, 1979, para 4.1). That was surely right. For matters such as the size and nature of the prison population, the capacity of the prison service to accommodate it, and the responsibilities for the security, control and treatment of inmates, were among those things to which the Committee was required by the Home Secretary to pay attention in making its recommendations. And such matters logically impose the question of what prison is for.

At one level, of course, there is scarcely room for disagreement about what prison is for. If prisons are to exist at all they must provide sufficiently secure custody to ensure that prisoners will remain inside until required by the courts or until their sentences are terminated. This serves at least either to protect the public or to punish the prisoner, and usually both of these purposes. But there is a persistent tendency to ask more of prisons than that they provide 'mere containment or custody' as the May Committee puts it (para 4.2). However, posing the question of what *else* is prison for may be easier than to answer it — at least in any satisfactory and non-contradictory fashion. Certainly the May Committee felt 'that no short statement of objectives is feasible' (para 4.3) even though, eventually, it went on to offer just such a statement.

There seem to be at least three reasons why answering the question should be difficult. First, it must be obvious that any answer is likely to be temporary. The most recent 'official' chronicler of the prison system, Sir Lionel Fox, for example, identified numerous separate answers linked to successive, and comparatively short, periods of prison administration (Fox, 1952). As social attitudes, standards of behaviour and morality, and the state of knowledge change, then the proper use of imprisonment, along with all other penal measures, is likely to need periodic review. Secondly, although answers must in some sense reflect the spirit of their times, it is unlikely in a complex and pluralistic society that they will ever reflect a genuine consensus of opinion. Thus Fox acknowledged the contradictory nature of competing claims for priority among the possible purposes of imprisonment in any given period. The need for compromise solutions in the intervening years has certainly not diminished. Thirdly, there is little point in seeking answers as to the objectives of a prison system without also addressing the task of specifying the means by which they should be pursued. This is not just a matter of reminding ourselves that there are many ways of killing a cat, though here again Fox's account demonstrates that historically much of the debate has been about means rather than ends. There is also the need to guard against the possibility that means intended to achieve one objective may unwittingly bring about other, and unwanted, results. In any event, unless some systematic attempt is made to match means to ends there is a definite probability that there will be a gap between the rhetoric of penal objectives and the reality of prison life.

Nevertheless, however difficult the task may be, and however much of a compromise — and a temporary one at that — the solution may be, an answer must be found that provides the best possible fit between prevailing attitudes and the contemporary state of knowledge. For the solution must be capable of sustaining a coherent policy on which all that happens in our prisons will depend.

The May Committee clearly recognised that the historic purposes of imprisonment had changed over the years (May, 1979, paras 4.4 to 4.7). It also recognised that current objectives were 'unclear or confused or both' (para 4.3) and that there was a need to achieve a compromise solution between competing alternatives. However, its sketchy review of 'treatment and training', and 'humane containment' (paras 4.8 to 4.24) as possible models suggests that the Committee, working against severe constraints of time, had developed only a tenuous grasp of the nature and meaning of these alternatives. In particular the Committee failed to realise the implications of these alternatives for penal policy and the organisation and staffing of the prison system. In the event the Committee rejected both models in favour of a vaguely worded formulation which it described as 'positive custody' (para 4.46). But the Committee seemed unaware that the rhetoric of 'positive custody' is susceptible to exactly the same interpretations as the 'treatment and training' model it was intended to replace, and enjoys none of the real benefits that could be associated with the 'humane containment' model.

It is to its credit that the May Committee recognised the need to diminish the gap between rhetoric and reality by considering the appropriateness of regimes that would give effect to positive custody (paras 4.29 to 4.44). But its consideration of these matters was rudimentary and naive. The Committee offered nothing new, and what it did offer is entirely consistent with existing Prison Department policies.

As a result we cannot accept that the May Committee's answer to the question of what is prison for is in keeping either with informed opinion in regard to law and order or with the contemporary state of knowledge on the effectiveness of penal sanctions. Above all we cannot accept that the policy it endorses is the right one to carry the prison system through the next two decades — for it is just such a policy that has brought the prison system to its present state of disorder, disillusion and disrepute.

To justify this conclusion we must review the recent history of prison policy and the meanings that have been attached to the supposed purposes of imprisonment, together with such evidence on these matters as was submitted to the May Committee and how the Committee evaluated it.

The myth of 'treatment and training'

We agree with the May Committee that the starting point for a consideration of the underlying philosophy of the modern prison system is the Report of the Gladstone Committee of 1895. Starting from the principle that imprisonment 'should have as its primary and concurrent objects deterrence and reformation', the Gladstone Committee was concerned to find ways of sending prisoners out as 'better men and women, physically and morally, than when they came in' (Gladstone, 1895, paras 25 and 47). The history of the prison system since 1895 has essentially been the history of attempts to give meaning and substance to the possibility of providing rehabilitative influences in prisons. As the May Committee puts it:

> Despite Paterson's paradox about trying to train men for freedom in conditions of captivity, the belief appeared firmly established that 'treatment' capable of changing men for the better was possible in penal institutions (May, 1979, para 4.7).

By 1949 the doctrine was formally stated as Rule Six of the Prison Rules in the following terms:

> The purposes of training and treatment of convicted prisoners shall be to establish in them the will to lead a good and useful life on discharge, and to fit them to do so (Home Office, 1949).

Nowhere was the faith in the possibility of providing effective prison treatment and training more forcefully stated than in the White Paper of February 1959, *Penal Practice in a Changing Society*. Widely acknowledged to be the work of the then Chairman of the Prison Commission, Sir Lionel Fox, the White Paper boldly stated the task of the prison system as follows: 'The constructive function of our prisons is to prevent the largest possible number of those committed to their care from offending again' (Home Office, 1959, para 44). And while the White Paper did not yet claim success in this task it knew from whence success would come: 'Through more precise methods of classification and continual search for improved techniques we must seek to reduce recidivism by more effective personal training' (para 51). Although the May Committee seemed unaware of its existence, let alone its historic significance, for *Penal Practice* gets no mention in their Report, the White Paper had a profound impact. In 1964 Rule Six was revised and elevated to Rule One to indicate its primacy: 'The purpose of the training and treatment of convicted prisoners shall be to encourage and assist them to lead a good and useful life' (Home Office, 1964).

The doctrine of treatment and training is of obvious appeal to the enlightened conscience. If prisons can be justified on the grounds that they make prisoners less likely to offend in future because they have been scientifically or clinically 'treated' and not merely 'deterred', then the social and economic costs of incarceration seem so much more worthwhile, and the retributive urge in ourselves and others can be clothed in a more palatable disguise. But embracing the doctrine of treatment and training has had important implications for penal policy. Until recent times the idea that prisons ought to be 'treatment-orientated' institutions has been a goal approved by criminologists and prison administrators alike. Indeed so important did it seem at one time that many argued against short sentences of imprisonment on the ground that these did not give the authorities sufficient time to do their remedial work. Not only were longer sentences preferred, but also indeterminate ones which would allow the authorities to release prisoners only when the treatment had had its appropriate effect. Moreover, as far as the organisation of the prison system is concerned, acceptance of treatment and training as the goal has led successive administrations since the Second World War to a peculiar use of resources. In essence the prison system has become committed to an arbitrary distinction between 'local' prisons which receive all prisoners from the courts, and 'training' prisons to which ideally all prisoners should be allocated for appropriate, specialised and differentiated regimes once their supposed 'needs' have received clinical 'diagnosis' and 'classification'.

Today the climate of opinion has changed and the optimism and confidence associated with the treatment and training philosophy has given way to disillusion. The disillusion is well founded. It is also world-wide. It is founded on a growing recognition of the gap between

14

rhetoric and reality, a reappraisal of the original conceptual basis of the philosophy, and the overwhelming evidence from numerous research studies as to its ineffectiveness.

As one observer of the English prison system observed (Morris, 1963, p.21) while the Prison Rules specify the purpose of treatment and training, there is nothing in the Rules which *requires* it to be carried out. As a result it is perfectly possible to argue that it has been honoured more in the heady rhetoric of administrators than it has in actual penal practice. Prison regimes do not differ all that widely from one another, even between the theoretical extremes (see Jones and Cornes, 1977; King, 1972; King and Morgan, 1976; King and Elliott, 1978). In so far as they do differ, the differences can rarely be attributed to specific programmes of treatment and training directed towards any well defined end. Over the last fifty years prisons have become more relaxed, and prisoners have spent a great deal more time out of their cells. Welfare officers, psychologists, psychotherapists and the like have been appointed, but their roles remain ill-defined and their services are not widely taken up. Occasionally, attempts have been made to introduce therapeutic programmes of 'group counselling' and so on, but they have soon lapsed. Vocational training and industrial training schemes have been tried over the years, but have never been available to more than a tiny fraction of the prison population. For the most part treatment and training amounts to the provision of work, educational classes and the opportunity for physical training — coupled with a loose exhortation to staff to adopt a quasi case-work relationship with their charges. In spite of valiant efforts to introduce work-study and incentive earnings schemes in recent years, the fact remains that most prisoners are under-employed, on tasks of little real value, in conditions that are a parody of the outside world. Productivity remains low, and earnings are pitiable. Education classes, like vocational training schemes, reach only a minority of the prison population. The training role of prison officers has been confusing to staff and prisoners alike. This is not to say that much good work has not been done in a number of prisons by remedial staff and under the banner of treatment and training. It is to say that what has been done scarcely amounts to a well thought out and co-ordinated implementation of the treatment and training philosophy.

The May Committee evidently accepts this analysis. While it wishes to dispense with the rhetoric of treatment and training, it intends: 'that the rhetoric alone should be changed and not all the admirable and constructive things that are done in its name' (May, 1979, paras 4.9 and 4.27). We too would wish to retain most, if not all, of these beneficial achievements, but we believe it to be of vital importance that they should be justified under a rubric that does not bring with it other, unwanted and harmful consequences. As we shall argue subsequently, to justify these developments under a philosophy of positive custody is so little different from justifying them under a philosophy of treatment and training, that harmful consequences will not be avoided. On the other hand, to justify them under the rubric of humane containment would be perfectly defensible, and would actually make it more likely that even more important and beneficial developments could take place.

The disillusionment with the treatment and training philosophy is not confined to the practical difficulties of devising and implementing appropriate regimes and programmes within the prisons. For the very assumptions that prisons ought to be about treatment or training, and that prisoners, however much they are incarcerated against their will, ought to want to receive it are based on insubstantial foundations. There is, in particular, no evidence to suggest that the reason why criminals are incarcerated in the first place is because they have previously lacked the programmes of treatment and training that prisons can provide. There is no reason, therefore, to believe that the provision of such programmes should have beneficial results in the prevention of future criminality. The problems of implementing Rule One are in any case much greater than is implied in Sir Alexander Paterson's famous paradox: 'It is impossible to train men for freedom in conditions of captivity'. For it is not captivity, as such, that constitutes the obstacle. Training *might* be provided in such circumstances if the trainees wanted to be trained and if the trainers knew what the training involved and how to do it. Unfortunately these conditions do not apply. Prisoners have always known that prisons are not really about training, they are really about captivity. There seems little to be gained from pretending otherwise.

As if this was not enough, the findings from research have given no comfort to the supporters of treatment and training. No satisfactory evidence has been found to suggest that the provision of treatment and training has done anything to reduce the rates of recidivism among prisoners. Nor to suggest that one type of prison treatment is better than any other. Nor that longer sentences are better than shorter sentences. The overwhelming conclusions to be drawn from the international research carried out on this subject are that prisons do not work as instruments of reform, and that the philosophy of treatment and training has been to no avail (see Lipton, Martinson and Wilks, 1975, and Brody, 1976, for detailed reviews of this evidence). Once again the May Committee acknowledges these failures, and even cites the official Home Office manual for sentencers (Home Office, 1978) and the recent Advisory Council Report on *Young Adult Offenders* (ACPS, 1974) as further evidence pointing in the same direction (May, 1979, para 4.11).

In spite of the philosophical doubts about the ethic of treatment and training, some observers conclude that the present evidence as to its failure simply indicates that the authorities should try harder: that more investment in research, personnel and the development of programmes is required before treatment and training can be properly assessed. The May Committee comes perilously close to such a position when it cautiously reminds us that:

> social scientists have *not* proved . . . that penal establishments have no reformative effect, nor that individual members of the staff exert no influence for good . . . (nor) . . . that inmates are invariably incapable of responding to whatever is provided (para 4.12).

At one level this represents a serious misunderstanding of the task of social science. At another it is a blinding glimpse of the obvious to which one can only respond, so what? Economists have not 'proved' that men are incapable of behaving altruistically in the market place — but who would base a prices and incomes policy on that?

Among the harmful consequences which may be directly attributed to the treatment and training philosophy are its effects on the public, prison staff, prisoners and the use of scarce prison resources.

As a direct consequence of the high sounding rhetoric of treatment and training, the public have been led to expect more than they have any right to expect about the possibilities of 'curing' crime and the part that prisons should play in this process. On close examination it soon becomes apparent that the public have only rather sketchy ideas as to how such cures are to be effected — how could it be otherwise in the present state of knowledge? — but they know that the treatment of offenders is entrusted, in part at least, to experts. Though the public may be rightly sceptical about extravagant claims in the face of apparently rising rates of crime, and especially recidivism, they can scarcely be blamed for thinking that more can and should be done. They are told repeatedly by prison administrators, prison reformers, leader writers and now by the May Committee (para 4.24) that it is no longer enough to lock prisoners away until they have served their terms. Some day, perhaps, prison officials, politicians and Committees of Inquiry will have the courage to educate the public to be optimistic only about those things that are actually possible.

For prison staff, especially uniformed officers, working under a philosophy of treatment and training constitutes a real dilemma. On the one hand they know that their function is essentially custodial. They have to maintain a constant vigilance to ensure the security of the establishment, and to maintain good order and discipline with it. In these activities their role is clear and their training unambiguous. Above all it is perfectly apparent to themselves and everyone else whether they are discharging these activities successfully or otherwise. On the other hand they have been persuaded by the press, the public, prison reformers and prison administrators to concern themselves with the training of prisoners. But here their roles are imprecisely specified — often no more than a vague injunction to be concerned with 'the whole man' — and their own training is short and ambiguous because nobody knows quite what they are being trained for. More or less elaborate procedures are devised to provide a framework within which the role may supposedly be fulfilled, but nobody is able to say at all clearly what the role actually consists of. The result is that staff are engaged in an endless charade of data collection, form filling, categorisation, allocation, interviewing and the development of plans that have form but no substance. Since nobody knows quite what is being done or why, staff equally have no way of knowing whether they are being successful or not. It is hardly surprising that they suffer from feelings of guilt, inadequacy or contempt. (For a fuller account of the collapse of confidence in treatment and training and its effects upon staff in what was once the showpiece prison of the system, see King and Elliott, 1978).

In 1963 a working party was set up, at the instigation of the Prison Officers' Association, to consider the role of the modern prison officer. Its output has been slender and real changes in the role of prison officers negligible. The working party is still in existence, but it has become, in effect, a sterile appendage to the Whitley Council. Disillusioned with the attempt to forge a more constructive role for themselves, and unable to comprehend the logistics of prison policy dictated by a distant headquarters organisation, it should be no surprise that prison officers have turned their attention to traditional trade union concerns with pay and conditions. In part at least, the very conditions of which they complain are a product of the attempt to implement Rule One.

Prisoners, too, soon learn the rhetoric and para-medical jargon of treatment and training. It encourages them to think of themselves in a quasi-patient role, and to expect some specific remedy for what ails them. If they detect the yawning chasm between rhetoric and reality — and most of them do — it arms them with grounds for the censure of staff and the authorities for failing to do what was never realistically possible (Mathieson, 1965). Prisoners frequently resent the intrusion of

18

untrained and incompetent staff into their privacy. As one typical prisoner noted, the end result of all the interviews, form filling, discussions and analysis was that he was allowed into the soft toys class (King and Elliott, 1978). Whether they see through the rhetoric or not, most prisoners know well enough that it will do no harm to go along with it while they are being considered for parole.

Important though these influences on the public, prison staff and prisoners are, they pale almost into significance when compared with the effect of the treatment and training philosophy on the use of scarce resources within the prison system. The attitude of Prison Department to Rule One might best be described as schizoid. Faced with the difficulties of giving treatment and training either an intelligible theoretical justification or a coherent substantive form in practice, and in the light of the evidence as to its ineffectiveness, the Department has played down its importance during the last decade. In large part this has been prompted by influences from outside the service. As we noted above, while substantive programmes have always been thin on the ground, the influence of the treatment and training philosophy has produced a general relaxation of prison regimes over the years. Indeed so persuasive had been the slogans about training men for freedom in conditions of captivity, that for a time it seemed as though 'captivity' was a regrettable impediment to the real work of training for freedom. It took a number of dramatic escapes in the 1960s and the cool gaze of Lord Mountbatten (1966) to restore a proper balance and to draw attention to the neglect of the security function of prisons. Since that time the concepts of treatment and training and their place in the functioning of prisons, have been the subject of much official heart-searching. Though it had been known since the late 1960s that Prison Department was looking for a new formulation for Rule One, none had emerged by the time of the establishment of the May Inquiry. Nevertheless, it is clear both from an examination of Prison Department statements in official publications and from observation of policy decisions that important shifts of emphasis have taken place. It will be instructive to review these shifts, for they have a direct bearing on the thinking of the May Committee.

The emergence of 'humane containment'

The White Paper of 1959, committed to the concept of treatment and training which would lead to the reduction of recidivism, advocated the establishment of sufficient remand and observation centres to accommodate all untried prisoners and 'such convicted prisoners as require observation before being classified' (Home Office, 1959, para 93). Once classified, the short sentence prisoner would remain in re-organised local prisons not 'because there is nowhere else to send him' but because in future they would contain training units 'to which he is allocated because that is the right place for him' (para 64). Such a future for local prisons was predicated upon the relief of overcrowding through the further development of open prisons which were conceived as 'a most effective instrument of training' (para 94) and the building of new closed prisons which would have specialist security or training functions. The general strategy for the prison system was clear — the task was to diagnose the problems of prisoners, to classify them according to their needs, and to allocate them to one or another of the diversified prison regimes where they would receive the appropriate form of treatment or training.

When the Prison Commission was merged into the Home Office as the Prison Department in 1963 the policy advocated in the White Paper had been put into practice and further developed. Grendon Underwood, the new psychiatric prison hospital, had been opened, and following the protest at the 'outdated' style of Everthorpe, the first closed prison to be built since the War, an expanded building programme of training prisons designed to foster the ideals of prison treatment had been inaugurated. The first of this new generation of closed training prisons was Blundeston, and when it was opened the optimism that had been generated by the White Paper four years earlier remained undimmed. Henry Brooke in his Foreword to *Prisons and Borstals* wrote as follows:

> We have indeed been well served by those whose good sense and imagination have helped to convert the punishment of loss of liberty from mere punitive detention to purposive treatment and rehabilitation (Home Office, 1964a, para 2).

He went on to argue that 'careful classification of prisoners, and facilities for separate treatment of the different classes' (para 23) is of vital importance in the attempt 'to reduce to a minimum the likelihood of each particular prisoner ever coming back into prison once he had been discharged' (para 24). The then Home Secretary claimed that in this country 'we are not unsuccessful' in that attempt, but that he 'set great store by research . . . into the causes and prevention of recidivism' (para 24) to improve matters still further.

By 1969, however, things had changed. The new generation of training prisons had not brought with them any dramatic breakthrough in methods of treatment and training, and negative research findings about the effectiveness of prison treatment were beginning to filter through from various parts of the world. The need for security had been rediscovered and had been given a new emphasis, first by the Mountbatten Report (1966) and then by the Radzinowicz Report (ACPS, 1968). Furthermore, the prison population continued to rise and no inroads had been made into the problems of overcrowding in spite of the prison building programme.

In a new White Paper, *People in Prison*, the aims of the prison service were subtly, but substantially, re-defined. The single overriding purpose of the prison system was said to be 'the protection of society' (Home Office, 1969, para 8). In fulfilling that purpose the first aim of the service was defined as the holding of those persons 'committed to custody and to provide conditions for their detention which are currently acceptable to society' (para 13). Treatment and training was not only relegated to second place, but was couched in less optimistic, even reluctant or dutiful terms:

> Second, in dealing with convicted offenders, there is an *obligation* on the service to do all that *may* be possible within the currency of the sentence to encourage and assist them to lead a good and useful life (para 13, emphasis added).

The White Paper employed, for the first time, the concept of 'humane containment' to describe the first task of the service. In doing so the Department admitted that the task is a prosaic one, acknowledged that the standards by which society lives should apply to offenders also, and confessed that 'in some respects the conditions of a prisoner's daily life fall short of what society would currently approve' (paras 11 and 15). Although the White Paper went on to state that 'humane containment cannot be the sole task of the prison service' (para 18) it took pains to re-define what it meant by treatment and training. Thus:

> . . . it is wrong to think of treatment as an item, or choice of items, that can be added at will to the daily regime . . . to meet the needs of offenders. Neither our capacity for the diagnosis of the needs of offenders nor the ability to effect a cure is at present as great as many advocates of this or that form of treatment have implied. We need a view of treatment that *embraces all that is done by or for the offender in custody* (para 32, emphasis added).

Having stripped the concepts of treatment and training of any precise or effective meaning in this way, the White Paper acknowledged that: 'there is also a place in the prison system for the use of the term in the alternative sense in which it relates to a diagnosis and to the possibility of a changed way of life' (para 32). But it was clear that treatment in this sense had a very minor role to play compared with what had been envisaged ten years earlier. Indeed it is hard to escape the conclusion that, however much it would have preferred to concentrate on humane containment, Prison Department was simply obliged to find some form of words to deal with treatment and training because of the existence of Rule One in the statutory Prison Rules.

One might have thought that this shift in the philosophical under-pinning of the work of the prison service would have led to a reconsideration of the policy of providing differentiated training regimes throughout the prison system. But in fact the White Paper remained committed to the process of classification according to 'needs' (now including security needs following the Mountbatten Report on prison security), and to the belief that 'ideally all prisoners would be sent to training prisons with a regime suited to their needs, and with a degree of security no greater than was necessary' (paras 167-171). Indeed the commitment to an expanding system of differentiated training prisons was perhaps increased by the continuing need to relieve overcrowding in the local prisons and the decision not to use local prisons for short term training but to limit their role to trial and remand, or closely allied functions (para 165).

It seems clear to us that by 1969 an effective contradiction had appeared between the expressed aims of humane containment, with a generalised and subsidiary role for treatment and training, on the one hand, and the continuing explicit use of local and training prisons in ways that seem more in keeping with the optimistic expectations that were held out a decade earlier. Moreover, the Prison Department had posed for itself a peculiar dilemma. The White Paper asserted that the general aims of the prison service should apply to 'all convicted offenders' (para 14) — that is, presumably, both those held in local and training establishments. Yet as a matter of policy, treatment and training was not to be attempted in the local prisons. And in order to implement it in the training prisons it was necessary to protect them from overcrowding. As a result the local prisons continued to absorb the burden of a rising prison population in more and more crowded conditions. In such circumstances was humane containment practicable in the local prisons?

If these contradictions were to be resolved something had to give, although by 1977 there was no sign, at least not officially, of any new developments. If anything the dilemma had got worse. In 1977 the Home Office published another account of the work of the prison service under the title *Prisons and the Prisoner*. The main tasks of the service were then defined as follows:

    i.   to provide various services to the courts;

ii.   to undertake the humane and secure containment of those committed to custody; and

iii.   within the currency of their sentences to do everything possible by way of treatment and training (Home Office, 1977, para 13).

There was nothing in *Prisons and the Prisoner* that could give any grounds for optimism about the effectiveness of treatment and training, but the Department apparently remained committed to the belief that 'the great majority of sentenced prisoners, apart from those serving very short sentences, ought to be in training prisons' (para 202). Moreover, once the requirements of legal status and security categorisation had been met, the purpose of classification was to ensure that each prisoner was allocated to a training prison 'where he will receive the treatment and training most appropriate to his individual aptitudes and needs' (para 26). So much for the theory, but in practice things work out rather differently. Something like a half of all prisoners received never get transferred out of the local prisons to that appropriate training regime (Sparks, 1971). And this does not just apply to short term prisoners, for 'one of the most unsatisfactory features of the present situation is that men serving up to four years imprisonment may have to serve the whole of their sentence in an overcrowded local prison' (Home Office, 1977, para 202).

This, then, was the official position by the time the May Committee was established. Rule One still existed, but treatment and training had been stripped of its medical connotation and given only a vague and generalised meaning. In any case treatment and training was accorded a lower, and residual, priority than humane containment in the aims of the prison service, although both were held to apply to all prisoners. In spite of this realignment of aims, the prison system continued to be organised as though nothing had happened, especially in regard to the distinction between local and training prisons. As a result, half of all prisoners, including some serving up to four years, were denied any access to institutions ostensibly offering treatment and training. At the same time these very prisoners, being held in overcrowded and old-fashioned prisons, were confined in conditions of custody that could least be described as humane containment.

The May Committee: evidence and conclusions

In our evidence to the May Committee we argued that Prison Department was right to turn the emphasis away from the unrealistic objectives of reform through treatment and training and on to the more

23

modest but realisable objective of humane containment. But we also argued that Prison Department should take humane containment much more seriously than it had treatment and training, and that it should ensure that genuinely humane conditions are achieved for all prisoners throughout the system. This would involve a major reorganisation with regard to the use of existing resources. In view of the evidence about the effectiveness of treatment and training, we argued that it was fruitless to follow a policy of allocating some prisoners to privileged conditions in differentiated training regimes — and wasteful of existing plant. It would be better to abandon the artificial and largely meaningless distinction between local and training prisons and to spread the overcrowding from the local prisons more evenly over the system as a whole.

The May Committee rejected our proposals in the following terms:

> Whilst we feel it has much force, particularly in its impatience with wishful thinking, there is a great danger that it may throw out the good with the unattainable and we are sceptical about the extent to which it may justify, as is claimed, sweeping changes in the allocation of resources in penal establishments. Further, as one group of witnesses pointed out to us, 'humane containment' suffers from the fatal defect that it is a means without an end. Our opinion is that it can only result in making prisons into human warehouses — for inmates and staff. It is not, therefore, a fit rule for hopeful life or responsible management (May, 1979, para 4.24).

It is worth commenting on this brief dismissal of our evidence before we go on to re-present the arguments here. First, we made it plain that we had no wish to 'throw out the good with the unobtainable' and indeed went to great lengths to show not only how the 'good' might be retained, but also extended, under a doctrine of humane containment. Secondly, if 'humane containment' does not justify the *abolition* of a distinction between local and training prisons, which condemns half the prison population to conditions of overcrowding, can the May Committee really have confidence that either 'treatment and training' or 'positive custody' justifies *retaining* such a distinction, when all the evidence shows that nothing actually works as far as reducing recidivism is concerned? Thirdly, why should humane containment be regarded as a means without an end? There is clearly no logical basis for such an assertion. It could be either a means to something else or an end in itself. If treated as an end then some welcome attention might be focused on the means by which it might be brought about. Lastly, the May Committee's opinion that humane containment can only result in making prisons into human warehouses is not so much wrong as naive.

Prisons have always been human warehouses and in some sense always must be. What the May Committee appears not to recognise is that prisons have sometimes been *inhuman* warehouses. The May Committee thinks that humane containment is not a fit rule for hopeful life or responsible management. That is, of course, a value position to which the Committee is entitled, though it would presumably have to be defended by some demonstration that something else — positive custody — was a more fit rule for hopeful life and responsible management. For our part we think the difference between inhuman warehouses and human warehouses is important. Moreover, establishing and maintaining the distinction between human warehouses and inhuman warehouses is sufficiently problematic that it frequently eludes responsible management. We would certainly feel more hopeful about the future of the prison system if we could feel satisfied that humane containment had been achieved.

It is clear that the May Committee did not receive much evidence on the objectives of the prison system, and what they did receive was largely 'unsystematic and rarely precise' (para 4.21). But two pieces of evidence are worth singling out, for we suspect that they were important influences on the Committee's verdict on humane containment.

The first is from the Home Office and shows the attempt by Prison Department to extricate itself from the requirement of providing both humane containment and treatment and training for all prisoners. In a paper on policy priorities the Department referred to an internal review conducted between 1971 and 1974. As a result of that review it was said that:

> Consideration was given to the division of the prison system into two parts. In some establishments there was to be a duty to provide a programme of treatment and training directed towards the offender's release, in the rest the duty was to be simply one of secure, humane containment. The proposal was intended to clarify the aims of different types of establishment and to make it easier to match resources to needs: it would not be altogether fair to characterise it as an attempt to re-introduce, in suitably modern form, the distinction between gaols and bridewells' (Home Office, Evidence, vol.I, paper IIA2, para 18).

That such a solution to the dilemmas we have outlined was considered at such length is of great interest. For it shows the willingness of the Home Office to manipulate the rhetoric of the system while leaving the realities unchanged. By restricting the treatment and training function to training prisons, the Department would have achieved nothing new. There was no suggestion that treatment and training would thereby become more effective. And the local prisons had long since ceased to pretend to do anything by way of treatment and training anyway. But what is alarming about the proposal is that it contains no suggestions for increasing the resources available to the local prisons that would actually make them *capable* of offering humane containment. To the myth that the training prisons *do provide* treatment and training, would have been added the myth that what was currently offered in the local prisons *did constitute* humane containment.

In fact the Home Office Paper went on to point out that 'this proposal forms no part of official policy, which remains that all establishments should have a treatment role with respect to convicted offenders' (para 19). But it is indicative of a further shift in thinking about humane containment since the concept was first introduced in the 1969 White Paper. For *People in Prison* had made it clear that humane containment was not an easy task (Home Office, 1969, para 15). It had acknowledged that the standards by which outside society lives should also apply to offenders in custody. And it conceded that in some respects prison conditions fell short of what society would currently approve. If we are correct in our analysis, and the Home Office effectively came to equate the concept of *humane* containment with the standards actually prevailing in the local prisons, that is with *mere* containment (or even *inhumane* containment?), then it is not hard to see why the May Committee should have rejected that as a goal for the prison service. Nevertheless, the concept of humane containment is capable of sustaining much more than mere custody, providing it is taken seriously and providing existing resources are re-allocated away from other, ineffective, priorities. We try to demonstrate how this can be done in chapter 4.

The second piece of evidence came from the British Association of Prison Governors. It is not unreasonable to assume that prison governors, or at least some of them, would have been familiar with these developments in official thinking at headquarters. In any case, since they have to implement policy in their own institutions, prison governors would be well aware that official faith in treatment and training had diminished and that humane containment as officially conceived amounted to no more than a tacit acceptance of the *status quo* in the most overcrowded of local prisons. Certainly the BAPG in their evidence reflected a profound feeling of disillusion. As the May Committee shows, the BAPG's call for the resurrection of treatment and training as the objective for the prison system regardless of its feasibility seems to be a counsel of despair (May, 1979, para 4.21). But since the May Committee's proposal for positive custody responds to the spirit of the BAPG's plea, if not the letter, some attention should be given to the governors' evidence.

The prison governors wrote as follows:

> The concept of treatment has changed to embrace almost everything that happens to a prisoner and the phrase humane containment is now commended as at least having the merit of truth. It does also have a number of de-merits (BAPG, Evidence, para 1.8).

Among the de-merits are the assertions that humane containment 'is so vague as to be almost meaningless' and that 'it can be used to rationalise virtually anything that is done to prisoners'. We think it much more likely that these charges apply to treatment and training than to humane containment. After all it was precisely the difficulty of giving meaning to the treatment concept that brought such widespread disillusion; and it might be noted that in some parts of the world both lobotomies and castrations have been justified under the treatment ethic. By contrast the concept of humane containment, if taken seriously, can be defined in reasonably objective terms and by reference to universally agreed standards; and by definition the inhumane aspects of imprisonment cannot be justified in its name.

What has to be remembered here is that the governors were responding to current Prison Department usage of the term humane containment. Small wonder, bearing in mind the state of the local prisons, that the governors felt that humane containment is morally neutral and that it fails to motivate staff. We suspect that this argument weighed heavily with the May Committee for in reaching the conclusion that positive custody should be the goal of the prison service it wrote: 'Prison staff cannot be asked to operate in a *moral vacuum* and the absence of real objectives can in the end only lead to the routine brutalisation of all the participants' (May, 1979, para 4.28, emphasis added). However, we cannot accept that the distinction between humane containment and inhumane containment is morally neutral; indeed in our view it is concepts like treatment and training or positive custody that are the more morally ambiguous, however well intentioned they may be. Moreover, we do not accept that the attempt to achieve humane containment is *not* a real objective, incapable of inspiring and motivating staff. It has one great advantage as a motivator over either treatment and training or positive custody – namely that it is capable of being defined in ways which enable staff (and the public) to know when they are achieving it or when they are falling short.

In part, at least, it may seem as though the differences between ourselves, the May Committee and the prison governors are mercly terminological. It is clear that we are all against mere custody of the kind that now prevails in the local prisons. We would also accept that much of what the May Committee regards as positive custody would be consistent with what we regard as humane containment. Certainly what the prison governors take to be the most important element in revitalising the existing Rule One — 'maintaining the quality of life in our penal establishments . . . based on the guiding principles laid down in the UN Standard Minimum Rules' (BAPG, Evidence, para 1.11) — we would see as one way of defining the proper basis of humane containment. We hope that our preference for a formulation in terms of humane containment will not be seen as a mere linguistic quibble, although given the history of the concepts of treatment and training it is vital that prison rhetoric should unambiguously mean what it says and say what it means. But it is more than that. Any serious statement of penal objectives has to be made in operational terms, by stating the procedures necessary to bring these objectives about. Any such statement necessarily carries with it implications about the appropriate ways of mobilising and distributing scarce resources. The treatment and training formulation of Rule One failed on all those counts: it was ambiguous, it failed to specify appropriate procedures, and it involved a wasteful use of scarce resources. The May Committee failed to appreciate these difficulties and its positive custody formulation suffers from exactly the same defects. What the May Committee has said, in effect, is 'Rule One is dead. Long live Rule One'. In so doing it has produced a blue print for the future of the prison system that is in no significant way different from the tattered plans of the past.

It is worth quoting the May Committee's attempt at re-writing Rule One in full. They wrote as follows:

> The purpose of the detention of convicted prisoners shall be to keep them in custody which is both secure and yet positive, and to that end the behaviour of all the responsible authorities and staff towards them shall be such as to:
>
> (a) create an environment which can assist them to respond and contribute to society as positively as possible;
> (b) preserve and promote their self respect;
> (c) minimise, to the degree of security necessary in each particular case, the harmful effects of their removal from normal life;
> (d) prepare them for and assist them on discharge.
>
> (May, 1979, para 4.26)

There are several problems with the May Committee formulation of positive custody. First, it is, of course, a loaded concept. For to disagree with it almost implies that one is in favour of negative custody, or that one approves of sin. But does it have any actual or obvious meaning? We think not. Certainly the use of the term 'positive' provides the hopeful quality that the May Committee was looking for. But more attention seems to have been paid to the generation of hope than to the generation of objectives. Ironically, in view of the Committee's dismissal of humane containment as a means without an end, the formulation of positive custody actually removes the one relatively clear statement of ultimate purpose — 'to encourage and assist (convicted prisoners) to lead a good and useful life' — that was enshrined in the original Rule One. The nearest the May Committee comes to stating an ultimate purpose for imprisonment — 'assist them to respond and contribute to society as positively as possible' — contrives to use the same term 'positive' to describe both means and ends without specifying what is meant in either context. As a result 'positive custody' becomes, indeed can only be, a rhetorical statement — though it was just this that the Committee set out to avoid.

Secondly, throughout its redrafting of Rule One, the May Committee has been content with an expression of *subjective intentions* and given no regard to the *objective standards* of living or behaviour that are to be achieved. The recent United States Commission on Criminal Justice Standards and Goals, in its report on *Corrections* (1973), made the point that a declaration of intent is not enough unless one also specifies standards against which actual performance may be measured, and a timetable within which standards should be achieved. We agree with that view. The May Committee gives no indication of how one 'creates an environment' which can assist prisoners to respond positively, nor any criteria against which to measure whether or not one has been successful in that endeavour. The same could be said of each of the features which are said to form part of positive custody. It is true that the May Committee looks towards useful work and education as a means 'to give life and effect to the new spirit embodied in the proposed new Rule One (para 4.29). But work and education are certainly not new to the prison system. Nor are the targets for the provision of work or education which the May Committee suggests. Moreover, the May Committee explicitly disclaims any responsibility for showing how, or demanding when, such targets should be achieved (paras 4.42 and 4.43). Thus the May Committee imposes no actual obligations on the prison authorities and confers no rights on prisoners. Indeed it would always be open to the authorities to justify any activity by intentions rather than results: 'We are being as positive as we can in the circumstances'. And so the May Committee's intentions will remain a pious hope.

Thirdly, although we have argued that positive custody has no real meaning, we suspect that it is capable of being made to mean anything by prison administrators and staff. In particular we suspect that the proponents of treatment and training will see in it a continued justification for much the same kinds of activities that have gone on in prisons in the past, and thus for the policies about local and training prisons that have lent support to those activities. Certainly the manner in which Mr Trevelyan, Director General of the prison service, so readily embraced the concept of positive custody at the NACRO Conference on the May Report on 30 November, 1979 (NACRO, 1980) suggests that this will be so.

The May Committee could have ensured that all the 'admirable and constructive things' that had been done in the name of treatment and training continued, without either committing the prison system to the wasteful use of resources that has been associated with that philosophy in the past, or setting up a vague, confusing and meaningless prison rhetoric. Indeed it could have grasped the opportunity of actually establishing many additional, and equally admirable and constructive, things as part of the prison system for the first time. The May Committee could have proposed duties for the prison authorities and rights for prisoners, that could, in time, have become enforceable. It could have shown the public precisely what it is reasonable to expect of a prison system and how to tell whether those expectations are being met or not. Moreover, much could have been achieved within existing resources. To have done so, however, the May Committee would have had to embrace the prosaic concept of humane containment and taken it seriously. It is to a brief enunciation of the principles associated with humane containment that we now turn.

Making humane containment a reality

When we gave oral evidence to the May Committee we were asked whether Rule One should be re-written to take account of our conception of humane containment. We agreed that it should. But much more is required than a new formulation of Rule One. Humane containment, as we see it, is clearly more than mere containment. Neither containment nor its humanity can be taken for granted. Both elements are problematic. There is a need to spell out objectives in each case, and the place for that is Rule One. But if the objectives are to mean anything in practice there is an even greater need to specify the standards against which they are to be measured, and the strategies to be used for achieving them. And that would involve the systematic review, and often the revision, of the Prison Rules as a whole. Indeed it would involve more than that, because as we have shown elsewhere (King and Morgan, 1976) some of the rights which presently do exist in the Prison Rules are qualified by the unpublished Standing Orders and Circular Instructions of Prison Department. Many of these Orders and Instructions are concerned with purely administrative matters. But where they are not these too would require review, revision and in this case publication.

Not everything in the Prison Rules needs throwing out. Usually the problem is that too much discretion is allowed in the way the Rules are interpreted. We accept that often the Department interprets the Rules generously, though this usually reflects the fact that the standards were pitched too low in the first place. Deciding the proper standards will not be easy. There will always be good reasons why in particular cases the standards cannot be applied. But there are too many Rules at present where no standards are specified, and there is clearly considerable scope for restricting discretion by a more careful drafting of the circumstances in which standards should be deemed not to apply.

All this may seem a daunting task. But it need not be as daunting as all that. In New York the Department of Correctional Services invited the Vera Institute to produce a comprehensive re-statement of the inmate rule book (Vera, 1977). That kind of approach does not seem likely to happen here, but the Home Office might consider the appointment of some appropriate body to undertake a review. After all the European Court of Human Rights has forced some changes in our Prison Rules already — as discussed by Professor Martin in chapter 6. It would surely embarrass the Government if that were to happen too often.

It is clearly beyond the scope of this volume to attempt a review of the Prison Rules, Standing Orders and Circular Instructions. What we can do is to explore the kinds of principles which would need to be implemented to make humane containment a reality; and to provide a rational context within which humane containment seems a meaningful objective. We are all too aware that the real task of translating principles into standards that will be achieved in practice remains to be done.

Humane containment refers explicitly to the prison system, which forms only a part of the wider criminal justice system. We believe that what we regard as humane containment is most compatible with what has come to be called the 'justice' or 'due process' model for dealing with offenders generally. Taken together they best fit the state of current knowledge about law and order and the effectiveness of criminal sanctions. They therefore offer the best basis at this time for the development of a coherent policy for the future of the prison system.

The May Committee itself acknowledges the growth of the justice model in its discussion of the decline of treatment and training (May, 1979, paras 4.16-4.18) but curiously the model does not seem to have been viewed with any favour, for although the issues are raised, they are not followed through.

The justice model is not, of course, new. Indeed it has been put forward in many and various forms by different generations (for recent discussions see American Friends Service Committee, 1971; Clarke, 1978; Von Hirsch, 1976). But the May Committee undoubtedly catches the essence of the matter when it notes that whereas the treatment model concentrates on the alleged needs of the offender, the justice model concentrates on his deeds. Under a justice model, whether or not imprisonment is appropriate, and if so for how long, should be determined by a court in consideration of the gravity of the offence, and not left to the discretion of the executive branch of government by reference to such matters as response to treatment or likelihood of re-offending. In other words, the punishment should fit the crime rather than the criminal. The re-emergence of the justice model in recent years is no more than an attempt to repair the erosion of this principle that had occurred under the guise of treatment and training, and to ensure that such erosion does not occur again.

As the May Committee points out, the justice model has been most developed in its contemporary form by academic lawyers in the United States. Until recently the American courts have respected what has become known as the 'hands off' doctrine with regard to the prison authorities — that is, once the courts had made a judicial determination of the case it was assumed that prisoners, by virtue of their criminality, had forfeited all civil rights and had become, in effect, slaves of the State. It was left to correctional authorities to decide how much of a sentence should be served in custody, under what conditions, and what criteria were to be met for release on parole and so on. Abuses have been documented with regard to, *inter alia*, classification and allocation procedures, parole and disciplinary hearings, methods of maintaining control, and compulsory treatments or treatments taken under duress (Mitford, 1973). In an effort to safeguard against such abuses proponents of the justice model argue that the executive should not normally have powers over inmates which cannot in some sense be supervised by the courts. In practice attempts have been made to make more and more of the decisions affecting prisoners subject to 'due process of law' through the limitation of executive discretion by the courts and, where discretion is inevitable, through the establishment of tribunals whereby prisoners get a fairer hearing, with a right to be represented and the possibility of appeal against decisions.

It is true that the demand for 'due process' has been most marked in the United States, where the recourse to indeterminate sentences which provide prison and parole authorities with massive powers over the release of prisoners has typically been much greater than in the United Kingdom. But it is surprising that a Committee of Inquiry, headed by an English High Court Judge, should appear to see the notion of 'due process' as a special reference to the American Constitution (May, 1979, para 4.18). The concept was enshrined in English common law long before it crossed the Atlantic with the founding fathers. As Abraham (1972) notes, chapter 39 of Magna Carta declares: 'No free man shall be taken, outlawed, banished, or in any way destroyed, nor will we proceed against or persecute him, except by the lawful judgement of his peers and by the law of the land'. By 1354 the words 'due process' were used in an English statute interpreting Magna Carta, and by the end of that century the terms 'due process of law' and 'law of the land' were interchangeable. In fact, in this country, the concept almost certainly goes back to the time of Henry II or even Henry I. As developed thereafter, and especially in the United States, due process of law has become the most valued restraint on the arbitrary exercise of powers of a Head of State, or any of the branches of government. In a word, it has become the defining attribute of the proper relationship between the State and the People in a democracy.

Imprisonment represents the supreme power of the State over the individual citizen, short of the death penalty. As such it is imperative that prison systems should command the respect of all citizens; that they should be above suspicion of the abuse of power. The safeguards afforded by the concept of due process would surely be welcomed by Academician Sakharov, as well as lesser known dissidents incarcerated as 'psychiatric cases', in the Soviet Union and other totalitarian states. But the safeguards are no less necessary in democracies. If the scope for abuses of power has been greater in American prisons there is certainly no room for complacency about the situation in the United Kingdom. One would not expect judges lightly to put such matters on one side. The response of the May Committee to the justice model and the concept of due process is, therefore, somewhat surprising. One detects for example, a slight air of regret in the recognition that 'prisoners and their representatives seek to rely' on the European Convention of Human Rights 'more and more in prisons in the United Kingdom' (May, 1979, para 4.18). Yet the fact that recourse to the European Convention on Human Rights is felt necessary, and has thus far resulted only in rebuffs to the existing policies of Prison Department, suggests that all is not well on human rights in British prisons.

Because imprisonment in the United Kingdom does represent the supreme power of the State over the individual citizen, perhaps the first safeguard against abuses should be that its use should be kept to the minimum consistent with public safety. Of course this is no more than the conventional wisdom. But it is still worth repeating the arguments. Imprisonment is the most expensive sanction available to the courts. And while imprisonment undoubtedly produces a measure of public protection for the duration of a sentence, there is no evidence to suggest that imprisonment is more effective at reducing crime in the longer term than other forms of disposal. Nor is there any evidence to suggest that longer sentences are more effective than shorter sentences. Indeed there are good reasons for thinking that the use of imprisonment, especially the excessive use of imprisonment, is likely to be counter-productive as a sanction against crime because of the inherently brutalising tendencies of incarceration.

Our first principle to govern the future of the prison system, in a society committed to the maintenance of justice as well as order, would be the *minimum use of custody*. This means, in effect, that imprisonment should be used only as a last resort, when other forms of sentence have been exhausted, or are clearly inappropriate having regard to the nature of the offence. It further means that custody should be used for the minimum length of time consistent with public safety. The May Committee took a similar view:

> We take it as axiomatic that imprisonment is bound to remain as the final sanction for imposing social discipline in our community under agreed rules of law. For the reasons which will appear here-after, we are forced to the conclusion that it should be used as little as possible (para 4.25).

Unfortunately, the May Committee was pessimistic about the extent to which imprisonment actually would be used, and offered little hope that anything would or could be done to control the size of prison populations. The problems of actually implementing a minimum use of custody principle are discussed in chapter 2.

One consequence of the attempt by advocates of the justice model to reverse the 'hands off' doctrine that for so long dominated the American prison system, has been the focusing of attention away from either the punishment or the reform of criminals and on to the protection of their human and civil rights whilst in custody. In so far as the same developments have occurred in this country, it is revealing that the May Committee should suggest that the justice model has not been attractive to the 'public at large, still less to prison officers who so often feel that more is always being done for inmates than for themselves' (para 4.16). Revealing, because it implies on the one hand that the justice model with its respect for human rights is in some sense a soft option; and on the other hand that alternative models — from punitive and deterrent, through treatment training and rehabilitative, or positive custody — involve elements which go beyond the justice of the case, yet do not require justification.

Actually we doubt that the public would find the justice model less attractive than other models. In so far as the public is concerned about these matters we would suppose that, once it was in possession of all the facts, it would be much more ready to endorse a policy of fairness to all prisoners than the arbitrary privileges, distinctions and inequities that are inherent to a policy based on treatment and training, or positive custody. Certainly the justice model, with its emphasis on the just deserts of an offender in relation to the nature and gravity of his offence, is both in rhetoric and reality less likely to involve a soft option as far as sentencing is concerned than has been the case in this country under the treatment and training model (cf Wilson, 1975). Indeed the problem of the justice model is one of finding safeguards that will minimise the tendency of the press, public and the courts to regard all offences as serious, and warranting resort to the use of imprisonment.

Unlike the public at large, prison officers are acutely aware of the implications of different models for what goes on in prisons. Their objection to the justice model would be the same as those of their masters at Prison Department, namely, that it would impose unwelcome obligations on the administration and staff to behave in minimally acceptable ways. Neither treatment and training, nor positive custody, would impose such obligations. Instead they would allow the authorities and staff to continue to hide behind the facade of high sounding verbiage and meaningless aphorisms. For example, Sir Alexander Paterson's famous assertion that men are sent to prison 'as a punishment, not for punishment' (Ruck, 1951, p.23) has long been held as a guiding principle in this country. In other words the punishment should comprise the loss of liberty itself, and not the imposition of additional hardships that were to be inflicted during the period of incarceration. But the apparent commitment to such a principle offered no real safeguards. Following Paterson's paternalistic approach the advocates of treatment and training wanted to use the period of incarceration as an opportunity to utilise reformative or rehabilitative programmes of one kind or another — even to the point whereby this became the purpose of imprisonment. Unfortunately many of the 'treatments' of the twentieth century involved inequities and hardships that can be regarded as the functional equivalents of the 'secondary punishments' of the nineteenth century.

Advocates of the justice model also take the view that criminals go to prison as, and not for, punishment. But in seeking to give this a meaning that would limit the excesses of both deterrence and reform they are more likely to look to the version of Paterson's dictum that has since been enshrined in the European *Standard Minimum Rules for the Treatment of Prisoners*. There it is expressed in the following terms:

> Imprisonment and other measures which result in cutting off an offender from the outside world are, by the deprivation of liberty, a punishment in themselves. Therefore the prison system should not, except as incidental to justifiable segregation or the maintenance of discipline, aggravate the suffering inherent in such a situation. The regime of the institution should seek to minimise any differences between prison life and life at liberty which tend to lessen the responsibility of the prisoners or the respect due to their dignity as human beings (Rule 58, Council of Europe, 1973).

Though this statement still leaves much to be specified it does appear to impose some duties on the prison authorities and to confer some rights on prisoners that would genuinely take prison systems in the direction of humane containment. While it was not enamoured of such a model, even the May Committee conceded that a prison system geared to ensuring that prisoners surrendered only those normal rights as are necessarily lost through the deprivation of liberty itself, could have a rehabilitative justification. For it can reasonably be contended 'that an offender can only be taught to respect the rights of society if it is demonstrated to him, whilst in prison, that his own rights are being respected' (May, 1979, para 4.16). In any event it seems to us that this formulation by the Council of Europe implies two further guiding principles which should govern the future of imprisonment and which together encapsulate most of what we mean by the notion of humane containment, namely the *minimum use of security*, and the *normalisation of the prison*.

Our second guiding principle, on the minimum use of security, is justified because security is expensive in plant, technology and manpower; and because in the nature of things security necessarily leads to constraints which exaggerate the differences between life inside and life outside of prisons. The higher the degree of security the more likely it is that prisoners will be deprived of autonomy, self-responsibility and contact with the outside community. Prisoners will not be rendered more responsible on release if they are deprived of all opportunity to exercise responsibility in prison; and if they are denied community contacts for an extended period they are likely to lose those very community ties which, on release, are most likely to influence their development and fulfilment as citizens.

We interpret the minimum use of security principle to mean that prisoners should be subject to only that degree of security necessary to safeguard the public against any realistic threat, and to ensure that prisoners complete their sentences in the prisons to which they are allocated. It must be obvious that not all prisoners require the same security conditions to prevent their escape, and that not all prisoners constitute the same risk to the public, the police or the State, should they be successful in escaping. In his report on prison security Lord Mountbatten (1966) proposed that prisoners should be categorised in terms of their security risk and sent to institutions offering security conditions appropriate to that risk. We consider that proposal, and its initial subsequent adoption, to have been sound. But in our view, Prison Department has, in recent years, embarked on policies which have over-emphasised the security of containment at the expense of its humanity; and which have meant that large numbers of prisoners are subjected to a measure of security which they do not individually merit. In practice the most important consideration now governing the conditions under which a prisoner serves his sentence is the security category to which he is assigned by Prison Department. Decisions on security categories have the most far reaching consequences, but are made by unknown persons, according to unpublished criteria, on the basis of evidence not made known to prisoners, and are not subject to appeal except through administrative petition. Official Prison Department publications suggest that the prison system is indeed guided by a principle of minimum security, though the realities of the Prison Department policies suggest that they are in breach of their expressed ideal. In chapter 3 we discuss these issues more fully and consider what changes are necessary to bring about the implementation of the minimum use of security principle.

Our third guiding principle is the *normalisation of the prison*. By this rather inelegant phrase we mean that as far as resources allow, and consistent with the constraints of secure custody, the same general standards which govern the life of offenders in the community should be held to apply to offenders in prison. Of course, the prison is necessarily set apart from the community in a geographical sense: security considerations dictate that. But the separation between the prison and the community has been social and cultural as well as physical, and has affected staff as well as prisoners, and the families and friends of both groups. There is no doubting the gap between the standards which prevail within the prison and those within the community, and this has been criticised by the Expenditure Committee (HMSO, 1978, 15th Report) and acknowledged by Prison Department (Home Office, 1969). But it is worth recalling that the gap between prison standards and those of the community is of long standing and one that has been deliberately cultivated through much of the history of prisons.

That the prison is a social and organisational enclave is in large measure due to the grandiose purposes which have infused its existence. The standards which prevail within the prison community are abnormal because historically the prison has been a place of special mission. In the nineteenth century the prevailing doctrine of deterrence and prisoner separation spawned an astonishingly elaborate organisation designed to subjugate the minutiae of everyday prison life to a master plan. More recently the doctrine of treatment and training, though largely rhetorical, nevertheless produced its own organisational devices. The more prosaic goals of social protection and humane containment demand no such special provision. They do not suggest that the prison be a place of special positive endeavour: nor do they impose extreme negative sanctions of a retributive or deterrent kind. Without drawing a veil over the punitive basis of imprisonment, humane containment suggests that the conditions within which the punishment (loss of liberty) is borne, should be humane, i.e. as normal as is consistent with the security which is necessary to ensure continued custody.

We still take the view which the May Committee quoted from our original evidence:

> that precisely because humane containment may fail to fire the imagination so it may prevent the excesses of the past. The function of imprisonment *is* a limited one and its use and administration should no longer be guided by claims which it cannot fulfil.

But we would like to reiterate something that the May Committee omitted to quote. Namely that the concept of humane containment, through the principle of normalisation of the prison, is not only capable of being achieved, but when achieved would actually offer many more practical and concrete advantages than are specified or implied in the illusory pursuit of either treatment and training or positive custody.

We consider the possibility of implementing the principle of normalisation of the prison system, and the resources required to achieve it in chapter 4. Here it is sufficient to state that such a principle would involve acceptance of the following guidelines:

i.   that prisoners should generally be held in the establishment closest to their community ties so as to maximise their opportunity to maintain family and other links which are the norm for persons in the community;

ii.   that prisoners should be permitted access to a similar range of health, welfare and educational facilities as they would have access to within the community;

iii.   services within the prison should be provided by the same commercial, voluntary or statutory agencies which normally provide them within the community;

iv.   that prisoners should be provided with a standard of accommodation (including normal services) food and clothing comparable to that provided by the State to persons in receipt of supplementary benefits;

v.   that prisoners, wherever possible, should be afforded the opportunity of gainful employment thereby enabling them to improve their standard of living and to meet some of their community obligations;

vi.   that prison affairs should be freed from official secrets legislation;

vii. that prisoners should be permitted to communicate on any matter with any persons or organisations that they choose, insofar as this does not make unreasonable demands upon staff time thereby prejudicing the welfare of other prisoners;

viii. that all serious disciplinary offences should be subject to adjudication according to due process of law;

ix. that all decisions which affect the date of a prisoner's release should be subject to judicial or some other independent form of review.

We recognise that security considerations and scarce resources necessarily impinge upon the quality of life which is provided for prisoners. We recognise too that reorganisation of existing facilities and services takes time. Many of the above guidelines could not be applied immediately to all prisoners. In the case of some prisoners facilities may have to remain at the existing level of provision for the foreseeable future. However, where this is the case the reasons for any shortcomings in the quality of life should be explained, and a timetable given for their rectification.

If the prison system were re-oriented, as we believe it should be, towards the principles of the minimum use of custody, the minimum use of security, and the normalisation of the prison, at least two sets of problems would remain. The first would relate to the appropriate forms of organisation at headquarters, regional and local levels. Such matters formed an important part of the remit of the May Committee, charged as it was with making recommendations to resolve a crisis of morale and industrial relations within the prison service. These problems are discussed by Dr Thomas in chapter 5. The second would relate to monitoring the work of the prison system within the broader context of the operation of a criminal justice system in a democratic society. The problems here involve striking a proper balance between the rights of the individual prisoner and the needs of the authorities to run a well ordered and disciplined prison system. Above all, since the prison constitutes the most stringent test of the proper use of power, it involves an examination of safeguards that would be sufficient to maintain a high degree of public confidence in the activities of the prison service. These issues are discussed by Professor Martin in chapter 6.

2 Minimum use of custody: controlling the prison population

The May Committee was *not* asked 'to examine and make recommendations' on 'the size and nature of the prison population'. But it *was* required to *have regard* to 'the size and nature of the prison population, and the capacity of the prison services to accommodate it' in making its examination of, and recommendations on, all the other matters that were within its brief (May, 1979, pp iii-iv). There was never any doubt, therefore, that the assumptions made concerning the future size of the prison population, as well as its changing composition, would be fundamental to the Committee's deliberations, and ultimately to its conclusions, about resources, staffing, organisation structure and the rest. Indeed it was the May Committee's handling of this issue which coloured everything else in the Report.

In the discussion which follows we shall be concerned to review four questions about the prison population. First, what was the nature of the evidence given to the May Committee? Second, what was the quality of the Home Office population forecasts? Third, what did the May Committee make of the evidence before them? Fourth, how might the Committee have interpreted its task? Central to all these questions, of course, is the curious nature of the Inquiry's terms of reference. In a concluding section we pose a fifth question. What, in the light of the May Report, now needs to be done if the prison population is to be controlled?

Evidence to the May Committee

A review of the evidence submitted to Mr Justice May by prison staff and outside groups reveals three types of response to the rather oblique role played by the 'size and nature of the prison population', in the Committee's terms of reference.

First, there was the technocratic or *management* stance. This was typical of the written submissions from most of the associations representing prison staff. The approach tended to ignore the detail of the May Committee's terms of reference and to treat the prison population in a relatively neutral fashion, as simply one factor in a larger equation which it was the Committee's task to solve. The argument generally took the following form. There is a mis-match between the tasks of the prison service and the resources provided. The prison population has risen without a commensurate increase in resources. Insofar as most, though not all, of the tasks of the prison service are directly related to the size of the prison population, there are two ways of bringing tasks and resources into line. Either tasks must be reduced, which effectively means that the prison population must be reduced, or resources increased. Population reduction or control was cited as a possible solution in several submissions. The Prison and Borstal Governors' Branch of the Society of Civil and Public Servants reiterated their suggestion, previously offered to the House of Commons Expenditure Committee in February 1978, 'that there should be restrictions on the powers of the courts to commit to prisons without first finding a vacancy' (SCPS, Evidence, para 9). The Prison Officers' Association proposed, albeit as a measure designed to provide incentives for prisoner compliance rather than population reduction, that the period of remission should be increased from one third to one half (POA, Evidence, p.143). However, no weight was attached to these management strategies. Indeed the recently reformed British Association of Prison Governors argued that further reductions in the use of custodial sentences was 'a matter for political judgement' and took the view that, given the increase in serious crime, 'the acceptability of a reduction in sentence lengths is therefore doubtful' (BAPG, Evidence, pp 4-5). In terms of the attention given to different arguments, the staff emphasis, despite the use of ostensibly impartial technical language, was decidedly in favour of the increased resources solution. For example, the Prison Governors' Branch stressed the connection between the high prison population, resource deficiency and other aspects of the Committee's terms of reference:

> When tasks and resources are hopelessly out of balance, it is extremely difficult to ensure the effectiveness of the organisation. It is also extremely difficult to hold management accountable at all levels. It follows that if the Inquiry wishes to reinforce the principle of accountable management, the present imbalance between tasks and resources must be rectified (SCPS, Evidence, para 10).

The Association of First Division Civil Servants echoed these sentiments.

> Major strains are placed on any administrative structure if it is required repeatedly to adjust its performance to meet an increasing workload and is given no scope either to reduce that load or to increase its resources (FDCS, Evidence, p.1).

Indeed so forcibly was the resources argument pressed that the prison staff groups created the impression that population reduction, even if it was politically feasible, could scarcely counterbalance the cumulative legacy of resource deprivation. We do not accept these arguments regarding resources but for the present we wish only to point out that the managerial posture adopted by representatives of prison staff treated the prison population of the future as a minor theme in a larger resources picture. We will analyse these assumptions concerning resources in chapter 4.

Secondly, and in contrast to the submissions from prison staff, the penal pressure groups adopted a *normative* position regarding the population issue. These contributors exhibited varying degrees of sophistication in interpreting the Committee's terms of reference. However, so concerted was their view that the prison population *ought* to be reduced, that they urged the Committee to make the most of their opportunities and to recommend bold initiatives for population reduction. These groups were heavily committed to a particular imprisonment policy. They took, in public at least, an optimistic view of the Committee's capacity and willingness to act as a vehicle for promoting that policy and sought to add weight to their approach by pointing out its expediency for resources. Thus, though the NACRO submission began by accepting Mr Justice May's announcement that his Committee was not empowered to review sentencing policy, it nevertheless went on to devote three pages to reasons and methods for reducing the prison population including changes in the sentencing powers and policies of the courts (NACRO, Evidence, paras 4-11). The assumption underpinning the NACRO submission seems to have been that the May Committee might *promote* the policy initiatives which would achieve population reduction by stating a general argument for the need to make prison places a scarce resource; to ration the use of imprisonment. Both the Howard League and NACRO sought to make this general review more likely by urging the Committee to think hard and long and to resist the pressures to report quickly. NACRO suggested that the decks might be cleared by means of an interim report in March 1979 (the date Merlyn Rees had suggested for the final report) thereby permitting a more thorough review of the long term population question.

Other groups concerned with penal policy were less circumspect concerning the constitution of the Inquiry and the part which Mr Justice May might play in achieving the solution of population reduction. Several were content to send in written submissions stating the imprisonment policy to which they were wedded, and urging the Committee to accept their arguments and to translate them into reality.

Thus the Haldane Society of Socialist Lawyers simply claimed that 'the prison population can and should be cut by half over the next five years' and set out the different ways in which this goal could be achieved (Haldane Society, Evidence, p.1); and the trustees of the Cadbury Trust submitted the interim report of a research project into the population of Birmingham Prison (Wilkins, 1979), claiming to show how men are needlessly imprisoned, and hoped that 'the Committee of Inquiry will see its way to making recommendations concerning relevant legislation and court procedures which will reduce the numbers of people given short sentences of imprisonment' (Cadbury Trust, Evidence, para vii).

The third and smallest group of contributors (for many written submissions made no reference at all to the size or composition of the prison population), adopted a more militant and, as subsequent events have demonstrated, a more accurate *political* assessment. They analysed the May Committee's population brief and sought to predict the manner in which the Committee would interpret that brief. The opening line of the NCCL evidence sought to persuade Mr Justice May that 'the crisis which has led to the setting up of this Inquiry is wider than your terms of reference might suggest', and went on to argue that an Inquiry conceived in haste and overshadowed by industrial action reflected 'a woeful way of running the prisons'. But, more significantly, NCCL suggested that if the Inquiry's terms of reference precluded consideration of 'the need for radical and drastic alternative sentencing programmes, both as an expedient to reduce immediate overcrowding and, more importantly, as a desirable end in themselves' then they concluded that the Committee's brief was too narrow to achieve the proper object of such an Inquiry' (NCCL, Evidence, p.1). Nevertheless, as far as NCCL were concerned there was scope for the May Committee to grasp aspects of the population nettle: whatever the implied constraints, NCCL's reading of the terms of reference suggested that it *was* open to the Inquiry 'to range widely into questions such as the suitability of types of custody in certain classes of case' (p.2). PROP, the National Prisoners' Movement, took a similar but, if anything, more sceptical view. In their evidence they complained that the Inquiry, by virtue of its restricted terms of reference, had been presented with a set of questions which were largely irrelevant to the problems confronting the prison system. The real issue, they asserted, concerned the use of imprisonment as a sentence and they pressed 'in the strongest terms, for a drastic reduction in the prison population and in the length of sentences' (PROP, Evidence, p.3). However, though they were encouraged to note that other bodies had flouted the Committee's terms of reference, and though they hoped the Committee would address themselves to the 'real issues', they were nevertheless resigned to the fact that growth of the prison system had been virtually built-in to the Inquiry's constitution. 'By continually stressing overcrowding' and, by implication, resources deprivation, PROP claimed that the Home Office and 'its propagandists are preparing public opinion for the financing of an accelerated programme of prison building. It is the logical response to a problem identified in such restricted terms' (pp 1-4). We return to this theme in our discussion of resources in chapter 4. However, it is worth noting at this stage that, whatever interpretation the Committee *might* have put on their terms of reference, the PROP prediction of a built-in expansionist outcome to the May Inquiry has proved to be wholly justified.

Whether optimistic or pessimistic about the May Committee's capacity and willingness to change the size of the future prison population, the written submissions of most external contributors canvassed very similar strategies for achieving their object. Drawing on the 1977 Interim Report of the Advisory Council on the Penal System on *The Length of Prison Sentences*, they argued that prison sentences should be significantly shorter. It was generally agreed that complex issues were raised by the need to reduce sentence lengths and that it would undoubtedly take some time before whatever measures were adopted made an impact on the prison population. Most contributors were content to state the arguments on this question and leave the solution to the May Committee. Thus NACRO argued that since the evidence suggested that longer sentences were 'no more effective in influencing the subsequent behaviour of offenders than short ones' (see Brody, 1976), then there were 'few arguments to support the imposition of long sentences when there is not a clear need to protect the public' (NACRO, Evidence, p.3). By pointing to the fact that 83 per cent of all persons received into prison under sentence in 1977 had been sentenced for offences *other* than violence against the person, a sexual offence or robbery, NACRO clearly took the view that the scope for reduction was considerable.

However, the penal pressure groups also pointed to measures which, they contended, were more straightforward and would have a more immediate effect on the size of the prison population. The Society of Friends, among others, proposed that certain offences — drunkenness, possession of some drugs, offences under the Vagrancy Acts, soliciting and petty theft — be made non-imprisonable (Society of Friends, Evidence, p.1). The Haldane Society, approaching the same question from a different angle, argued that no person should be imprisoned for any offence which did not carry the right of jury trial and contended that though 'it may be necessary to retain some coercive powers for refusal to comply with reasonable orders of the court . . . in general terms prison should only be a matter for the Crown Court' (Haldane Society, Evidence, p.4). Although all contributors agreed that coercive imprisonment would have to be retained for *refusal* to meet certain community responsibilities — fine and maintenance payments — there was substantial agreement that current legislation and court practice resulted in the excessive use of imprisonment for persons whose failure to pay owed more to want of means than refusal. NCCL pointed to the fact that of 16,040 fine defaulters received into prison in 1977, no fewer than 2,256 were in default of fines for drunkenness. This implicit reference to lack of means was corroborated by the research findings submitted by the Cadbury Trust (Cadbury Trust, Evidence; Wilkins, 1979). In a similar vein a number of written submissions suggested that despite the changes introduced by the 1976 Bail Act, many persons were needlessly remanded in custody prior to conviction or sentence who could and should receive bail. NCCL argued that the presumption of bail should be strengthened by making it an unqualified right for all persons charged with a non-imprisonable offence; that in the case of imprisonable offences tried summarily there should be a right to bail except for persons who had previously absconded and were likely to do so again; and that 'no person should be remanded in custody for social inquiry and medical reports unless a social worker or medical practitioner certifies that it is necessary' (NCCL, Evidence, pp 9-10).

Moving closer to the area within which the May Committee might have exercised more direct influence, the penal reform groups pointed out that though the Home Office is *largely* captive to the sentencing decisions of the courts it is not *without* control over the size of the population with which it has to deal. Reference was made to the way in which Borstal training, technically a partially open-ended sentence in which release from custody depends on the response of the trainee, has in practice become a determinate and even shorter sentence as overcrowding has made increased throughput administratively convenient. The Howard League argued that this expedient should be pushed further (Howard League, Evidence, p.1). Similar precedents were found in the use of remission and parole. Like several other contributors, NACRO suggested that remission could be increased from one third to one half of the original sentence and pointed out that this measure had already been introduced in junior detention centres and in Northern Ireland (NACRO, Evidence, p.4). Several submissions proposed that the scope of parole should be widened and the criteria for granting it relaxed. The Howard League also pressed for the extension of several existing schemes which, they claimed, would ease the pressure on bed spaces or workshop and other facilities. Home leave, for example, could become an entitlement; the Hollesley Bay Borstal hostel scheme could be extended; and the pre-release employment scheme, introduced in 1953, could be developed on a scale that Prison Department seemed unwilling to contemplate (Howard League, Evidence, pp 1-2). Many of these strategies, their proponents argued, could be employed by the executive, without resort to extensive consultation or legislation. They would bring immediate benefit in reducing the size of the prison population.

In the face of this considerable volume of prescriptive evidence, on aspects of the prison population which Mr Justice May had argued were really outside the Committee's terms of reference, the May Report somewhat illogically devoted a considerable proportion of its chapter on 'The Prison Populations' to an examination of 'ways in which the populations might be reduced'. But before considering the Committee's analysis of this question we must first review the most detailed and apparently authoritative population evidence available to the Inquiry: that from the Home Office.

The Home Office population forecasts

Whereas the population evidence from external contributors was prescriptive and forward looking, that from the Home Office was predominantly descriptive and historical. It was also brief: nine pages. Although six pages were accounted for by fourteen tables and graphs, only two of these included population projections. It may seem contradictory to describe a paper, half of which was sub-titled 'the future', as historical in its emphasis. But the contradiction is more apparent than real. In order that we may establish an argument, which we shall develop later, it may be appropriate to make some general observations about forecasting techniques before explaining the nature of the Home Office evidence.

Most forecasts involve no more than the *extrapolation* of an existing trend or trends. The assumption is made that the factors underpinning existing behaviour will remain the same and that changes evident from the records of recent years will continue in the same direction and at a similar rate, or rate of change, in the future. Extrapolation may be more or less naive. Methods are available which permit the values of interrelated variables to be estimated and for establishing underlying movements in situations where the data fluctuate. But no matter how sophisticated the mathematical techniques employed, the assumptions remain relatively crude. In so far as they assume that the *status quo* will continue largely unchanged, it follows that extrapolation forecasts reflect essentially conservative views of the world; and since the world *does* change, then the longer-term the forecasts are, the less accurate they are likely to be.

A second approach is generally termed *scenario* forecasting. In this case the purpose is to examine a hypothetical situation; to examine the probable consequence of some change or event which is *not* evident from existing trends. The change may comprise some catastrophe, for example, or a scientific invention or a political initiative. The distinction between straightforward extrapolation and scenario forecasting is relative rather than fundamental. For scenario forecasting rests upon the assumption that most variables other than the nominated stimulus or stimuli will behave very much as they do at present. But though extrapolation remains the basis of scenario forecasting it is, by definition, a less conservative technique in the sense that predicted or planned change is incorporated into the very nature of the exercise. However, we must be clear that where forecasts, of whatever type, are used as the foundation for policy formation, they are never the value-free, scientific tools their advocates sometimes suggest (Miles and Irvine, 1979). Forecasts always tell us more about the present, or more accurately the past, than they do about the future. Existing trends reflect past and present priorities and choices. Extrapolating those trends is not to portray, in a non-political fashion, a pattern of behaviour over which we have no control. Rather it portrays the continuation of past and present political choices. If those extrapolations become the basis of future resource allocation then, to a greater or lesser extent, the perpetuation of those choices becomes a self-fulfilling prophecy.

For present purposes perhaps the crucial distinction between extrapolative forecasting and scenario forecasting is that the former tends to be 'policy blind' in that it disregards alternative policy choices, whereas the latter tries to be 'policy informed' and sets out to take policy choices into account. A good example of attempted policy informed scenario forecasting is in the recent study carried out for the United States Department of Justice, *Prison Population and Policy Choices* (Abt Associates, 1977).

The Home Office population evidence to the May Committee was divided into two parts. The first described the present composition of the prison population and the second comprised a forecast of the population to 1982. Because the material in the first part will be well known to persons familiar with the annual reports of Prison Department and other Home Office publications we need do no more than briefly summarise it here. The average daily prison population consists largely of males (97 per cent) and of persons sentenced to an immediate custodial sentence (83 per cent). The majority (61 per cent) of these offenders are sentenced for property offences. The average number of persons in custody has, except in the immediate aftermath of new legislation, risen fairly steadily since 1945 and this rise reflects both an increase in the number of persons received and the average length of time for which they are held. In fact the *proportion* of persons receiving custodial sentences has fallen during the same period but the increase in the *number* of persons convicted has been sufficient to produce a real rise in prison receptions. The contribution of longer sentences is reflected in the fact that whereas there was a one-and-a half-fold increase in the average daily prison *population* between 1947 and 1977, the number of sentenced prisoners *received* rose by only one fifth. During these years the number of fine defaulters received increased five-fold and the number of unconvicted prisoners received on remand increased more than three-fold. The average length of sentences *imposed* by the courts increased by three-fifths between 1947 and 1977 though the increase in the length of sentences *served* was rather less because of the introduction of parole in 1967 and other factors.

Because of 'marked differences in the growth in the numbers of receptions and of the prison population in different categories' the Home Office population forecast was produced by adding the forecasts made for each of the prisoner groups referred to above (Home Office, Evidence, vol.I paper IIC1, para 12). In each case the forecast comprised a simple extrapolation of existing trends, though sometimes it was 'adjusted for the effect of any changes which are known and likely to affect the figures' (para 12). The general assumption underpinning the forecasts was that the *status quo*, including current trends, would be maintained; and there would be a steady increase in the number of persons coming before the courts and that organisational factors and sentencing practice would continue unchanged. Thus it was tentatively assumed that the working of the 1976 Bail Act would marginally reduce the proportion of defendants remanded in custody, but that this would be offset by the increased number of defendants coming before the courts and so prison receptions for this group would remain steady. The numbers of remand prisoners in the population, however, would continue to rise because the length of time spent in custody before trial was 'predicted' to continue increasing. In this example, as in other sections of the forecast, what is really of interest is the way in which past policy decisions or anticipated policy decisions are allowed to masquerade as 'trends'. For the projected rise in the remand population presumably reflects a decision *not* to increase the number of courts or court personnel which might reduce the time spent awaiting trial.

In most sections of the forecast the important *status quo* assumptions were those concerning sentencing and Home Office release policies. Thus it was assumed that the proportion of adult males receiving custodial sentences would continue to fall but that the reverse would be true in the case of male offenders aged 14-16 years. Nowhere in the forecast was any allowance made for proposed or planned changes in release policy, either with regard to remission periods or the easing of parole criteria. Nor was there any reference to these aspects of executive policy. The largest projected increase (24 per cent) was in the number of female prisoners and the overall forecast was of a 3½ per cent rise in the total prison population from 41,570 in 1977 to 43,000 in 1982 (a figure reached, in fact, early in 1980).

There are three points which ought to be made about the Home Office population forecast before we consider what the May Committee made of it. First, it was submitted to the Committee at a relatively early stage in the Inquiry, February 1979. Had the Committee so wished, there was ample time to digest the data, to request supplementary evidence, and for that additional evidence to be provided. Secondly, the evidence was almost exclusively limited to extrapolations. Only two changes not already reflected in current trends were allowed for. One was the hypothesised impact of the 1976 Bail Act already referred to. The other concerned the detention centre population. It was assumed that sentences of detention would continue to increase in number but would not be allowed to exceed the accommodation available: the effect of this limitation in holding down the detention centre population was said to be small (para 16). Thirdly, it seems to follow that in February 1979 at least, the Government had no plans whatsoever for any policy — in policing, criminal law, sentencing powers, or the administration of the penal system — which the Home Office considered would have any impact on the numbers of persons held in custody during the period to 1982. Had there been tentative plans for such policy initiatives there would have been no reason to omit them out of deference to the Committee's deliberations for, as Mr Justice May had already agreed, recommendations regarding such matters were not within the Committee's terms of reference.

The May Committee's interpretation of the evidence

Because of the tensions implicit in the May Committee's terms of reference it was to be expected that criticisms of its findings would focus on the manner in which it dealt with the population issue. In that sense the critical tone in what follows is unsurprising. But we should make it clear that our criticisms of the May Committee do not arise simply because it came to the wrong conclusions on the basis of the evidence before it — though in several instances we consider that to be the case. Nor even because it failed to make what might have been made of its terms of reference. Rather, our major criticism is that the Committee vacillated over its terms of reference and that, as a direct consequence, chapter 3 of the Report, on 'The Prison Populations' is a confused muddle of contradictory statements, of viewpoints half-stated, of connections implied but not made and finally, of indecision as to the proper direction of future policy. We will first try to substantiate these charges before considering the reasons for, and the consequences of, the Committee's findings.

A strictly legalistic view of the Inquiry's terms of reference would be that since the Committee was *not* actually asked to examine and make recommendations on 'the size and nature of the prison population, and the capacity of the prison service to accommodate it', but only to have regard to these factors, then it was no part of the Committee's task to take up any position on the questions as to who, or how many persons, should be in prison. Rather, the Committee should simply have taken note of the present prison population and the estimates of its probable future size and composition. The gaps in resources for dealing with that population — accommodation, facilities, expertise and the like — would then have led to recommendations about what additional resources, if any, should be made available. This is not an interpretation which would have appealed to most of those who gave evidence to the Committee, but it would have had the virtue of logical consistency. Readers of the May Report could even be forgiven for thinking that this is just what the Committee did. After all, the chapter on population concluded with the observation that 'the population forecasts offered by the Home Department are well founded' and if anything 'more likely to underestimate than exaggerate current trends' (May, 1979, para 3.69). The Committee certainly went on to use them as the basis for recommending a massive prison building programme in its subsequent examination of resources. But in fact the Committee accepted the Home Office forecasts as the basis for its discussion of resources having *first* engaged in what purported to be a review of the scope for population reduction.

Technically the May Committee did in relation to the prison population what the penal pressure groups had wanted it to do: it departed from the letter of its terms of reference. As we have already seen in chapter 1 the Committee acted similarly in relation to Rule One of the Prison Rules. Its brief specified that it should have regard to 'the responsibilities of the prison services for the security, control and treatment of inmates'. In effect its task was to assess the adequacy of resources for the realisation of the Prison Rules as laid down by Parliament and not to recommend the reformulation of those Rules as it did. However, in the same way that we argued that the Committee's concept of 'positive custody' was little more than 'treatment and training' refurbished, so the Committee's ostensible departure from its terms of reference in relation to the prison population led it to the conclusion that present trends are, at least in the short term, immutable.

In its discussion of the prison population the May Committee takes two rather different stances which it does not seem to realise are contradictory. On the one hand crime rates, sentencing decisions, prison receptions and the like are treated as though they are the products of external social forces over which no control is possible. This impression of a wholly apolitical penal policy is imperceptibly built up as the past is merged, through the population projections, into the future. Thus, in introducing a description of prison population trends since 1945 (almost entirely a recapitulation of the Home Office evidence to which we have already referred), the May Report blandly suggests that the significant increase '*reflects* . . . the post war rise in crime' (para 3.4). Or later, noting that the decline in the proportionate use of imprisonment has exhibited a modest reversal since 1975, the Committee concludes that this 'suggests that *trends* towards reducing the use of custodial sentences are now exhausted' (para 3.7). And, most tellingly, at the end of their population chapter Mr Justice May and his colleagues accept the Home Office projections on the basis that they represent the current '*penal momentum*' (para 3.69) (our emphasis throughout). In these sections the reader is shown a purely mechanical relationship between criminal behaviour and sentencing policy. It is as if the past had not been determined, and the future could not be determined, by human will at all. Thus the further use of non-custodial options in dealing with crime is spoken of in negative terms analogous to a debate on energy policy in which there are said to be finite and exhaustible supplies of coal and gas. The forecast is not unlike a weather forecast: the 'penal momentum' the equivalent of a cold front moving in from the Atlantic.

On the other hand, the May Committee seemed to be well aware that the size and composition of the prison population *is* partly a matter of choice. For example, the Report noted that the population in detention centres had been determined by the availability of accommodation and increases in remission — from one sixth to one third in

1968 and, in junior centres, from one third to one half in 1975 — at least as much as by alleged increases in criminality. Moreover, the Committee evidently agreed that too many persons are in custody and for too long, and recommended the removal or diversion of some categories of offenders. Thus the Committee was 'unanimous and emphatic' in endorsing the conclusions of the Advisory Council on the Penal System:

> that a large number of sentences of imprisonment passed by the courts, especially the short and medium term band of sentences, are longer than they need be, in the interest either of society or of the offender (ACPS, 1977, para 3, quoted in May, 1979, paras 3.63-4).

The Committee asserted that 'Dutch and Scandinavian experience demonstrates that civilised society can co-exist with significantly lower sentencing tariffs' and hoped that the proposals of the 1978 Advisory Council Report 'would be acted upon by the courts now as far as possible and, ultimately, by Parliament' (paras 3.64-5).

In relation to other segments of the prison population the Committee were categorical in stating population policy objectives. Although, according to Home Office evidence, only five or six hundred, out of forty-two thousand prisoners, are said to be capable of benefiting from psychiatric hospital care, the May Report was highly critical of the lack of commitment represented by repeated failures to remove these prisoners to NHS hospitals (paras 3.35-44). Having castigated the health service for failing 'to measure up to its responsibilities' the Committee was unequivocal about the solution:

> We think the best way to achieve change is for the DHSS to press regional health authorities as a matter of priority to bring to fruition plans already made and to continue to press them until success crowns their efforts after so many years (para 3.43).

Since this is no more than an endorsement of existing policy it may be argued that it is scarcely an example of the May Committee adopting a prescriptive posture on a population question. But in relation to drunken offenders the May Committee specifically recommended a policy which, for want of financial support, exists in only experimental form and, at the time of writing, looks as if it may be scrapped entirely. The Committee took the view that the existence of only two detoxification centres, and those currently threatened, indicated a need for 'greater determination' in 'developing alternative disposals' to custody for drunken offenders:

> We think that voluntary endeavour could play a substantial part in this area, provided that grants from government to start and

maintain such schemes were made available. We recommend that the DHSS should do so: relatively speaking the sums needed would not be large (para 3.45).

Occasionally these two stances are brought face to face. The reader is drawn beyond the terms-of-reference-boundary, given a glimpse of the prescriptive promised land and then, in the next sentence or paragraph, dragged back to the automated trends. Take, for example, the question of remands on bail or in custody. The Committee expressed concern over the dramatic increase in the number of remand prisoners since 1945 and the fact

> that as many as 44 per cent of those remanded in custody do not receive an immediate sentence of imprisonment and, further, that remand periods in England and Wales are frequently excessively long and have generally been increasing (para 3.66).

It was also disturbed to note that though the immediate effect of the Bail Act 1976 seemed to have been a reduction in the percentage of persons committed for trial in custody this had not been sustained in 1978: 'we hope this does not represent a new trend and that no effort will be spared to minimise custodial remand in future' (para 3.66). Points of possible effort were highlighted. The growth of bail hostels was commended and, as a way 'of doing everything possible to bring defendants remanded in custody to trial as soon as possible', the Committee wondered whether the Scottish legal requirement that all persons remanded in custody must be brought to trial within one hundred and ten days might be copied in England and Wales. But the Home Office comment 'that a mere statutory requirement without the simultaneous provision of court and judicial resources to respond to it would achieve nothing' seems to have been sufficient to nullify the thought and the Committee lamely concludes that 'the scope for less remand in custody may, at least for the moment, be exhausted' (paras 3.68-9). In the very next sentence the 'penal momentum' and the Home Office population projections which, as we have seen, assume even longer remand periods in custody, are accepted as the resource planning base.

Had the May Committee stuck resolutely to its terms of reference it would have been disappointing but, as we have argued, logical. As it is, we are presented with a Report which describes, quite misleadingly and damagingly, the worst of all worlds. There is the *appearance* of a discussion on the scope for population reduction but this is allied to a predicted increase in that population. The impression left is not that these matters lay outside the Committee's remit, but that there *is* little or no scope for reduction. The danger now is that when population questions are raised in the future it may be claimed that Mr Justice May dealt with them. He did not.

What the May Committee might have done

We are by no means unmindful of the urgent response required by the events leading up to the May Inquiry. In our view the pressure over industrial relations might best have been alleviated by the publication of an interim report. However, accepting the approach and timing which the Committee adopted, there are a number of fundamental points which it should have recognised and which it had a duty, even within a strict interpretation of its terms of reference, to state in unequivocal terms. First, the size and composition of the prison population *is* a matter of choice. It happens neither by chance nor is it the product of forces over which the government exercises little control. It may be that some of the controls are indirect and that the outcome of policy initiatives is difficult to predict, but it is misleading to suggest that the prison population is anything other than politically determined. Second, there is a trade-off between prisons and other forms of social policy expenditure. This is not to adopt the sort of simplistic financial transfer argument — one prisoner removed from prison will *not* save sufficient money for the employment of one extra probation officer — of which the penal pressure groups have been guilty in the past. Nor is it to suggest that the nature of the trade-offs can always be precisely determined. It is simply to argue that any committee *seriously* concerned to examine the scope for prison population reduction would try to take the economic, as well as the social, costs and benefits into account in evaluating different strategies. Third, the case for adopting alternative population reduction strategies needs to be well grounded. It requires an appreciation of current sentencing policy, a statement of realistic sentencing objectives, practicable disposal alternatives, and the best possible forecasts of likely effects. Lastly, no strategy for reducing the prison population is likely to succeed in the long term unless it operates at the legislative and sentencing level.

At the very least the May Committee could and should have laid these facts on the line, placed the choices squarely before the Government and the public, and stated quite clearly the tasks that remained to be done. Instead, the Committee chose a compromise path. It breached its terms of reference and began to undertake an investigation which, however necessary we may think it, the Minister had not requested of it and which it had neither the time nor the expertise to carry out. Indeed, as we will argue, it did not even have the appropriate evidence before it. We sympathise with the Committee in the dilemma it must have faced. Despite the unanimity of its final report we suspect that there may have been considerable debate within the group, about the proper scope of the Committee's remit to review the prison population as well as other issues. Nevertheless, and paradoxical though it may seem, the further the May Committee breached its terms of reference, the more it managed to cloud the issues which, no doubt, had prompted the breach in the first place.

We have already noted the confused picture which the Committee conveyed as to the determination of the prison population. Several options for population reduction were briefly discussed which involved the redirection of certain offenders, the development of non-custodial alternatives, executive intervention and changes in sentencing and remand practice. But in almost all cases the Committee was concerned to point out disadvantages and uncertainties as to the outcome. The overall result was one of general pessimism and indecision, and the reader was left unclear as to whether the paucity of recommendations had been dictated by the Committee's restricted terms of reference or its negative appraisal of the available options. The Committee's concluding remarks seemed to suggest the latter.

> Although everyone who comes to it for the first time may think so, in fact none of this ground is new. Redirection is in principle desirable, especially for mentally disordered offenders, but will not be productive of much relief to present population levels either by itself or in respect of other groups. New non-custodial disposals are highly desirable, but only where they can be calculated not ultimately to make the problems of prisons worse. Executive intervention is available, but chiefly perhaps to cope with a condition of actual as opposed to imminent crisis. The result of changed sentencing practice can only be realised over a long period and without predictable population effects (para 3.69).

Its conclusion was that the prison population must be expected to go on rising.

Two points must be made about the Committee's review. First, it was a review of only *some* of the options. With the important exception of its endorsement of the Advisory Council recommendations the Committee made no reference to the various proposals for new criminal law legislation which, whatever the original object, might have an impact upon the size and composition of the prison population. Several of these proposals, as we noted earlier in this chapter, were discussed in evidence submitted to the May Committee. For example, there is no

56

reference in the May Report to the possibility that certain offences might be decriminalised, cease to be imprisonable, or cease to be imprisonable if tried summarily. Nor is there any suggestion that the short-comings of the 1976 Bail Act, might be removed by a new, and tighter, Bail Act as NCCL proposed (NCCL, Evidence, pp 9-10). No discussion of the scope for population reduction which failed to include these possibilities can reasonably claim to be adequate.

Secondly, the Committee's review appears to have been conducted without the benefit of any systematic evidence or technical support. No doubt the penal pressure groups, those most anxious to press the case for population reduction, would have backed their arguments with very much more detailed evidence had they considered it likely that the May Committee would have taken such matters seriously. And the Home Office, as we have noted, presented no written evidence at all on the scope for reduction. It seems likely that during the course of oral evidence members of the Department were invited to offer their opinion as to the possible impact of adopting various alternative strategies. We imagine, to take but one example, that the Committee's reference to the fact that the creation of detoxification centres may 'only encourage greater police involvement without decreasing the involvement of the criminal justice system as a whole' (para 3.48), may have been the product of just such an *ad hoc* process, for nowhere is this point pursued in the written evidence. Nor did the Committee request the Home Office to provide what we have called *scenario* forecasts that would have taken *different* assumptions into account, despite the fact that there was ample time for them to have done so. The Home Office population paper was completed in February, and other papers *requested* by the Committee on matters as urgent as staff working conditions were not received until May 1979.

Of course, it will be argued that scenario forecasts take time to prepare and, at the end of the day, are of limited value. We accept that it would not have been possible for the Home Office to develop sophisticated estimates of the impact of all the possible options. And the May Committee hardly had the expertise to specify the alternatives, or priorities among them. But one might have expected that the Home Office, as part of its normal long-term planning arrangements, would have undertaken some such exercises in the past, and that these could have been brought forward in evidence. In any event it was certainly open to Mr Justice May to suggest that scenario forecasting *should* be carried out if the Government were to make well informed policy choices. And there was absolutely no reason why the Committee should not have sought detailed estimates of the population and expenditure implications of those options which it *did* consider.

The fact that the Prison Medical Service had, unsolicited, provided figures on the number of prisoners likely to benefit from psychiatric hospital care enabled the Committee to conclude that even were such prisoners removed to NHS hospitals this would do no more than dent the overall prison population. But there were no similar figures to assess, for example, the consequences of increasing remission from one third to one half; of counting pre-sentence custody as part of Borstal training and of further reducing the average length of that sentence; of making prisoners eligible for parole at an earlier stage in their sentence; of easing the release criteria on parole; or of adopting the Scottish provision for a maximum custodial remand of one hundred and ten days. Although estimates could have been made speedily from existing Prison Department data, the Committee did not even ask for them. We fully recognise that estimates of the short-term impact of these strategies could scarcely be described as scenario forecasts. A sophisticated forecast, to take the parole or remission examples, would need to gauge the likelihood of courts discounting their effect by passing longer sentences. But we would contend that any estimates, however short-term or crude, would have better enabled the readers of the May Report to assess the potential for population reduction of the strategies reviewed. Certainly they could have been set against the quite arbitrary selection of possible disadvantages to which the Committee made reference.

Much the same deficiencies are to be found throughout the May Committee's discussions of finance. In chapter 4 we will have more to say on the implications of the May Committee's recommendation that current overcrowding, and a projected population increase, should be absorbed by a massive prison building programme. We think, and certainly hope, that successive governments will *not* be prepared to spend the sums suggested. But whatever the case there is something strangely illogical about the May Committee's assumption that governments should give a relatively free hand to prisons expenditure but will inevitably hold back spending on other, closely related services. The Committee contended that prisons expenditure is a special case when it comes to restrictions on spending in the social services: in its view the same limitations should not apply to prisons because they are the last line of defence against disruptive forces (May, 1979, paras 6.94-100). This argument would be more convincing if the Committee really believed that all those persons currently held in prisons needed actually to be there for the protection of the public. But, as we have seen, this is not the case. In fact the Committee had already concluded that certain categories of offenders would be better dealt with by other services. And it had endorsed the general argument of the Advisory Council on the Penal System for a lowering of tariffs.

Yet, by accepting an embargo on extra spending elsewhere, the Committee seems at once to deny that other services have a function in preventing crime or protecting the public, and to ignore the *relationship* between spending on these services and spending on prisons. Thus, when discussing the probation service, important for both the operation of non-custodial alternatives to imprisonment (community service as well as probation orders) and the supervision of prisoners released on parole, the Committee concluded 'we understand . . . that there are no large scale resources available for such a shift back to the probation order' (para 3.51). In this context it is worth pointing out that the annual increase in capital expenditure on prisons recommended by the May Committee, £25 million, represents one third of the total amount spend annually on the probation service! Nor should it go unnoticed that whereas the May Committee was happy to recommend the compulsory purchase of land for new prisons, they simply noted that 'an expansion (of probation hostels and day training centres) would seem desirable but, again, they seem expensive facilities and they are difficult to establish in the face of resistance from the local community' (para 3.52). Increased, but undefined, costs were also presented as an objection to any expansion of the parole scheme (para 3.61) and it was argued that a statutory limitation on the length of custodial remands would achieve nothing because 'the simultaneous provision of court and judicial resources to respond to it' would presumably not be forthcoming (para 3.68). No estimate was made of the obvious expenditure trade-offs in *any* of these examples.

Lest we be misunderstood, let us make it clear that we are not arguing that the May Committee should have undertaken the task of forecasting the implications of alternative penal strategies for population reduction or finance. Had the Committee kept to its terms of reference all that would have been required was an indication of the proper basis on which informed penal policy choices ought to be made. But having decided to go beyond its terms of reference, the Committee had an obligation either to review the population question systematically — and that would have meant calling a great deal more evidence — or to admit that they did not have the time, the expertise or the resources to do the job properly. Our criticism of the May Committee is that it did neither of those things. The question now is how can progress best be made on these tasks?

Developing a prison population policy

The May Committee's excursions into possible ways of reducing the prison population did not permit it to challenge the Home Office projections about the future. There is reason to think, however, that this failure resulted more from constitutional inhibitions about its terms of reference, and from lack of time, resources and statistical expertise, than from inclination. For there can be no doubt that the May Committee accepted the minimum use of custody principle, and believed that imprisonment 'should be used as little as possible' (May, 1979, para 4.25). In spite of the confusions to which we have alluded in its Report, the May Committee would surely welcome any policy initiatives which had a real chance of reducing the prison population.

It would have been surprising had the Committee come to any other conclusion. Surprising because we know of no statement of informed opinion suggesting anything other than that our prison population is unnecessarily large and that a substantial number of persons currently receiving custodial sentences could be adequately controlled or better treated in the community. Indeed this view has been expressed by successive Home Secretaries, by both major political parties, by the all-party House of Commons Expenditure Committee, by the Home Office, by prison governors and officers, by penal reform groups and by academic specialists. Even those groups, such as the Justices' Clerks Society, which have traditionally argued that if prisons are overcrowded then the proper response is to build more prisons, have nevertheless conceded that many petty offenders are needlessly sent to prison (Justice's Clerks, Evidence, paras 14-15). Clearly the vast majority of commentators would accept the *minimum use of custody* principle. So much is it the conventional wisdom that there is no need to argue the case further here. Nor is there any need to search for methods to reduce the prison population. A catalogue of strategies, all too familiar to the Home Office and to everyone conversant with the penal system, and many of which have been referred to earlier in this chapter, have been canvassed for several years. The problem lies in deciding on the most effective package of initiatives, for it is doubtful whether any single innovation would confer substantial or long-term benefit, and in stimulating the political will to implement it.

It seems clear to us that insufficient attention has been paid to the *process* by which prison population change can be achieved or to the *assessment* of the costs and benefits involved. Because we believe the formation of opinion to be a crucial variable it may be wise to begin with those points which we have raised in criticism of the May Committee. Too much of the discussion on the prison population has foundered for lack of basic data. Speculation as to the impact of policy innovations and the transferability of funds for the creation of community facilities is no substitute for research. The May Committee very properly exposed some of the speculation but failed to provide the evidence that would eliminate the need for further speculation.

In our view, the Home Office should give the highest priority to the development of four types of estimates. First, of the number of persons in the prison system who might be diverted from custodial disposals by one means or another. In many cases this is a simple head-counting exercise. Establishing how many persons are currently incarcerated for offences that might be de-criminalised or made non-imprisonable are of this type. Other estimates which fall under this heading, however, involve much more complex issues. A much discussed example, referred to by the May Committee, is that of the petty persistent offender. The adoption of marginally different operational definitions, in terms of the number of previous convictions and length of current sentence, can produce startlingly different results (Fairhead and Marshall, 1979). The usefulness of one definition against another very much depends upon the nature of the policy initiative intended — be it the creation of community facilities to deal with attendant social problems or sentencing guidelines — and even then the heterogeneity of prisoner characteristics is such that the impact of any innovation must be uncertain. However, the Home Office Research Unit has undertaken, or has in hand, studies which should enable estimates to be made of the numbers of prisoners with 'diversion potential', based on a variety of operational definitions (Banks and Fairhead, 1976; Fairhead and Marshall, 1979).

Secondly, the Home Office should prepare estimates of the short-term effects of what the May Committee termed executive intervention. Calculations under this heading would do no more than report the immediate consequences of, for example, counting periods spent on remand as part of the sentence to Borstal training, or increasing remission for prisoners serving determinate periods of imprisonment. The rather more gradual population consequences of advancing parole eligibility dates, or easing release criteria, should also be calculated on this simple short-term basis without speculating on the possible feedback repercussions for sentencing policy.

Thirdly, we need much more information on the budgetary implications of penal policy change. Both the May Committee and the Home Office have been at pains to point out that despite the high costs of imprisonment it is untrue, though often naively implied, that great savings are to be derived from reducing the prison population (Bailey, 1979, p.18). The Home Office has pointed out that since buildings and staff account for most of the prisons budget the marginal savings derived from having fewer prisoners is small (Home Office, 1977a, para 8). If this be the case, and we broadly accept the argument, we need to know at what point the savings become significant. To what extent does the prison population have to be reduced before it becomes feasible to think of closing establishments and reducing staff? Or, to take an example referred to earlier, how many more courts, involving what costs, have to be provided in order to achieve a significant reduction in the average duration of custodial remands? In conducting this type of exercise it should be remembered that the Home Office low marginal cost argument applies only to cut-backs in the use of *existing* facilities. And that the May Committee has argued that much *more* money should be spent on prisons to raise standards – a factor that will alter these equations if implemented. The low marginal cost argument has no relevance to the creation of *new* facilities of the sort recommended by the May Committee. Of course, if the Home Office is in fact applying the low marginal cost argument for future planning on the basis that increased use can be made of existing facilities – greater system overcrowding than currently exists – then this should be stated quite clearly. Whatever the case, we need to know more about the assumptions upon which vague statements of relative costs are made.

Finally, we consider that both Parliament and the general public would be better able to make judgements on the population issues if the Home Office were to prepare and publish scenario forecasts based on a number of alternative policy packages. Since 1945 the use of custody, as a proportion of all disposals, has fallen substantially. But it is not easy to say precisely why. The repeated assertion that imprisonment is costly and of minimal value in terms of either deterrence or rehabilitation may have been more powerful an influence than the various legislative restrictions on the powers of the courts to resort to custody. The experience of other countries suggests that the creation of a battery of non-custodial sentences is not a prerequisite for the minimum use of custody (Tulkens, 1979). Certainly the introduction of measures designed to reduce custody in the United Kingdom have had limited direct success. A few may even have been counter-productive. The proportionate use of Borstal and detention has increased since the passing of the Children and Young Persons Act, 1969; and the history of suspended sentences has been cautionary enough to inhibit the introduction of the provision for partially suspended sentences in the Criminal Law Act 1977 (Bottoms, 1977a; and Barnard and Bottoms, 1979). It would be naive to look to a single policy initiative to achieve any lasting reduction in the prison population. The issue must be tackled from several directions at once, each pressure reinforcing the others. For example, it would not do to interfere with the tariff or other sentencing powers of the courts without simultaneously increasing the credibility and availability of treatment and control facilities in the community. In this field of social policy scenario forecasts can provide only a rough guide to the long-term impact of initiatives. But if we are consciously to shape the future they have a vital educational as well as informative role. The preparation of scenarios alerts all those who plan and participate in penal policy to the likely problems. Scenarios also signal commitment for change. They are a symbolic statement of our unwillingness to be led by the nose. They cultivate the opinion that the future does not have to be like the past. In that sense they are the exact opposite of the population projections which were given to the May Committee.

Getting the information is one thing: making the right decisions is another. Although our next suggestion will almost certainly be greeted with widespread impatience, we see no alternative to the creation of another committee, this time with specific terms of reference to analyse and make recommendations on the size and composition of the prison population. We suggest that it be a small inter-departmental committee composed of civil servants from the Home Office, DHSS, and Lord Chancellor's Department. It could be supplemented by a few external experts broadly representing relevant constituencies such as the judiciary, police and voluntary organisations providing community facilities for offenders, and serviced by capable researchers and, if necessary, academic consultants. We think it reasonable to expect the committee to report within twelve months.

We sympathise with those who may argue that our proposal for yet another committee will only serve further to delay policy initiatives which are urgently required now. Nevertheless, we believe the objection to be unfounded. Our reply involves two arguments. First, there is no reason why the existence of a committee should preclude the nearly immediate adoption of limited measures designed to ease current population pressure within the prison system: such matters might be the first items on its agenda. Secondly, it should be apparent to all those acquainted with penal policy that changes of the order required to achieve long-term population reduction can only result from the creation of a policy package which involves few political, as well as economic and social costs. There is no shortage of strategies which *will* reduce the prison population. The problem is to design a strategy which is politically as well as financially cost-effective; a policy which will meet deep-seated fears and objections and which can be marketed by a Government whose manifesto had 'law and order' as a major theme.

Our proposal for an inter-departmental committee is based on the following considerations. We do not believe that the Home Office, through its internal policy planning structure, is capable of developing the intiatives we seek. After all, experience suggests that previous attempts have been too easily submerged under the exigencies to which the Home Office is peculiarly prone: the demise of the Crime Policy Planning Unit as a source of innovation is a case in point (Train, 1977, p.382). In any case the Home Office simply does not exercise operational or advisory control over all of the agencies vital to decisions to imprison. The relevance of the Lord Chancellor's Department to sentencing is self-evident. The DHSS would be involved because of the departmental wrestling match over the location of mentally abnormal offenders (Butler, 1975; May, 1979, paras 3.34-44). Moreover, its ability and willingness to finance a range of community facilities is likely to be a major factor in satisfying the courts that a non-custodial response is adequate in dealing with certain classes of offenders (see May, 1979, paras 3.47-9 on detoxification centres for example).

It may also be objected that a committee dominated by representatives of the major departments is unlikely to produce the radical initiatives for which we have argued. We accept that this is a danger but we can see no realistic alternative to the proposal outlined. A recent White Paper has generally stated the Government's objections to so-called QUANGOs and announced the abolition of the prestigious Advisory Council on the Penal System (Prime Minister, 1980). We are hopeful that the new House of Commons Select Committee on Home Affairs will follow up their precursor's excellent report on *The Reduction of Pressure on the Prison System* (Expenditure Committee, 1978); but as one of us has argued elsewhere, it is unrealistic to look to Parliamentary committees for detailed and operational policy recommendations of the sort that are to be expected from a departmental working party (Morgan and Smith, 1979; Morgan, 1979, p.25). We can only reiterate that the problem lies not in the shortage of radical ideas but rather in mobilising their acceptance by government and the major departments.

Finally, and briefly, we turn to the agenda for our proposed inter-departmental committee. Inevitably the committee would face two issues. What can be done to give immediate relief to the population pressure on the prison system; and in the longer term, which strategies offer the best prospects for a substantial programme of decarceration? In our evidence to the May Committee, and consistent with our emphasis on the justice model in chapter 1, we argued that the decision as to how long a person should spend in custody is best determined by the courts according to agreed and publicly pronounced criteria and procedures laid down by Parliament. We consider that there are great dangers attached to broadening the gap between the length of sentences passed and the length of sentences served. It not only grants excessive power to the executive, whose decisions seldom meet the standards of due process, but also invites sentencers to discount the effects of possible early release when fixing new sentences. In our judgement there is no good reason, other than political or administrative expediency, for increasing the discretion of the executive in making release decisions. However, since the prison population has reached a new peak of over 43,000 (February, 1980), it may be that the time for expediency has come. Accordingly, the first task of the inter-departmental committee would be to make immediate recommendations for modest executive intervention.

In the longer term, although it is hard to predict the consequences of new policies, it is clear that many of the standard items on the de-carceration advocate's list would only have a marginal impact on the total number of prison receptions and still less on the average daily population. This is not to suggest that initiatives be judged *solely* in terms of their numerical potential: there may be other, equally important, or more important, reasons for adopting them. For example, it is clear that there are relatively few prisoners 'in need of and capable of gaining benefit from, psychiatric hospital care' (May, 1979, para 3.39) but their removal would result in benefits far beyond the numbers involved. The prisoners might receive treatment that the prison service is ill-equipped to provide and a source of considerable tension and alleged disruption, for prisoners and staff alike, would be eliminated. A similar case can be made out for the removal of other groups of offenders, including remands and fine defaulters, who are vagrants or have problems associated with alcoholism. For these and other reasons we are in favour of:—

i.   decriminalising certain minor offences, such as drunkenness, soliciting and the possession of small quantities of marijuana;

ii.   removing the power to imprison for certain offences such as theft of less than a certain value (say £50);

iii. further restricting the power of courts to imprison for fine or maintenance default;

iv.   further restricting the power of courts to refuse bail (on the lines of the recommendations advanced by NCCL).

However, we have come to the conclusion that these measures, important though they may be, are no substitute for a major initiative involving a two-pronged attack on the size of the prison population.

Sentences must be shortened and a whole range of caring and controlling facilities created in the community.

The evidence suggests that the reason why the British prison population is so large compared to that of most other European countries lies less in the *proportion* of offenders committed to prison and more in the average *duration* of custody. Reducing the length of sentences rather than the number of committals seems to offer the greater scope for prison population relief. The House of Commons Expenditure Committee (1978) and the Advisory Council on the Penal System (1977, 1978) have both endorsed this view and in recent years the Home Office and the Lord Chancellor have urged the courts to pass shorter sentences (Home Office, 1977a). Like many others, however, we have grave doubts about the Advisory Council (1978) proposal to reduce the length of sentences on ordinary offenders by two-tier sentencing (see Radzinowicz and Hood, 1978, and Bottomley, 1979). In any case we doubt the political feasibility, at least in the short term, of any proposal involving the broad legislative revision of sentence maxima. In our judgement the best prospect for an acceptable and effective reduction of sentencing tariffs will be through the development of sentence guidelines. In essence this need involve no new mechanisms. The Lord Chief Justice already offers Practice Directions, and rules of guidance are set down in cases decided by the Court of Appeal. In principle there is no reason why the Lord Chief Justice should not be equipped with a staff so as to develop more formal guidelines (Barnard and Bottoms, 1979). Moreover, we agree with Ashworth's (1979) contention that, if there is a gap between Parliament's intentions and judicial practice, there could be no proper constitutional objection to the Government promulgating a sentencing policy in order to stimulate the emergence of practice guidelines. Were the courts to fail to respond to clear statements of Parliamentary intention then there would be no alternative but to legislate for change. As several commentators have noted, the promulgation of guidelines would not fetter the discretion of the courts; would be consistent with a justice approach; and would probably encounter less opposition amongst the judiciary and public at large than any alternative strategy (Barnard and Bottoms, 1979; Ashworth, 1979).

Last, but not least, there is the possibility of committing fewer persons to prison. The category of prisoners generally referred to as petty persistent offenders are both the most obvious and also the most intractable target for community initiatives. We doubt whether the creation of new non-custodial sentences will make inroads into this section of the custodial population. Nor does it seem appropriate for existing sentences, such as community service, to be applied to those fine defaulters and petty offenders whose long developed habits make a positive response highly unlikely. Research studies suggest that the best prospect lies in creating enough community resources to meet those basic social and physical needs — accommodation in particular — which lead so many disadvantaged offenders to seek refuge in prison; a solution in which, given the absence of alternatives, the courts understandably collude (Banks and Fairhead, 1976; Corden, Kuipers and Wilson, 1978; Fairhead and Marshall, 1979).

We conclude this chapter by repeating our main contentions. There is no disagreement about the wisdom of reducing the prison population. Nor is there any shortage of ideas on how it can be done. What is needed is a programme of action, based on informed policy choices. Because the size of the prison population is so profoundly consequential for everything else that happens in a prison system, the need is urgent. Until we have a programme of action, however, there can be little point in putting more resources into the prison service except on a short term, palliative basis. In any case much can be done to improve our prisons within existing resource levels, providing new priorities are adopted in internal Prison Department policies. It is to these matters that we turn in chapters 3 and 4.

3 Minimum use of security: a strategy for 'dangerous' prisoners

We noted in chapter 1 that the public statements of Prison Department appear to embrace the idea of the minimum use of security. Thus the 1969 White Paper, *People in Prison*, stated that all prisoners should be sent to prisons offering regimes and a degree of security appropriate to their needs (Home Office, 1969, para 171). In spite of this we consider the prison authorities to be in flagrant breach of the minimum security principle.

In one respect Prison Department is aware of the deficiency and it is a matter of official regret. Thus the Department claims that resources have not permitted the development of enough training prison places for prisoners who could be housed in semi-secure or medium-secure institutions. As a result many thousands of prisoners have to spend the duration of their sentences in overcrowded local prisons which, because they have to receive all prisoners from the courts, necessarily have to provide a degree of security higher than most of their inmates actually require. Whilst we do not accept the logic of this position, the Department can at least claim that this breach is a result of the mis-match of resources and population. In another and more important respect, however, the breach of the minimum security principle is a matter of deliberate policy. It concerns the strategy for dealing with what are conceived to be the highest security risk or 'dangerous' prisoners.

In a recent paper, Bottoms (1977) has argued that one consequence of the worldwide decline in the rehabilitative ideal has been an increased emphasis on the incapacitation of offenders and the prevention of crime (see especially Wilson, 1975). In this country, against a background of ever rising costs and a need to determine priorities, argues Bottoms, there has been a bifurcation in penal policy. On the one hand there is an attempt to isolate the 'mad' and the 'bad' as groups of dangerous offenders whose psychopathic or calculative approach to crime requires indeterminate, or at least very long, preventive sentences of imprisonment (Butler, 1975; Scottish Council on Crime, 1975; Home Office, 1976; ACPS, 1977, 1978). On the other hand are more ordinary, run of the mill offenders, for whose offences some situational explanation seems more plausible and in respect of whom society can afford to take a more lenient line, even by reducing sentences (Rees, 1976).

In fact, even when the rehabilitative ideal was most widely accepted there were preventive measures available for those who were deemed untreatable. But there is no doubt that there has been a heightened interest in the concept of dangerousness in recent years. The 'justice model' which, as we discussed in chapter 1, has come to replace a rehabilitative model in thinking about sentencing policy, can easily fall prey to a hard line 'law and order' approach because of its focus on the deeds rather than the needs of the offenders. We accept that one implication of the justice model will be that long sentences will be imposed on retrospective, retributive grounds for grave offences — though to guard against the worst excesses we would like to see the powers of the courts firmly restricted as to an upper limit. We are, however, entirely against the use of long or indeterminate sentences imposed prospectively and preventively on offenders, defined in advance as likely to be dangerous, when such sentences could not be justified by reference to the gravity of the current offence. Like Bottoms, our opposition would be on the grounds that 'dangerousness' is likely to be defined in rather arbitrary ways, and that the dangers cannot be predicted with sufficient accuracy to justify such Draconian measures. The use of preventive imprisonment has obvious dangers for civil liberties and would clearly be in breach of our minimum use of custody principle.

Nevertheless, it remains a fact that the courts have been sentencing an increasing number of offenders either to indeterminate life sentences or very long fixed terms of imprisonment. Not surprisingly prison staff and the Home Office have expressed increasing concern about the custody of 'dangerous' offenders. The concern has been expressed in two ways. One is over the problem of security: how to ensure that 'dangerous' prisoners do not escape. The other is over the problem of internal control: how to ensure that 'dangerous' prisoners do not disrupt the smooth running of prison regimes, or threaten life or property in prison. Problems of security and control are inherent to any prison system. Though the problems are analytically, and often empirically, separable, there has been a persistent tendency in this country to confuse them. In fact the security and control problems derive from different roots; and dangerous prisoners from a security point of view are not necessarily the same prisoners who constitute dangerous control problems. But because the problems have been confused, more and more prisoners are caught up in the elaborate procedures designed to ensure security in British prisons.

Ironically, in the light of Bottoms' analysis of the bifurcation tendency in sentencing policy, it is arguably the case that in the prison context the process of bifurcation has not gone far enough. For bifurcation is indeed implied in the very conception of the minimum use of security. All prison systems distinguish different degrees of security which are thought to be appropriate for different groups of prisoners, and in our view it would be unrealistic and unjustifiable for them to do otherwise. But the higher the degree of security, and especially with the paraphernalia of maximum security, the more likely is it that regime disadvantages will accrue to prisoners. In these circumstances the task must be to minimise the disadvantages. This requires careful attention to the definition of dangerousness on both security and control grounds. But it also requires attention to the provision of safe-guards against the consequences of having been defined as dangerous. In order to consider how well the United Kingdom has fared on these matters it is necessary to review some recent history on the handling of security and control problems.

The background

Fifteen years ago when the Prison Commission was merged into the Home Office as the Prison Department, there was no talk of dangerous prisoners in this country, and no maximum security accommodation in the prison system. In so far as the Prison Commission concerned itself with thoughts of providing maximum security conditions, it did so only in respect of life sentence prisoners, not at all for prisoners serving determinate sentences. In the last full year of the Prison Commission there were some three-hundred or so lifers in the prison population — most of whom were domestic murderers — and the numbers were growing slowly. Then, as now, life sentence prisoners were distributed among a number of prisons, for most of them were not high security risks either in terms of their likelihood of escaping or of their danger to the community if they were successful in so doing. For those who did constitute such risks, a maximum security block, to house between thirty and sixty lifers, was planned for the Isle of Wight. The block has never been built. As far as the new generation of closed prisons was concerned, security was to be provided for in the buildings themselves rather than in the strength of the perimeter. According to Peterson (1961), the then Chairman of the Prison Commission, in a clear state-ment of the minimum use of security principle, security in such prisons should not be 'excessive having regard to the purpose for which the establishment is intended'.

In the early 1960s, however, public recognition was given to a new class, or classes, of long sentence prisoners. They ranged from sophisti-cated and large scale thieves and robbers, through violent and ruthless

70

gang members and racketeers, to a variety of amateur and professional spies. Whether any of these really represented a new class of criminal is still a moot point, but perhaps no longer the most relevant issue.

What is important is that they were almost universally regarded as such and were sentenced accordingly, many of them to very long fixed terms that would last longer than the average life sentence. Later, as the impact of the abolition of the death penalty was realised, a number of child and police-murderers were added for whom the life sentence might have to mean just that. More recently still, of course, the courts have passed very long sentences on terrorists, most notably associated with the IRA, and these undoubtedly do constitute a new problem, if only because of the possibility of their claiming a political motive for their actions.

The response of Prison Department to the reception of these long sentence prisoners, a response greatly heightened by the dramatic escape of the train robbers Wilson (1964) and Biggs (1965), was the provision of the 'special wings' — at Durham, Leicester, Parkhurst and Chelmsford. These were ordinary wings at old prisons, hastily converted to provide a very high degree of security but, by general consent, at the cost of producing intolerable living conditions. The plans for the maximum security block on the Isle of Wight had been inherited by Prison Department, but little headway had been made apart from increasing the planned accommodation to eighty places.

With the escape of George Blake on 22 October 1966, matters came to a head and the then Home Secretary, Roy Jenkins, appointed Lord Mountbatten to conduct an immediate Inquiry into prison security. He reported his findings in just six weeks. His conclusions and recommendations are well known and require only the briefest summary here:

i.   that there was no really secure prison in the country (Mountbatten, 1966, para 14);

ii. that prisoners should be classified into four categories according to security risk and sent to prisons suitable for their containment. Category A prisoners were those whose escape would constitute a danger to the public, the police or the security of the State; Category B were those for whom escape should be made very difficult but without recourse to the highest security conditions; Category C should be housed in semi-secure closed prisons; and Category D were those suitable for open prisons (paras 212, 217);

iii. that all prisoners in Category A should be concentrated in a new maximum security prison, Vectis, to be built with all possible speed on the Isle of Wight site earmarked for the lifers' block (paras 212, 215);

iv. that the Home Office plans for eighty maximum security places were inadequate and that the new prison should accommodate up to one hundred and twenty prisoners, and a second such prison should be built in due course if the need arose (para 214);

v. that the new prison should utilise physical barriers as well as televisual and electronic aids together with guard dogs to prevent escapes, and that staff should be specially trained in security matters (paras 232, 274, 295).

Mountbatten's approach was entirely in keeping with existing Prison Department policy. In effect it advocated the isolation from the normal population, in a single prison, of those high security risk prisoners who were then isolated in the special wings. As for the normal population his recommendations simply made more explicit the Peterson principle that security should not be 'excessive having regard to the purpose for which the establishment is intended'. Nevertheless, the report was greeted with reserve, even hostility. Whilst many of its recommendations, including the classification of prisoners into four security categories, were adopted, the main proposal, to build Vectis, later renamed Alvington, was at first accepted, then deferred and finally abandoned. Within two months of publication the Home Secretary had invited the Advisory Council on the Penal System to consider the related matter of the regime for long-term prisoners in conditions of maximum security. The Advisory Council appointed a sub-committee under the Chairmanship of Professor Radzinowicz for this purpose.

Once again the conclusions and recommendations of the Radzinowicz sub-committee are well known and require only a brief summary here:

i. that there needed to be an increase in the 'coefficient of security' in closed prisons (ACPS, 1968, para 45);

ii. that Category A prisoners should not be concentrated in a single prison but be dispersed among (para 62) and occasionally transferred between (para 154) a number of secure prisons;

iii. that there should be a liberal regime within a secure perimeter (para 48) which would include observation towers (para 53) manned by armed officers (para 61);

iv. that recalcitrant prisoners should be moved, as necessary, into specially constructed segregation units within each dispersal prison (para 164).

The Radzinowicz sub-committee advised against the building of Alvington on several, and in our view largely erroneous, grounds: that Mountbatten's plans were regarded by the Americans as retrograde; that to lock up all the high security prisoners in one prison would reinforce their feelings that they were 'special' cases who had reached the 'end of the road'; and that the resultant 'excessively custodial', 'repressive' and 'potentially explosive' environment would pose insuperable problems of control. The sub-committee further argued, somewhat illogically and in any case ironically as events have shown, that since it would be impossible to assign prisoners to security categories with complete accuracy, the authorities might be tempted to play safe and greatly expand their use of the maximum security classification.

The alternative which the Advisory Council preferred was dispersal. Instead of concentrating high security risk prisoners in a single establishment, it was argued, it would be better to disperse them in smaller groups among the general population of three or four dispersal prisons. By treating them as 'normal' rather than 'special' prisoners it was hoped to neutralise the notoriety attaching to their crimes, to reduce their prestige within the prison community and to avoid the 'nothing to lose' mentality that supposedly accompanied an 'end of the road' environment. The sub-committee pinned its hopes for the stability of the dispersal prisons on the possibility of providing a civilised and relaxed regime within a secure perimeter. Any residual problems of control would be dealt with by withdrawing troublesome prisoners from the general population and placing them in the segregation units. An incidental advantage of dispersal would be the prospect of transfer between equally secure prisons, but which would offer prisoners a change of scene to break up very long periods of imprisonment. A final reason for advocating a dispersal policy was that it was thought to be cheaper to upgrade the security in three or four dispersal prisons than to build a new maximum security prison from scratch.

The Radzinowicz proposals represented a radical departure from existing policy. In particular, by insisting that Category A prisoners be dispersed among Category B and Category C prisoners who would all be subject to conditions of maximum security, they reversed the Peterson commitment to the minimum use of security principle. Nevertheless with the exception of the recommendation about armed guards, the proposals were accepted and implemented by the new Home Secretary, James Callaghan.

When the dispersal policy was introduced in 1968 some of the Category A prisoners were taken from the special wings and placed in small numbers amongst Category B and Category C prisoners in three existing but newly strengthened prisons — Parkhurst, Wakefield and Wormwood Scrubs. After a massive programme of security work had been carried out, Gartree and Hull were added to the dispersal system in 1969, and Albany in 1970. At first, in these six prisons, a genuine attempt was made to make the system work. Considerable freedom of movement was allowed within the security perimeter, and a standard Category A regime was operated which, though constrained by security considerations, was not very different from that to be found in other closed training prisons.

Nobody escaped from the dispersal prisons, but they soon provided the locations for some of the most serious disturbances and riots in the modern history of the UK prison service — at Parkhurst in 1969, Albany in 1971 and 1972 and Gartree in 1972. As the problems of control mounted so the relaxed and civilised regime was whittled away. The strengthening of security that was initially geared to perimeter defences was extended to internal buildings, cells and workshops, as well as the segregation units. Many Category C prisoners were either removed from the dispersal prisons or reclassified as Category B prisoners. Movement within and between halls and wings was restricted and subjected to surveillance by closed circuit television. Time spent in association was reduced and limits were placed on the number of prisoners who might congregate together. Communal dining facilities were abandoned in favour of providing meals in cells. Electronic locking and unlocking procedures were introduced and extended. All of this was additional to the double security fences, barbed wire, geophonic alarms, high-mast flood lighting, perimeter defence forces, dog patrols, UHF radio systems, emergency control rooms, and links with local police forces and so on, which comprised the normal security barriers at such establishments.

Some of these measures were introduced as a result of two reviews set up by the Home Secretary, Robert Carr, in the wake of the Albany and Gartree riots of 1972. Some had already been acted on before then. Both reviews reported in 1973. One of them was on the dispersal policy itself and concluded that the dispersal policy was right, but that a dilution of the control problems might be achieved by the spreading of 'prisoners who are most likely to cause trouble and who are in the highest security Category' among a larger number of high security prisons (*Hansard*, vol.856, cols 215-6). The other review was of the system of rewards and punishments in prisons, and led eventually to the setting up of 'control units'. The control units were intended for the 'deliberate and persistent troublemaker' who could be confined for 'substantial periods' under an 'intentionally austere' regime until 'able to show his willingness to behave himself and the ability to sustain that good behaviour that would justify a return to normal conditions' (Home Office, 1974). By the end of 1973 Long Lartin was brought into use as a seventh dispersal prison. Two control units were established, at Wakefield in 1974 and Wormwood Scrubs in 1975, but following a storm of protest the Home Secretary announced that one had not been used at all and the other would be discontinued (Fowler, 1977, Appendix 15). Even now the legality of control units under the Prison Rules is being tested in the courts.

The net effect of these measures, apart from tightening security, was to heighten tension in the dispersal prisons. A series of fires and incidents involving the taking of hostages occurred in Albany at the end of 1973, and the dispersal prisons continued to simmer. In 1976 Hull prison erupted into violence which caused damage to the fabric estimated at three-quarters of a million pounds. The Hull riot resulted in some severe sentences imposed by the Board of Visitors. But it also produced some disturbing allegations of reprisals carried out by staff. Although allegations of reprisals following prison riots are common, they are also commonly dismissed — as was the case at Parkhurst in 1969. Some of the allegations associated with the Hull riot, however, were upheld by the courts two years later, when several prison officers were prosecuted, convicted and given suspended sentences. Moreover, for the first time in history, some of the sentences passed by the Board of Visitors were subsequently overturned by the courts on appeal (see chapter 6 for a further discussion on these matters).

By then, though, the official Home Office Inquiry, carried out by Fowler, the Chief Inspector of Prisons, had already exonerated staff from accusations of 'brutality' and 'harshness' although some had exhibited 'unnecessary zeal' in their handling of prisoners' property (Fowler, 1977, paras 8 and 317). And the Fowler Report reinforced the conclusions of Robert Carr's review of dispersal. In particular, Fowler argued that yet more dispersal prisons were required, and that dispersal prison staff should receive special, though unspecified, training (para 364). Already Low Newton, soon to be renamed Frankland, was planned to be the first purpose-built dispersal prison and, in 1980, it would bring the total number of maximum security establishments to eight. Presumably Fowler was pressing for the reinstatement of the project for a second purpose-built dispersal prison at Full Sutton, which had been deferred as one of the cuts to the building programme.

It soon became clear what the special training was that Fowler referred to when the Prison Department, under the direction of the then Home Secretary Merlyn Rees, established the so called MUFTI (Minimum Use of Force — Tactical Intervention) squads which were specially equipped to deal with riots. Though the troubles in the dispersal prisons did not go away, the disturbances at Gartree in 1978, were at least handled in a peaceful manner (see Martin, 1980; and chapter 6). But the MUFTI squads were evidently used in what, at the time of writing, seems to have been a massive over-response to a passive demonstration in Wormwood Scrubs which occurred at the very time the May Committee was preparing to hand the findings of its Inquiry into the UK prison services to the new Home Secretary, Mr Whitelaw.

Evidence to the May Committee

In spite of the dramatic events that had occurred in the dispersal prisons throughout the 1970s, the May Committee devoted just four of its three-hundred and thirty-seven pages to the problem of how to deal with dangerous prisoners (May 1979, paras 6.62-72). It is only fair to add, however, that not many of the bodies which gave evidence to the May Committee spent much time on it either.

The POA briefly reiterated its long-standing objection to dispersal and called for a return to Mountbatten's proposal for concentrating high security risk prisoners in a fortress prison. It declared its belief that a substantial minority of mentally disordered inmates were at the fore-front of the riots and demonstrations of the 1970s, and that they would be better housed in secure, mental institutions. And it called for the reintroduction of control units (POA, Evidence, Section 12, paras 9, 10, 25 and 59). The effect of the POA's call for a return to a concentration policy was somewhat vitiated, however, by the inclusion of a memorandum from the General Secretary to the membership about the Fowler Report on the Hull Riot (Appendix B). In this document the POA, faced with the repeated rejection of the concentration policy first by Radzinowicz, then by Carr and finally by Fowler, had sought to come to terms with what must have seemed the inevitable, and made various suggestions for making dispersal more workable.

The British Association of Prison Governors, on the other hand, took the official Home Office line on dispersal: 'It would be simplistic to suggest that these problems could be overcome by the provision of more dispersal prisons, although we feel that this is undoubtedly a necessity and sooner rather than later' (BAPG, Evidence, p.25). Quite why more dispersal prisons were 'necessary' when there was evidently little faith that they would overcome the problems, was no better explained by the prison governors than it had been by Fowler or indeed any of the earlier policy reviews. The governors were in agreement with their uniformed colleagues about the disruption caused by mentally disturbed offenders who ought to be in secure hospitals. In the absence of the DHSS accepting responsibility for these inmates, the governors called for extra psychiatrists to be appointed to the dispersal prisons. The governors also agreed about the necessity of control units — though they adopted a cynical stance when they argued that 'in view of the fiasco' over their previous introduction 'the terminology may be critical in the success or failure of such units' were they to be re-introduced (pp 23-4, 28).

While NACRO recognised that 'the difficulties caused by the dispersal policy are clear' it was not able to make a recommendation on the alternative policy of concentration. Instead it sought a 'way forward' through the closer examination and independent evaluation of the work of the Barlinnie Special Unit for long-term prisoners. It also proposed a number of reforms on security classification procedures (NACRO, Evidence, paras 18 and 19). The Howard League for Penal Reform argued that the definition of Category A should be more narrowly drawn, and warned that an excessive concern with security could endanger human rights. The League also called for a review of the security apparatus and said that its 'potential for causing aggravation' should be weighed against 'the needs of security': presumably an implicit commitment to the minimum use of security principle (Howard League, Evidence, paras 10 and 11). Neither organisation had anything new to say to the May Committee about control units: one supposes because it seemed inconceivable that there would be any serious intention of resurrecting them.

The National Prisoners' Movement (PROP) offered some observations about the control problem in prisons. In particular they exposed the popular fallacy that it is the notorious long sentence, or life sentence, prisoner who has 'nothing to lose' in prison riots. They argued:

> The life sentence prisoner, has in fact everything to lose. In contrast prisoners with fixed sentences, and particularly short fixed sentences, can quantify the possible loss of remission when deciding whether to participate in prisoner protests (PROP, Evidence, p.6; see also King and Elliott, 1978, for a similar analysis).

PROP, however, also rejected the Mountbatten proposals for a single fortress prison, though it seems likely that this was because they believed it would be used for control purposes — as a place 'into which "troublemakers" can be herded' (p.4) — rather than simply for security purposes.

A few other witnesses referred to security issues, but in the end the only substantial independent evidence the May Committee had to consider was from ourselves (King, Evidence, reproduced with amendments in King and Morgan, 1979, chapter 2). Only a summary of that evidence is possible here.

We argued that the dispersal policy had been illogical and wrong-headed from the outset because it was based on a misunderstanding of the relationship between the security and the control problems. In any case the way in which it came to be implemented seriously undermined the spirit of the original Radzinowicz proposals. None of the claimed advantages had actually accrued from dispersal and all the evidence pointed to the fact that it had been a costly mistake. Moreover it was a mistake the Prison Department seemed unable or unwilling to rectify, for all its actions served only to compound the error. A return to the Mountbatten proposal of concentrating high security risk prisoners was advocated as a solution to the security problem, with separate measures to deal with the control problem (King, Evidence, paras 6-7, 55-6; and King and Morgan, 1979, paras 85-6, 128-9).

More particularly it was argued that dispersal was vastly more expensive than concentration would have been. At the time that Alvington was abandoned it was estimated to cost £2.6 million — only a little more than the eventual cost of upgrading the security in Albany, just one of the seven dispersal prisons. Yet having rejected a purpose-built prison to concentrate Category A prisoners the Home Office was now building one to disperse them (Frankland) at an estimated cost of £11.9 million. True, if Mountbatten's policy had been adopted a second Alvington would have been required, but if Fowler had his way, so would there be a second purpose-built dispersal prison at Full Sutton at an even higher price. To this had to be added the costs of repairing riot damage and the higher running costs of such a large system of maximum security prisons (King, Evidence, paras 13-15; King and Morgan, 1979, paras 88-90).

These costs were largely attributable to the phenomenal growth in high security accommodation. On the face of it between 1962 and 1977 maximum security had grown by 6,666 per cent: from the planned block for 60 lifers to 4,000 planned places in eight dispersal prisons (including Frankland but excluding Full Sutton). It was acknowledged that it was difficult to establish precisely how many places were actually available for use. Some places were lost to maximum security through riot damage, the multiple functions of Wakefield and Wormwood Scrubs, and the deliberate choice to keep some dispersal prisons under-used in the interest of maintaining a reasonable regime in the face of control problems. Given different assumptions about usage the actual number of maximum security places could be as low as 2,000 (an increase of a mere 3,333 per cent) or as high as 3,500 (an increase of 5,833 per cent) (King, Evidence, paras 22-5; King and Morgan, 1979, paras 97-9). What was certain was that the operation of the dispersal policy involved a deliberate and profligate waste of accommodation at a time when the prison system was supposedly cracking under the pressures of overcrowding. Thus, as a matter of policy, some 500 or 600 places in Albany, Gartree, Long Lartin and Parkhurst were kept permanently empty. These places, many of them in new prisons, could be released to relieve overcrowding if there was a return to the policy of concentrating high security risks (King, Evidence, paras 36-8; King and Morgan, 1979, paras 110-12).

It was equally certain that the growth in maximum security accommodation could not be accounted for by the growth in the long-term prison population or the changes in the quality of that population. The numbers of what Prison Department regarded as significant long-term prisoners grew by only 41 per cent over the same period: from 3,678 in 1962 to 5,196 in 1977. The most important changes in the long-term prison population were in respect of life sentence prisoners. These numbered 300 to 350 in 1962, mostly domestic murderers, of whom 17 to 20 per cent were deemed suitable for the planned lifers block. Since the abolition of the death penalty the lifer population has grown dramatically, from 551 in 1968 to 1,286 in 1977, or 233 per cent in a decade. Over the same period the numbers serving very long fixed sentences remained constant. Although the life sentence population now contains more 'dangerous' prisoners than formerly, most are still domestic murderers and the qualitative changes should not be exaggerated. Life sentence prisoners are distributed through more than twenty establishments including open prisons. In 1977 only 141 or 11 per cent of the lifers were classified by Prison Department as Category A security risks. Indeed, what is supremely ironic in any analysis of the changes in the prison population is that the number of prisoners actually classified by Prison Department as needing the highest degree of security, 257 in 1977, are entirely consistent with Mountbatten's estimates as long ago as 1966. All could be accommodated in two small maximum security prisons (King, Evidence, paras 24-31; King and Morgan, 1979, paras 98-105).

The only conceivable justification for this growth in maximum security accommodation was that put forward by the Radzinowicz Committee, namely that dispersal would dilute the control problems that were anticipated if Category A prisoners were all housed together.

The cost of keeping Category B or Category C prisoners in conditions of security which, by definition they did not require, was the price the Home Office was prepared to pay for a liberal and humane approach to the custody of high security prisoners serving very long sentences. It *might* have been acceptable had the relaxed regime within a secure perimeter become a reality, and had the control problems actually been avoided. But in fact, with each review of the policy, the dispersal prisons became more and more like the Mountbatten fortress in security and regime. Anyone who supported the dispersal policy because of fears about fortress security and impoverished regimes must now face up to these realities (King, Evidence, paras 16-19; King and Morgan, 1979, paras 91-4). And the record of the dispersal prisons on control problems could scarcely be worse. Even when not in situations of outright violence, such as has been seen in Parkhurst, Albany, Gartree, Hull (and now Wormwood Scrubs), the dispersal prisons ticked over for most of the 1970s with an undercurrent of tension and aggravation that made life acutely uncomfortable for staff and prisoners alike (King, Evidence, para 39; King and Morgan, 1979, para 113). Only Wakefield and Long Lartin have been free from overt disturbances, and able to operate reasonably harmonious regimes — though the threat of an alert situation has never been far away.

The failure to maintain discipline and control under the dispersal policy arises out of a fundamental confusion of security risk problems with control problems; and out of a failure on the part of the Radzinowicz sub-committee and Prison Department to appreciate how prisoners actually do respond to the experience of imprisonment.

The notion of 'dangerous' prisoners contains two analytically distinct categories. The first embodies the idea of high security risk — those prisoners who are capable of engineering a successful escape and who would constitute an intolerable risk to the public, the police or the security of the State if they were unlawfully at large. The second embodies the idea of control risk — those 'subversive' prisoners who, while contained within the prison, constitute a threat by reason of their manipulative, intimidatory or enforcement powers, to the good order and discipline of the prison community and the authority of the staff. It is now widely recognised that although there may be some overlap between the two categories — that is some prisoners may be both security risks and control risks — generally they are far from forming a unitary group. If these categories are analytically and empirically separate there is everything to be said for adopting separate policies to deal with each problem. Regrettably, under the dispersal policy, these problems have been appallingly confused. Initially Prison Department, following the Radzinowicz sub-committee, allocated high security risk prisoners to the dispersal prisons in the hope that control problems would be avoided. Indeed it was the express function of Category B and Category C prisoners to neutralise the notoriety of Category A prisoners and thus to de-fuse those situations which allegedly would have exploded had the Category A prisoners been housed together. As the policy developed, however, and control problems became rife within the dispersal system, staff at all levels came to see the dispersal prisons as an appropriate disposal for subversive prisoners from any security category.

Because security risk and control problems are not co-terminous the Radzinowicz fears of an explosive environment under concentration were as unrealistic as their hopes for a relaxed and civilised atmosphere under dispersal. The ways in which prisoners do react to their imprisonment are complex, and cannot be dealt with adequately here (see, however, Cohen and Taylor, 1972; King and Elliott, 1978). Suffice it to say that the great mistake of the Radzinowicz policy was to pretend that high security risk prisoners were no more special than the general population amongst whom they were dispersed. Category A men knew different, whatever the policy of Prison Department, because the courts had left them in no doubt about that. They were quite aware that the paraphernalia of security under the dispersal system was intended just for them and not for the general population. All that dispersal did was to enhance the prestige of ex-Borstal boys who would otherwise never have been brought into contact with their illustrious colleagues. Indeed it was just these short term prisoners who really had little to lose in terms of loss of remission if they made trouble, and the dispersal policy gave them every opportunity. As one dispersal governor said of the population in his prison: 'Sentences range from twelve months to life, the ages from 19 to 70, security categories from A to D, the widest range of social backgrounds is represented and every kind of offence.' He did not expect it to work without trouble. And he was right (King, Evidence, paras 39-50; King and Morgan, 1979, paras 113-121).

One of the most insidious effects of the dispersal policy is that it unwarrantably taints the long-term population with the high security or dangerous prisoner label. In recent years the Home Office claims it has removed most Category C prisoners from dispersal prisons. If that is true it has undermined the spirit of the Radzinowicz proposals, for Category C prisoners were supposed to normalise the regime. But there is reason to suppose that Category C prisoners were not so much removed as re-classified in Category B. Thus at the South East Regional Conference for Assistant Governors in March 1979, it was reported that a headquarters survey had shown that 30 per cent of the Category B prisoners in one dispersal prison could more properly be regarded as

Category C prisoners. At the same Conference it became clear that the dispersal prisons were seen as appropriate allocations for Category B prisoners 'who required dispersal security'; for Category B 'control problems'; and for long-term prisoners who would otherwise remain in the local prisons. What all this suggests is that whoever is put into dispersal prisons, and for whatever reasons originally, they soon come to be seen as needing or deserving maximum security. It is not hard to see how this happens. The places in the dispersal prisons have to be filled somehow. And it is of the essence of the policy that once in there prisoners are treated in basically the same way. Security categorisation becomes virtually meaningless under the dispersal policy. It makes no material difference, either to Prison Department or to prisoners, what security category is assigned: all prisoners are subjected to the same high degree of security, and the same basic regime which was designed for Category A prisoners. This then has a knock-on effect throughout the prison system as a whole — for if Category B prisoners 'deserve' maximum security, can Category C prisoners be left in semi-secure prisons and anyone be trusted in open conditions? In a real sense this obsessive, almost paranoid, concern with security is a product of Prison Department's own policies which constantly serve to amplify their own fears.

Ironically this charge of increasing security throughout the system was levelled at Mountbatten's proposal even though it could scarcely be less likely under a policy of concentrating security risks. For had Mountbatten's proposal been adopted maximum security accommodation would always have been a scarce resource. As a result Prison Department would have had to think very carefully before assigning anyone to Category A, to make sure that they did not take up a place required by someone who was a greater security risk. Under concentration the pressure would be to review and downgrade security ratings and the downgrading would make a difference. Under dispersal there is still room for over 3,000 prisoners in maximum security even though they are not assigned to Category A. Indeed the possibility could not be ruled out that, if the accommodation continued to grow, and the labelling process continued to develop, then one day *all* long term prisoners might be held in conditions of maximum security. Already it was *possible* to have 80 per cent of the long term population in the dispersal prisons (King, Evidence, paras 21-2; King and Morgan, 1979, paras 95-6, 106-9, 127).

The dispersal policy had never gained the confidence of prison officers. In spite of the Radzinowicz and Home Office fears, about it being impossible to staff prisons containing only high security risk prisoners, the POA had always preferred Mountbatten's solution. There is no reason to suppose that the problems of handling high security risk prisoners would be greater under concentration than they are under dispersal, and thus no reason why a concentration policy should be more difficult to staff. Indeed fewer staff would be required for such duties than at present (King, Evidence, paras 51-3, 76; King and Morgan, 1979, paras 122-4, 174).

Given the weight of all this evidence there seemed no good reason for continuing with the dispersal policy and we proposed a return to a policy of concentrating high security risk prisoners. In deciding high security risk a balance has to be struck between the likelihood of a successful escape and the risk to the community that such an escape would produce. This assessment of what we called the 'escape-catastrophe quotient' should be very like what happens now in deciding allocation to Category A. But we argued that if a concentration policy were adopted then Prison Department might wish to play safe, and re-classify some Category B prisoners as Category A prisoners. As a result, the numbers in the highest security category might rise from about 250 to perhaps 400-500 prisoners. We argued that there would be no need to build any new special security prison because each of the dispersal prisons had already been proved to be sufficiently secure. The likely numbers of Category A prisoners could comfortably be accommodated in two existing dispersal prisons — Albany and Long Lartin (or Frankland if that proved more suitable when completed). The remaining dispersal prisons with their elaborate security arrangements dismantled, would be released for other purposes in the prison system. It was acknowledged that with only two high security prisons there would be fewer opportunities for transfers to break up long sentences than there were under dispersal; but it was also noted that transfers had as often been used for controlling allegedly disruptive prisoners as they had for providing a change of scenery. High security risk prisoners serving very long sentences would be given as many compensating privileges as possible. These would acknowledge their special status, help make their sentences easier to bear, and ensure that they *do* have something to lose. Among these privileges would be the possibility of unsupervised family visits.

Having dealt with the security risk problem in this way, we argued, the control problem would have to be tackled separately but directly. It should be clear that control problems are found in all prisons, not just in high security prisons, although the operation of the dispersal policy made dispersal prisons particularly prone to incidents of sub-version and intimidation. Tackling control problems could best be done through the processes of classification and allocation. Deciding control risks involves an assessment of a prisoner's willingness and ability to

subvert authority or to enforce his will on other prisoners: an assessment of what we called the 'subversive-enforcement quotient'. The
great majority of prisoners would have a low subversive and a low
enforcement potential. Some would be high on one dimension and low
on the other. A few would be high on both dimensions. Prisoners who
were classified into different categories on control grounds would then,
as far as possible, be kept separate from one another in whatever
prisons they had been allocated to on security or other grounds.

This separation of different groups of prisoners within the same
prison was not intended to involve solitary confinement, nor confinement in segregation units, nor even any special kind of regime, and
certainly not anything involving the kind of sanctions applied in control
units. It was simply intended as a judicious allocation policy, in much
the same way that males are separated from females, and to which no
regime disadvantages would be attached. It was recognised, however,
that this classification would be in some degree subjective, and possibly
open to abuse. But that is the case with the present practice of
removing allegedly subversive prisoners to segregation units: and
removal to segregation units is both more consequential, because of the
regime disadvantages entailed, and more provocative of further trouble,
because of the suspicion that surrounds the procedure.

We concluded our evidence by arguing that both the security and
control classifications should be subject to review, and the possibility
of appeal. The high security prisons and those sections of all prisons
where control risk prisoners were housed, should also have higher than
normal staff ratios (King, Evidence, paras 55-77; King and Morgan,
1979, paras 165-175).

The Home Office evidence

The response of the May Committee to this submission was to pass it to
the Home Office for comment and then, on request, to provide an
opportunity for us to reply in the course of oral evidence.

The Home Office took the line that attack was the best form of
defence alleging that our assessment was by turns speculative (Home
Office, Evidence, vol.II, paper III(9), para 2), exaggerated (paras 9 and
24), mistaken (paras 6, 7 and 25) and out of date (para 18). Broadly
speaking the Home Office assessment was that few, if any, of the
catalogue of problems associated with high security risk or subversive
prisoners could directly be attributed to the operation of the dispersal
policy itself. They reiterated the Radzinowicz arguments against
concentration and implied that the problems would have occurred

84

whether or not dispersal had been adopted and would actually be worse if dispersal was abandoned (paras 7, 29, 33-4). But throughout their evidence the Home Office continued to confuse the security and control problems, and slipped from one to the other in an attempt to justify the *status quo*. They offered no convincing evidence to substantiate their position. Ultimately the Home Office rejection of concentration rested on a reluctance to introduce major changes in the use of establishments (para 61) and the problems it would create for dealing with IRA prisoners (paras 57-9).

The Home Office paper was marginally longer than the one to which it constituted a reply. But, at the risk of prolonging the debate still further, it is necessary to correct some of the official distortions, and to highlight some rather dramatic weaknesses, in what one must assume was a considered and definitive Prison Department statement.

On two occasions (para 45 and 55) the Home Office suggested we had called for a 'third prison specialising in subversives'. There was, of course, no call for anything of the kind in the original evidence (nor by us on any occasion before or since). What was proposed was that subversive prisoners should be kept separate from the general population 'in whatever prisons they had been allocated to on security risk or other grounds' (King, Evidence, para 60). Whether intentionally or not the Home Office evidence confused the issue by implying a similarity between our proposals and those sometimes advocated by prison officers — to put all the subversive control problems together in a fortress prison, with or without the high security risk prisoners. That would be a recipe for disaster. On other occasions (paper III(9), para 7) the Home Office implied that we advocated the use of a purpose-built Mountbatten fortress for the concentration of security risk prisoners, and they even went to the trouble of including a detailed critique of Mountbatten's design brief as an Appendix. In fact we also rejected the purpose-built fortress both on design grounds and because it is unnecessary (King, Evidence, para 68). Others will appreciate, as apparently the Home Office did not, that a critique of the design of the Mountbatten fortress is not the same as a critique of the principle of concentration.

Much of the Home Office evidence was concerned with the extent of maximum security accommodation, its cost, and who needs or uses it. Although the Home Office preferred to see the expansion of maximum security accommodation as the unfolding of developments that had been planned since the policy was adopted, they did not deny that this was indeed a dramatic growth over and above what the Radzinowicz sub-committee envisaged (paper III(9), para 5). Nor, in spite of many assertions about 'inflated' figures and 'misunderstandings' was there any disagreement about the extent of that growth from 60 to 3,500 places (para 9).

The Home Office took issue over the costs of dispersal, arguing that concentration would have been more expensive on capital costs (para 34) partly because there would have been 'significant expenditure' to improve the security for Category B prisoners anyway (para 20). They further claimed that concentration would not have eliminated the need to repair riot damage (para 33). The paucity of figures offered by the Home Office suggests that they were just as guilty of the speculation over costs with which they charged us.

We would be inclined to accept the Home Office view that the debate is sterile because 'the expenditure cannot be recovered' (para 34) were it not for two things. First, the Home Office said nothing about running costs, especially staffing. And secondly, the Treasury, Civil Service Department and Central Policy Review Staff (the Central Departments) were clearly uneasy about the costs of security in their evidence to the May Committee. The Home Office claimed that although the 'record of the dispersal prisons in avoiding escapes has been extremely good . . . the security provision is not excessive' (para 20). The Central Departments, however, noted that 'prison security and control account for the largest increase in staff numbers' (Central Departments, Evidence, vol.III, paper V(3), para 9). The increase in staff numbers had been, by any standards, extraordinary: since 1965 prisoners had increased by 37 per cent and officers by 88 per cent. Four in every ten of the extra officers were accounted for by increments in security. Not surprisingly the Central Departments asked:

> What risks would the system run by reducing the present level of security? Would those risks be justified in relation to the likely savings that would follow? Are there any international comparisons which would be helpful? (para 9).

We believe these to be good questions.

The elaborate Home Office discussion of who needs maximum security accommodation, intended to reassure the May Committee about the propriety of the dispersal policy, actually contains three remarkable statements. The first involves one of the very few admissions of failure in the Home Office paper. Clearly no-one would deny that Category A prisoners need maximum security — for presumably without Category A there would be no maximum security. But according to the Home Office:

> There is a number of extremely dangerous prisoners who have shown great propensity to escape, or whose escape would be absolutely unacceptable to the public and whom as a consequence

it has been decided not to risk including in the dispersal prison regime. They number 13 at present and are normally housed in the two remaining special security wings (para 41, emphasis added).

Thus even the vast accommodation in the dispersal prisons cannot handle all the high security risk prisoners. That the Department finds it necessary to distinguish between Category A prisoners who can be detained in dispersal prisons, and 'super' Category A prisoners who cannot, suggests that there is something radically wrong with the dispersal solution to the security risk problem.

The second statement concerns security categorisation:

The Department recognises *a need to re-examine the process by which people are placed in security categories and the rigour with which a prisoner's security category is reviewed* . . . and for that reason a working party has been appointed to study categorisation and re-categorisation (para 25, emphasis added).

The setting up of a working party to look into this ten years after the establishment of the policy might be considered by some to be long overdue. The admission that there *is* a problem about assigning security categories comes at the end of a paragraph which seeks to deny that Prison Department has attempted to make the dispersal system look like a more reasonable use of high security accommodation by re-assigning Category C prisoners into Category B. Indeed the Home Office claims that it would be pointless to do this because of a shortage of Category B accommodation generally. According to the Home Office reply to our evidence only 100 prisoners or 4 per cent of the dispersal population are in Category C and they are there to do work that cannot be entrusted to higher risk prisoners (para 19). In an attempt at re-writing history the Home Office further argues that it was never the intention that Category A men should be dispersed among Category C prisoners (para 17). Unfortunately, as is so often the case with revisionist histories, this new version has yet to percolate down even to quite senior levels of the administration. Thus at the March 1979 South East Regional Conference for Assistant Governors, to which we referred earlier, the Regional Director made an impassioned plea for a return to the 'original' policy whereby up to a third of the prisoners in a dispersal prison were drawn from Category C.

In any case the Home Office assurances would be easier to accept were it not for the fact that elsewhere in their evidence — in their paper analysing the prison population — they list 539 Category C prisoners and 124 Category D prisoners with a further 627 unclassified, as all being held in dispersal prisons! (Home Office, Evidence, vol.1, paper IIc(1), table 9). There is everything to be said for publishing the criteria by which security allocations are made, together with the number of places available in different levels of security accommodation, and the procedures for upgrading and down-grading security status. Especially as the Home Office gives the game away in a euphemistic reference to the fact that: 'the availability of places (in Category B and Category C accommodation) is to some extent distorting these processes' (of re-classification) (Home Office, Evidence, vol.II, paper III(9), para 25). Anyone with a nodding acquaintance with the processes of allocation in prison (and there were no such persons on the May Committee) will recognise that what this means is that the most important element in any classification decision (other than Category A status) is the availability of accommodation.

As it happens we obviously agree that Category C prisoners should not be in maximum security. The 100 (or 539) such prisoners officially admitted to be in dispersal prisons should be removed — and any jobs that cannot be entrusted to higher risk prisoners should be done by staff. But the Home Office cannot have it both ways, and if Category C prisoners have been removed then they should admit that this has undermined the spirit of the dispersal policy.

The third statement is one of the most damaging, but since it is deeply buried in the Home Office evidence we need to spend some time digging it out. If there are only 257 Category A prisoners in the dispersal prisons (plus or minus 13 who have to remain in the special wings) and 100 Category C prisoners (to take the lowest Home Office figure and ignoring any who may have been mis-classified as Category B) then it follows that the dispersal prisons are predominantly for Category B prisoners whose escape should be made 'very difficult'. The Home Office agrees and states that the dispersal prisons provide places for 'some 2,000 Category B prisoners' (para 10). This is hard to interpret for even using Home Office figures the numbers should be around 2,500 on existing accommodation and 3,000 on planned accommodation. Do they need maximum security? If so on what grounds?

Our arguments against dispersal are based, in part, on the fact that it makes little difference whether one is in Category A, B or C: so long as one is in a dispersal prison the conditions are much the same. The Home Office contest this by saying that Category A status demands greater restriction, and Category C status less restriction, within the dispersal prisons. They argue that this is much the same sort of thing as the special status traditionally given to 'redbands' in all prisons (para 11). We cannot accept that this is realistic. Mountbatten insisted that the really crucial division in the prison population was between Category A prisoners — for whom escape should be made impossible —

and the rest. It was precisely for this reason that he proposed their separation into a maximum security prison. Having checked and re-checked this with Lord Mountbatten we know that this remained his view until his death, whatever the Home Office now say about the general applicability of Mountbatten's findings for Category B prisoners. We are sure that Mountbatten was right. And we are no less sure that maximum security conditions exercise a dominating, all embracing influence on regimes, that far outweigh any fine distinctions of status that may be applied within the dispersal prisons.

If a policy of concentration was adopted, with a consequent lessening of security for Category B prisoners throughout the system, it would not be unreasonable for Prison Department to cast their Category A net a little wider. We would expect about 150 or so, even a little more at first, of the Category B prisoners to be re-classified as Category A prisoners. But once again the complete confusion produced by the dispersal policy is revealed as the Home Office, in their evidence, find themselves supporting two contradictory positions. On the one hand they argue that classification criteria are strictly applied and that the numbers of Category A prisoners would remain the same under concentration or dispersal (para 16). On the other hand they are happy to talk about Category B prisoners 'needing maximum security'. Surely it would be more easily understandable for everyone if we could agree that Category A prisoners need maximum security and Category B do not?

The Home Office say they 'do not believe there to be any grounds' for the assumption that only 150 or so Category B prisoners might really need maximum security. But they offer no counter arguments, give no alternative figures, and ask the world to believe that the Home Office, in its wisdom, has got some good reason for keeping 2,000 (2,500?, 3,000?) Category B prisoners in maximum security. Once again the game is given away, however, when the Home Office say:

> The Department does not accept Dr King's assumption that the majority of the population of dispersal prisons do not need this level of security, *but this may well be true of some Category B prisoners and the Department has recognised a lack of reliable information on which to base a judgement* (para 26, emphasis added).

This prompts several vital questions. If there is no basis for making a judgement, on what basis do they dispute the assumption? Is it not surprising that there is no reliable information after ten years of operating the policy? On what basis did the Home Office justify the extension of the dispersal system to its present size? And how can the

Home Office now say that 'there is no reason to think that the intended addition of two purpose-built dispersal prisons as envisaged in 1973 will be over-provision' (para 60)?

The whole question of which Category B prisoners do need maximum security is evidently an enormously grey area. If the Home Office do seek to argue that the great majority of Category B prisoners now held in dispersal prisons are there on genuine security grounds, then we are already in the situation where well over half of our long-term prisoners are defined as 'needing' maximum security. This was something the Home Office was at pains to deny (para 16). It is high time that the grey areas of supposition are turned into black and white statistics.

Meanwhile constant public vigilance will be required if these Home Office arguments are not to lead to a quite unwarrantable extension in what is already one of the most oppressive systems of high security imprisonment in the world. When we gave oral evidence to the Committee, Mr Justice May put to us, purely as a matter of conjecture, the following argument. That if there has been no proper Category A prison so far, and if the Home Office regard Category B prisoners as needing dispersal prison security, then the introduction of a concentration policy would do nothing to reduce security levels elsewhere in the system. All that would happen would be that security for Category A prisoners would shift into an even higher gear. This may well have reflected discussions with Prison Department officials as to future policy. On 31 March 1978, Lord Harris, then Minister of State, canvassed the idea that a new prison, built to even higher standards of security than the dispersal prisons, should receive only Category A prisoners, but should not house the whole of the Category A population. In their evidence the Home Office made it clear that some dispersal prisons would continue to receive Category A prisoners, while others would cease to do so under this proposal (para 2). What was not said, but must be inferred, was that there would be no diminution of security in those dispersal prisons which no longer housed Category A prisoners. That kind of development could only be explained by the extraordinary power of Prison Department's own labelling procedures which constantly reinforce their fears about security.

Fortunately, it seems likely from the evidence we have already quoted from the Central Departments, that the Treasury would want to look very closely indeed at any such development on cost effectiveness grounds. But sometimes such proposals can get converted into action unannounced. It would seem wise to keep a close eye on the use to which Frankland is put, in relation to the rest of the system, when that prison is brought into use.

Clear cut answers on the question of who needs maximum security will not emerge until this matter is disentangled from the control problem. In the Home Office pronouncements there is continual slippage between the need for security and the need for control as the justification for the dispersal system. The Home Office do not deny the troubled history of dispersal but they do assert that things might have been worse under a policy of concentration (para 33). Since concentration has not been tried in this country such a view must be total speculation. The Home Office repeat all the fears expressed by the Radzinowicz sub-committee about concentration, and say that these arguments have never been answered (paras 7 and 29). They conveniently forget that when the Radzinowicz sub-committee reported, the Advisory Council could only speculate about *both* dispersal *and* concentration. Since their optimism about dispersal was so ill-founded why should any confidence be placed in their pessimistic analysis of the control problems under concentration? Even the Home Office now freely admit that: 'the disturbances in dispersal prisons cannot be shown to have been due to the presence of Category A prisoners' (para 33). If so, why should Category A prisoners constitute such a threat if housed together? In any case it is just not true that the Radzinowicz fears have not been answered. One of the most eloquent answers is that the Federal Bureau of Prisons in the USA, whose decision to close Alcatraz convinced the Radzinowicz sub-committee that building Vectis was a retrograde step, has returned to a policy of concentrating high security risk prisoners in Marion Prison, Illinois.

Our proposals for dealing with the control problem received rather short shrift from the Home Office, though apparently following the publication of *Albany* (King and Elliott, 1978) they had been given some brief consideration by the Dispersal Prison Steering Group (para 53). The Home Office objections arose mainly because the propensities of prisoners to be control problems were not considered 'sufficiently stable characteristics to be a foundation for categorisation' (para 51). We never suggested that they were stable characteristics. Indeed we went to some lengths to argue that subversion is but one possible response to regimes, and that it was particularly likely in dispersal prisons. Much could be done through our principle of normalisation of the prison as discussed in chapter 4, and through the provision of safeguards for prisoners as discussed by Professor Martin in chapter 6, that would make control problems less likely to arise. But it is strange that the Home Office should say on the one hand, that subversion is not a sufficiently stable characteristic to be a foundation for categorisation, and on the other that some prisoners 'may *by their character and personality* tend to be the means by which disorder is promoted' . . . and that *'there are unstable prisoners* who readily become excited if a disturbance occurs' (para 28, emphasis added). In any case it is quite clear that the Home Office *do* categorise prisoners in this way. The Home Office, in a revealing passage, ruefully admit, as indeed we had alleged, that: *'There has clearly been a tendency for dispersal prisons to be regarded by allocation centres as appropriate locations for difficult prisoners in Category B who are arguably unsuitable for the regime'* (para 42, emphasis added). At least the Home Office have the grace to confess that 'it is doubtful whether this is a wise policy'. But if it is possible to identify control risks and send them to the dispersal prisons we do not see why it should be so difficult to identify control risks and keep them in *separate* parts of *any* prison.

In the final analysis the real objections to the concentration policy, as far as the Home Office are concerned, are the administrative difficulties of reorganisation, especially concerning life prisoners (paras 27 and 61) and the adequacy of alternative accommodation for Category B prisoners (paras 20 and 26); and, of course, the thorny problem of what to do with the IRA and other 'terrorist' groups (paras 41, 57-9). There is not a great deal to be said about the administrative difficulties, except to note that what the Home Office actually say is rather obscure (para 61), and to observe that no administration welcomes change. If there are real problems about life sentence prisoners then obviously this would have to be taken into account. As far as most of the Category B prisoners are concerned, once they were removed from maximum security the fears generated by the labelling tendency inherent to the dispersal policy would gradually diminish.

Much the most serious reservation must concern the IRA and other quasi-political terrorist groups. It has to be said that these scarcely figured, if at all, in the thinking of Lord Mountbatten or the Radzinowicz sub-committee. While we regard this problem from a different perspective to that of the Home Office, we do not dismiss it lightly. Whereas we think a concerted attack on one or more prisons by the IRA is rather unlikely, we conclude that it would be irresponsible of the Home Office to ignore such a possibility, however remote. We understand, though we do not share, the determination of successive governments not to treat such prisoners as though they had a political status. Nevertheless, failing to differentiate them from more conventional criminal prisoners is unrealistic, and in any case has unfortunate consequences for the prison system. Whether or not one concedes a formal political status there is still everything to be said for dealing with these prisoners separately from the general run of

Category A prisoners.

Whatever the Home Office *says* about political status such prisoners will see themselves as *occupying* a political status. This will greatly influence the way in which they adapt to imprisonment. For them 'being disruptive' must take on a quite different meaning from that understood by other, non-politically motivated, prisoners. For the former there is some philosophical underpinning, however much one may disparage it, while for the latter there usually is not. Although our direct contact with IRA prisoners is slight, we would expect that for a substantial number, though by no means all of them, the *security* problem and the *control* problem would indeed coincide. This has two conflicting implications. First, that it would be unwise to concentrate them all together because, unlike other Category A prisoners who could reasonably be expected to 'do their own bird', the prospect of banding together in a co-ordinated way must be very high. Secondly, that to disperse such prisoners in, for example, the existing dispersal prisons, must run a very high risk of disrupting the regime, and also of 'politicising' other prisoners in ways that would otherwise not occur.

It is important to stress that while 'terrorist' groups constitute a severe problem for the prison system, there is a distinct possibility, if not probability, that it will be a temporary problem. Just as hard cases make bad law, it would seem disastrous to allow these prisoners to dictate the shape of our prison system. The response to the IRA must be a flexible, pragmatic one, not one which constrains the solution to the much more pervasive problem of coping with our conventionally defined criminal prisoners.

It seems to us that the IRA prisoners should neither be concentrated with other Category A prisoners, nor placed within the general population of dispersal prisons. According to the Home Office, IRA and similar prisoners account for about one third of the Category A population — some 80 to 90 prisoners (para 57). As the Home Office say it would be quite unacceptable to house them in conditions of lesser security than for other Category A prisoners (para 59). In these circumstances we see no alternative but to accommodate them all in some variant of the special security wings. The Home Office still maintain two special wings — at Parkhurst and Leicester — and they imply that the thirteen Category A prisoners said to be held in them are indeed 'terrorist' prisoners (para 41). The Home Office say it would be regrettable to proliferate such units, but they do not say why (para 59). Yet the Home Office nonetheless claim that the facilities in the special wings have improved considerably since the days when they were criticised by Lord Mountbatten and the Radzinowicz sub-committee (para 41). It is worth emphasising, however, that there were only ever four special wings. Dispersal was supposed to replace them. But in spite of developing seven dispersal prisons only two special wings have been closed.

Since the dispersal policy cannot cope without having special wings at present, can there really be any objection to a concentration policy that operates with special wings also? How many would be required and where they should be is obviously a matter for discussion. Whether it is possible or desirable, to bring the special wings formerly at Durham and Chelmsford back into use we are not in a position to say. One possible solution would be to create special wings within some of the existing dispersal prisons, in addition to those at Leicester and Parkhurst. After the dispersal prisons are phased out the special wings could be retained for as long as they are deemed necessary.

The May Committee conclusions and the future

Though the May Committee raised some of these issues it scarcely did justice to them in its brief discussion of categorisation, allocation and the dispersal system. It is perhaps not surprising that the May Committee concluded:

> Whatever the arguments in favour of concentration — and we acknowledge some raise important issues which no prison system should ignore — they do not in *present operational conditions* add up to justifying either a partial or a total reversal of dispersal policy (May, 1979, para 6.72, emphasis added).

It reached this conclusion 'not by the strength of the arguments in favour of dispersal but of those against concentration'. In fact it cites only two arguments. First, that severe problems of control would arise from terrorist prisoners. We understand this fear but, as we have argued, it is a great pity that such a numerically insignificant group should be allowed to distort the real problems of the prison system and condemn thousands of prisoners needlessly to the highest standards of maximum security. We do not accept that this is necessary, but we note that the May Committee's conclusion is linked to 'present operational conditions'. Once these particular circumstances change we assume that the way will be open for a move away from dispersal which will be long overdue.

The second argument concerns whether or not it would be possible to staff one or two prisons holding only maximum security risk prisoners. The May Committee thought not. Again this can only make sense in relation to the 'present operational conditions'. For IRA prisoners apart, the May Committee (para 6.71) like the Home Office eventually accepts that security and control problems are not the same. As far as conventional Category A prisoners are concerned, the control problem, and therefore the staffing problem, should be no greater under concentration than under dispersal. And it must be evident that the POA do not share the same fears about staffing.

Great credit is reflected on the May Committee for its statement that *'we are not satisfied that the Home Office has struck the right security balance'* (para 6.70, emphasis added). After weighing up the numbers of escapes the Committee poses the question of 'whether all inmates in the dispersal prisons do really need to be there'. The Committee rightly notes that 'the issue is not just one of categorisation (i.e. are the right people in Category A), but also whether all the dispersal prison Category B inmates are in the right kind of prisons'. The Committee 'do not think that question has been convincingly answered' (para 6.70) and it recommends that the Home Office Working Party should give it their full attention. We wholly welcome this attempt by the May Committee to throw light on this exceedingly grey area to which we have repeatedly drawn attention. But it is difficult to have much confidence in the outcome of the Working Party's deliberations when so much of what they are looking into seems to have been pre-judged by the Home Office evidence. Could a Home Office Working Party now come up with conclusions radically at variance with what the Department has already asserted to be the case, and what Ministers have already defended in Parliament? We take some comfort, however, from the fact that the Treasury seems likely to be vigilant on these matters.

If the May Committee's dissatisfaction with the Home Office over the right security balance is to be remedied, then at the very least the deliberations of the Working Party must be made public so that some independent evaluation can take place. The Home Office should publish in full what it calls its 'precise and clear' criteria and instructions for the processes of classifying and re-classifying prisoners into security categories, and for allocating and re-allocating prisoners to prisons of different security standards. The Home Office should also publish a detailed breakdown of the available accommodation by security standard, and of the numbers of prisoners classified into each security category together with the reasons for their classification. Finally the Home Office should indicate which prisoners are actually held in inappropriate security conditions and why they are so held. If this were done we doubt very much whether the Home Office could justify either the existing security categories or the dispersal policy any longer. In that case the way would be open for a reorganisation along the following lines.

We suspect that in the longer term it may be more sensible for Prison Department to move towards a three-fold, rather than a four-fold, classification of security. This would produce a much more selective approach to high security risk prisoners, and a general de-escalation of the emphasis on security elsewhere in the system. In other words it would produce just the kind of bifurcation in the prison system that Bottoms (1977) talked about with regard to sentencing policy.

Under such a scheme Category A prisoners would be those whose escape would be highly dangerous to the public or police or the security of the State. We would suppose, as a rule of thumb, that only prisoners serving longer than, say seven years, should ever be eligible for this category. Numbers would be somewhat higher than at present, perhaps as many as 500, because some Category B prisoners would be re-classified, but only on security grounds. These prisoners would be housed in Albany and Long Lartin (or perhaps Frankland). Security status would be subject to appeal, and extra privileges would be provided. Special wings might have to be retained for as long as terrorist prisoners constituted a significant problem.

Category B would constitute a new group, effectively incorporating a high proportion of existing Category B and Category C prisoners. This would be the normal, and numerically most important category, for whom the highest conditions of security are not necessary but who could not, as a matter of routine, be trusted beyond the prison perimeter. Category C would constitute those prisoners whose escape would not be dangerous and who could be trusted outside the prison. This would embrace some Category C prisoners and all Category D prisoners. We suggest that, in addition to the selection of low risk prisoners for this Category, that all prisoners should normally become Category C prior to their release.

In our view Categories B and C do not demand a proliferation of specialist establishments with carefully graduated variations in their security precuations. Some prisons, perhaps the down-graded dispersal prisons stripped of some of their security paraphernalia, might be predominantly for Category B usage. But most prisoners in the system could be accommodated within a range of more general-purpose, secure establishments. Allocation to those prisons would be primarily on a locality basis. Assignment of security ratings B and C would then define certain limitations on access, or privileged access, to various facilities inside and outside these prisons. Most open prisons, as we know them today, and which in any case are something of a contradiction in terms, would either be closed in or closed down.

Once some common sense had been introduced into the handling of the security and control problems, attention could be devoted to the appropriate regime for maximum security prisons. Broadly speaking we take the view that subject to some extra restrictions compensated for by extra privileges, the regime for maximum security prisoners should be governed by the same general principles that should govern all prison regimes. We discuss this in chapter 4.

4 Normalisation of the prison: the use of scarce resources

Throughout our discussion there has been a tension between what is and what ought to be; between what the May Committee recommended and the conclusions to which it might have come. In this chapter, more so than in previous ones, these tensions become paramount. The use to which one puts scarce resources is so predicated on the aims of the prison system, the size and composition of the population, and the resort to security, that it is barely feasible to plan the future in the absence of substantial agreement on these prior conditions.

In our own evidence to the Committee we adopted a position very similar, in one respect at least, to that taken by the May Report. We urged that our evidence be seen as a whole. We stressed the relationship between our analysis of what it is realistically possible to do in prisons and our statement of the principles which should govern their use. Our discussion of resources was grounded on these principles as well as the premise that it was not penologically, socially or economically defensible either to increase or maintain the rate at which we currently use imprisonment. As we have seen, the May Committee, though rightly describing its Report as a package (May, 1979, para 1.19) took different views on these opening issues. It conceded the need critically to reappraise the security categorisation of prisoners. But, the Committee argued that future planning should assume an *increased* population in a system geared to aims which, though worded differently from the present Rule One, implied a similar *distribution* of resources to that which currently obtains. Which is to say that by the time the May Committee reached the issue of resources it had already agreed a framework which suggested that the only question about resources was 'how much more is needed?'.

It goes without saying, having parted company with the May Committee well before this point, that we reject the growth assumption. As a consequence we have faced a dilemma in writing about resources. On the one hand we wished to take issue with the May Committee's analysis. On the other we did not wish to confine our discussion within the constraints of that analysis: to have done so would have been implicitly to accept the reality of those constraints. As a result this chapter is divided into two parts. In the first we provide a general review of the evidence regarding resources together with a critique of the May Committee's conclusions. In the second we elaborate our manifesto for the implementation of our last principle — *the normalisation of the prison* — which we outlined in chapter 1. This section is concerned with the use and distribution of resources assuming — in our view, quite realistically — that there will be no great increase available.

It may be objected that to devote a large proportion of this chapter to a view presented to, and rejected by, the May Committee is unwarranted — a stubborn failure on our part to recognise the impracticability of our proposals. However, our conviction is based on more than mere attachment to our original formulation. We have grave doubts about whether the Government, even were it to accept the arguments advanced by the May Committee, will be able or willing to allocate the extra funds which those recommendations involve. If that proves to be the case — and there are already signs that it is so — then the May package cannot be implemented. Other solutions to the resources and standards questions will have to be sought. We believe that the Government will be forced to adopt strategies which, given other economic circumstances, it might not have chosen. Necessity is the mother of invention. We suggest that, in the long run, our admittedly radical proposals are both politically and economically more realistic than the May Committee's seal of approval on current policy would appear to indicate.

The general nature of the evidence on resources

On one issue practically all who gave evidence to Mr Justice May were agreed: the prison system has long been under-financed and most of the problems besetting Prison Department are the consequence of increasing demands, most of them beyond the control of the Department, being made on inadequate resources. Insofar as staff disputes over pay and conditions were the immediate cause of the Committee's appointment, it could be argued that resources — the overall size of the prison budget and the Government imposition of cash limits — were central to the Inquiry's deliberations. The prison system is manpower intensive. The cost of staff, just over £169 million out of a little over £244 million in the 1979-80 Supply Estimates, is the largest component in prison expenditure (May, 1979, para 6.79). But putting staff pay on one side it has also been a repeated claim that the whole system has been consistently under-financed and that long-term neglect, particularly of capital equipment, has resulted in a gradual build up of problems.

The first of the Committee's terms of reference requested that they examine and make recommendations upon the adequacy, management and use of the resources in the prison services. On this topic the various staff associations spoke in thunderous unison. The POA submission opened a chapter devoted to the question of resources with the claim that 'the Prison Service has been a poor relation amongst the social services for as long as anybody can remember' — and following a fairly muted discussion of manpower (concerned more with the quality than number of officers which should be recruited), supported a call for the resumption of the prison building programme with the assertion that 'the development of new buildings has come nowhere near matching the increases in the prison population' (POA, Evidence, section 13, pp 164-8). In developing this theme, reference was made to the 'scandalous' and 'chronic overcrowding' in local prisons involving the housing of three prisoners in cells designed for one more than a century ago such as 'no civilised society should tolerate' (p.166). This diagnosis was endorsed by the Home Office Branch of the Association of First Division Civil Servants. Referring to the open-ended commitment of the prison service, without 'commensurate flexibility in the provision of resources' the Association argued that the 'problems of the prison service are most immediately the result of the shortage of resources' and placed particular emphasis on the reliance 'to an excessive degree on nineteenth century buildings with nineteenth century facilities' (FDCS, Evidence, p.1).

Prison governors took a similar line. They argued that were resources not brought into line with tasks then staff might well place restrictions on the tasks performed (SCPS, Evidence, para 9). To this threat of industrial action was added a more ominous warning. The newly formed British Association of Prison Governors argued that overcrowding reduced staff capacity to control prisoners and suggested 'that we cannot build new prisons as quickly as inmates can knock them down' (BAPG, Evidence, p.5). Restating evidence previously submitted to the House of Commons Expenditure Committee, the Prison and Borstal Governors branch argued for an open cheque book to accompany 'the open door', claiming that the 'building stock must be amongst the worst of any public service' and describing current overcrowding and recent cuts in the building programme as indefensible (SCPS, para 12). The reduction of living standards consequent on the expenditure cuts was, they argued, 'intolerable for inmates, staff and management' (para 12). The BAPG were more specific. The building programme must be such as to permit replacement of all institutions 'which have passed or are approaching the end of their useful lives'. A not inconsiderable matter since for them it meant the replacement 'of nearly all our present institutions, all the Victorian prisons and most of the open institutions built during the Second World War' (BAPG, p.4), an aim later described in the same submission as unrealistic (p.19).

Though the tendency was to offer rather different solutions, most of the external organisations submitting evidence to the Inquiry agreed with this picture of severe overcrowding, antiquated buildings and facilities, and low living standards. As we have seen in chapter 2 the penal pressure groups vigorously proclaimed the need to reduce the prison population and, anticipating the possibility of a new building programme, argued that increased accommodation would probably result in a further increase in persons imprisoned. One or two questions were also raised about the use made of existing resources. Though most of the organisations would probably agree with NACRO's rather resigned confession — 'it is clear that the system has been neglected over the years and in the short term some money will have to be spent on raising the basic standards' (NACRO, Evidence, p.5) — some contributors, for example the probation officers, suggested that, population reduction apart, existing resources 'could be more flexibly and effectively used' (NAPO, Evidence, para 2.2). In particular the Howard League argued that many establishments, closed as well as open prisons, were under-utilised; and that more prisons might be designated local establishments; that single occupancy of cells was not necessarily the ideal, and that current security arrangements should be reviewed. (Howard League, Evidence, pp 3-4). These points were discussed in greater detail in our own evidence and we return to them later in this chapter.

Apart from these few rather halting challenges the 'resource deficiency' arguments, which have for many years mesmerised most participants in the penal debate, swept the field. The penal pressure groups anticipated the consequences but based their opposition to an expanded prisons budget, or at least to a new building programme, almost entirely on the population reduction argument. The use of current resources, went virtually unchallenged; the associations of prison personnel relying apparently on the self-evident character of their claim, did not bother to document the gap between existing provision and alleged needs; and Mr Justice May and his colleagues who, as we have seen from chapter 2, saw population reduction initiatives as beyond their brief, were nicely prepared, to the accompaniment of staff chorus, to receive the Home Office diagnosis.

Our own submission to the May Committee appears to have been the only one which made a real attempt to question the lengthy, complex and very detailed arguments which the Committee received from the Home Office. Indeed the May Report quotes our submission on several occasions, describing it variously as thoughtful, interesting and challenging (May, 1979, paras 4.23, 6.38, 6.52). Despite appearances, we are not concerned to emphasise this point because we conceive our contribution to have been exceptional in terms of its analytical or innovatory content. On the contrary we are only too well aware of its shortcomings, although given the fact that it had to be completed within four weeks, without the benefit of seeing the Home Office evidence, some shortcomings might be forgiven. However, having made some flattering references to our evidence the May Committee went on to ignore it completely. The Home Office account was accepted without being subject to any more external appraisal than that derived from what Mr Justice May later described as 'the good sense of the Committee' (NACRO, 1980).

This near unanimity from the prison service itself on the question of resources, coupled with the meagre quality of advice received by Mr Justice May from outside, lies at the root of the Committee's failure seriously to appraise existing Prison Department policy. For, as we shall argue, what the May Report has recommended in relation to buildings, overcrowdings and regime standards, is in effect simply an endorsement of what Prison Department is already committed to.

The May Committee conclusions and their implications

Because, in most respects, the Inquiry's recommendations on resources follow from acceptance of the Home Office account it may be sensible to begin with the conclusions before embarking on a detailed scrutiny of the evidence.

Of its three hundred and thirty seven page Report the Committee devoted a single chapter, comprising forty-five pages, to resources. A quarter of those pages were taken up with tables of statistics, graphs and accounts transcribed from Home Office evidence. An appendix, comprising Home Office descriptions of existing accommodation was also included. It is a modest discourse on the first, and arguably the most important, of the long-term issues on which the Committee was specifically requested to make recommendations. But, as we have seen, by the time the Committee reached the resources question, the stage had already been set. Having broadly endorsed the population projections, Rule One (despite its new clothing), and the framework for security, the Committee had left itself precious little space for critical manoeuvre.

Under the resources heading, three questions, manpower, buildings and overcrowding, were reviewed by the May Committee prior to a general discussion of the prisons budget. Regarding manpower, the

102

Home Office staffing data were sufficient to stimulate the most dormant critical faculty. They showed an 88 per cent increase in personnel, without any diminution in the very high levels of overtime worked, during a thirteen year period when the prison population increased by only 38 per cent. Indeed, in a brief but tightly argued paper jointly prepared by the Treasury, Civil Service Department and Central Policy Review Staff (Central Departments, Evidence, vol.III, paper V(3), pp 14-16), the Committee was provided with ammunition that enabled it to make trenchant comments on manning levels, dock escorts, and the arrangement of working rotas and overtime. Nevertheless, though the Committee judged there to be scope for manpower savings, it concluded that more staff were needed. Since the question of staff pay would have to be settled by Government, and since the Committee referred several disputed staffing questions back to the Home Office negotiating machinery, no attempt was made to calculate the financial implications of these observations.

A different view was taken of capital expenditure. Here the Committee made calculations and arrived at specific financial recommendations. Having concluded that the prison population greatly exceeds existing accommodation; having assumed that 'whilst every effort should continue to be made to reduce the prison populations, for the foreseeable future they can be expected to rise gradually' (May, 1979, para 6.101); having assessed the condition of the penal estate to be very run-down; and being convinced that no redistribution of the population would either eliminate overcrowding or substantially improve living conditions; the Committee then endorsed the Home Office call for a building programme so massive as to be comparable with that which followed the construction of Pentonville in 1842.

The Committee recommended that annual capital expenditure be doubled to £50 million, at current survey prices. This would permit the Department to embark on a new building programme designed:

> to reduce overcrowding to the extent that there shall in no circumstances, except for dormitories or specially enlarged cells, be more than one inmate in any one cell, and either by modernisation or replacement produce integral sanitation and washing facilities progressively throughout the system' (para 6.105).

The Committee took the view that no attempt to repair the neglect of the penal estate would be credible unless it involved either the replacement or effective rebuilding of all the older Victorian prisons. In this Mr Justice May and his colleagues seem to have accepted the Home Office assessment that the programme would not be completed for twenty-five years (para 6.84). Integral sanitation, it was estimated, would mean the replacement of 5,500 cells lost in the course of modernising the Victorian prisons. The elimination of cell sharing required the provision of 8,500 new places. Four prisons providing 1,000 places were said to be so run down as to necessitate replacement within a decade. In addition a further sixty-six establishments were said to require redevelopment. Although this accommodation increase of 15,000 places in thirty-six new prisons, plus the refurbishment of other establishments, would cost about £720 million, the Committee strenuously advocated that future governments should not, like their predecessors, permit the building programme to be held back by short-term needs to cut public expenditure.

Since there appears to be so much agreement between Home Office, prison personnel and outside commentators, on the poor condition of the penal estate, some readers may interpret our scrutiny of the Home Office evidence which follows as nitpicking. Others may consider it irrelevant. After all, it might be argued, the prison system is largely about people. Manpower is the major cost; even were the May Committee's capital expenditure recommendations carried out it would remain a modest part, some 17 per cent, of the annual prison budget, less than 3 per cent of the total law and order expenditure. And though buildings do not dictate regimes they do constrain what is possible: the physical conditions in many prisons are indisputably squalid. Furthermore, given that twenty-five years will pass, according to the Home Office estimates, before the estate is modernised and overcrowding eradicated, there will be, as the May Committee argued, ample opportunity to review the programme should political initiatives be taken which successfully reduce the prison population (para 6.107).

All these arguments have substance but they ignore the more significant aspects of prison buildings. Prisons, by definition, are substantial edifices built, as the current stock amply demonstrates, to endure. They take up a large amount of space: they are not easily accommodated in urban areas. At one time they were deliberately constructed with the intention of striking deterrent fear into the hearts of the population that gazed on their walls: today they awaken rather different anxieties. New prisons are opposed on the grounds that they threaten the security or social tone of neighbourhoods: yet the closure of existing prisons is also opposed on grounds of loss of employment and loss of trade. No more graphic example of the enduring quality of prisons need be sought than the instant local opposition to the May Committee's recommendation that Dartmoor be closed and Mr Whitelaw's immediate assurance that it would not be so. About one third of our existing establishments were built on the Pentonville model in the nineteenth century by counties, boroughs or the convict authority. We rather doubt that prisons built today are as physically robust, but we must assume that establishments planned now — and about ten years elapses between conception and birth — will be in use until well into the second half of the twenty-first century. Given these considerations no new prison should lightly be contemplated. It is not simply that a new prison is a substantial investment: it is rather that the physical commitment of resources itself generates a pressure that those resources be used.

What then are the issues we should bear in mind when considering the May Committee's building programme? In our judgement the fundamental questions are those which we discussed in chapters 1 and 2. What are the proper uses of imprisonment and how large ought the prison population of the future to be? Since it is almost universally agreed, by those who have given the character of the prison population careful consideration, that too many people are in prison, then our first aim must be to inhibit the courts' use of custody. No matter how humane custodial conditions might be made, the loss of liberty remains unalterable; it will always be indefensible for a person needlessly to be deprived of his or her liberty. We contend that until the courts significantly reduce their use of custodial sentences it would be fundamentally wrong to adopt any policy which might reduce rather than increase sentencers' inhibitions.

Recent evidence from the United States suggests that the degree to which we resort to custody, and to high security custody in particular, may be as much a function of expanded supply as increased demand. In chapter 3 we argued that this had proved to be the case with regard to our own use of high security prisons. Similar observations have been made regarding the use of secure accommodation for juvenile offenders (Cawson, 1975; Martell and Cawson, 1975; Millham, Bullock and Hosie, 1978). A comparative study of incarceration in the United States has demonstrated that the availability of prison cells is as significant a determinant of prison population size as crime rates and other social and economic factors (Rutherford, personal communication). Old prisons are seldom closed: those States with the largest building programmes in recent years also recorded the largest rise in prison population (Nagel, 1977).

It would clearly be unwise to draw conclusions from American data for this country and, as yet, we know too little of the experience of other European countries. The criminal justice and penal systems in the USA and UK are very different: variations in the scope of executive discretion and in the prosecution process mean that there are real differences in the degree to which demand-push and supply-pull mechanisms *can* affect the size of the prison population. Obviously, where some rationing system operates, the use of custody is *necessarily* dictated by supply. This has been the case, as the May Committee noted, in relation to detention centres 'receptions . . . rose during the period (1974 to 1978), as accommodation became available' (May, 1979, para 3.9). Strangely, however, the Committee merely notes that 'the largest proportionate increase in the numbers received into custody over the period (1974 to 1978), was in the number of young people received under sentence of Borstal training or detention' (para 3.9). It does not appear to have considered that this may have had less to do with the too readily accepted explanation of the 'post war rise in crime' (para 3.4), and rather more with the greatly expanded accommodation available. After all, the rise in adult crime has been broadly similar to that for juveniles and the rise in the proportion of juveniles receiving custodial sentences during recent years has been very much faster than the increase in juvenile crime (New Approaches, 1980).

These considerations should promote some scepticism over claims that new buildings will replace old ones, or at least lead to less intensive use of them. Indeed the assumptions underpinning the Home Secretary's current policy suggests that the May Committee's proposal to expand accommodation *and* greatly improve living conditions will, in the absence of any restriction on the sentencing power of the courts, almost certainly increase the resort to custody. Part of Mr Whitelaw's justification for introducing tougher 'short sharp shock' regimes is that they might make shorter sentences more acceptable. Presumably the reverse is equally true. No one should be beguiled by those penal historians who argue that since seventy to eighty prisons have been closed in England and Wales during the last century there is no evidence of reluctance to close establishments in this country. Those prisons were closed after 1878 when the control of all prisons passed from the local authorities to central government. It was the consequence of very considerable over-capacity which, prior to the administrative change, could not have been readily eliminated. It was a closure programme dictated by factors which will never be repeated. Only two prisons have been closed since 1945, both of them temporary open camps.

There is one other lesson which the experience of other countries and our own history suggests. Let us suppose that the May Committee's optimism is well founded; that during the course of their projected building programme new political initiatives stabilise or reduce the prison population and that replacement and closure of establishments takes place. What then will be the building stock carried through into the twenty-first century? 'Only rarely' the Committee argued 'would on site redevelopment seem practicable' (para 6.108). We must assume then that the Holloway experiment – the only Victorian urban prison to have been completely rebuilt this century – is not likely to be repeated. If Mr Justice May's thirty-six new prisons are built, almost all will be on new sites. These sites will inevitably be distant from the areas from which most prisoners are drawn and they will be large, on average over four hundred prisoners in each, if they are to create fifteen thousand places.

To be fair, the May Committee recognised this problem and in no way advocated the use of those rural and inaccessible sites characteristic of practically all new establishments opened since 1945. On the contrary it suggested 'it will be necessary for the government seriously to contemplate resort to their undoubted powers of compulsory purchase' if urban sites are to be obtained and construction times and costs kept within reasonable levels (para 6.109). But the Committee's claim that 'this is not to advocate arbitrary expropriation and brushing aside local objections' (para 6.109) is not convincing. It is a common-place among prison administrators that if they could reconstruct the system *de novo*, unfettered by cost and planning considerations, it would consist of relatively small urban prisons. But the cost and planning restrictions are such that, inexorably, the reverse is always the case. If one recalls the prisons closed after 1878 — Cambridge, Ilford, Southampton, Bath, Ipswich, Northampton, Taunton, Chester, Kirkdale, Dover, Woking, Hereford, Knutsford, Brecon, Derby — and some of those retained — Dartmoor, Parkhurst, Rochester, Portland — the pattern is clear. Which prisons might be phased out as the May generation of establishments arises? Presumably the oldest, whose potential is said to be poor — Oxford, Bedford, Canterbury, Gloucester, Leeds, Leicester, Shrewsbury, Swansea and Winchester — generally the smaller urban local prisons. Indeed if the May Committee's proposals were adopted, and initial building priority given to remand accommodation, it seems likely that the *raison d'etre* of these prisons, their geographical proximity to Crown Courts, would be removed.

Our own view, elaborated in the second part of this chapter, is that the local prisons should continue to form the hub of the prison system. Indeed their number and importance should be increased rather than diminished. Locality of custody is an integral part of what we mean by the normalisation of the prison.

The Home Office evidence

1. Buildings

The official evidence as to the condition of prison buildings was incorporated in a Home Office paper devoted to accommodation and compiled by the Prison Department Directorate of Works (Home Office, Evidence, vol.I, paper IIC(2), pp 129-48). A table setting out the use, size, age, physical condition and future potential of each establishment was reproduced as Appendix 6 to the May Report and formed the basis of the Committee's assessment of future needs. There are a number of discrepancies in the Home Office data — for example, one more camp, described as in poor condition, is referred to in the summary tables (para 11, table 21) than is listed in the appendix — but, since these make only a marginal impact on the final picture, it is pointless to enumerate them. However, in two respects the building stock was misleadingly presented.

First, under the sub-heading 'age', each establishment was categorised as pre-1930, post 1930 or camp. The date referred to was that for the construction of the building; camp referred mostly to open institutions developed from former service camps taken over since 1945. The year 1930 was chosen as the dividing line to distinguish 'between the new purpose-built prisons, which are expected to have a life at least to the end of the century, and older buildings' (para 8). This suggested that the older buildings had no such life expectancy, an impression reinforced by the summary statement that 'the physical state of the older prisons and most of the wartime accommodation gives serious cause for concern' (para 15). According to this assessment only 32, or 27 per cent of all establishments, and only 22 per cent of all certified accommodation, could be relied upon to carry us into the twenty-first century. That is plainly nonsense.

There is, as we shall see, a poor fit between the Directorate of Works assessment of the physical condition of the buildings and the explanation given for the dating method. We do not find this surprising. In the past, Prison Department has dated its establishments by the year when first used for offenders. In the case of converted premises, this was followed by a description of the origins of the buildings (Home Office, 1969, pp 82-7; Home Office, 1977, pp 145-9). In our own evidence to the May Committee we pointed out that, according to the previously published Home Office data 82 or 61 per cent of the 135 separate functional units operational in 1977 were purpose-built, or converted for penal use since 1945; and they provided 47 per cent of all certified accommodation (King and Morgan, 1979, paras 21-24). This is a rather different picture from that derived from the Home Office evidence. The May Report described this as 'an interesting perspective but . . . vitiated by the fact that date of first penal use is a poor guide to condition' (May, 1979, para 6.38). We agree, but we venture to suggest that, in the absence of more detailed information, it is likely to be a very much better guide than date of construction. Assessment by date of construction presents the *most aged* impression possible: it verges on distortion to use a method which, for example, places Moor Court, a converted mansion opened in 1957, in the same category as the local prison at Oxford, the main building of which remains almost unchanged since 1858.

Secondly, and more seriously misleading because it significantly reduced the reliability of both age and condition assessments, was the Home Office's decision to categorise not buildings, nor even functional units, but penal complexes. By way of illustration we may take the example of Winchester. In the Home Office evidence Winchester is described as a local prison, with certified accommodation for 484 men, pre-1930 in age, fair in physical condition, and with poor future potential. In reality, Winchester is a Prison Department complex comprising two distinct institutions, a local prison and a remand centre. The local prison, of Victorian radial design behind a high wall, was the old County Gaol built in 1846. Although the perimeter wall now encompasses a recently built visiting and educational block the accommodation wings remain virtually unchanged from the nineteenth century. However, the remand centre, with certified accommodation for 60-80 boys is a modern purpose-built prison opened in 1965. It occupies its own compound to the rear of the local prison site, is surrounded by a modern high security fence and has its own entrance. How this substantial complex, incorporating several modern buildings, ideally located to serve the Hampshire region, convenient to the city centre for both the Crown Court and, more importantly, visitors using public transport, can be described as having poor potential is beyond our comprehension. This example could be repeated several times over.

In our own evidence to the May Committee we described Winchester, as does Prison Department in its annual reports, as two functional units. It is difficult to interpret the Home Office decision to reduce 135 such functional units to the 117 complexes listed in their evidence as anything but deliberate obfuscation of the facts. By so doing it actually submitted to the May Committee a less accurate set of buildings data than can be gleaned from *Prisons and the Prisoner* (Home Office, 1977). What one might have expected on the occasion of so important an inquiry into resources would have been a breakdown, by age and condition, of the accommodation *within* prisons. What the Home Office has done, however, is to conceal the modern accommodation units built on older sites conveniently from view. Thus Camp Hill, described as pre-1930, in fact includes a block for 160 prisoners opened in 1976. Bristol, described as a pre-1930 prison in fair condition, contains a block for 100 prisoners, opened in 1967 and a second for 192 prisoners opened in 1975. Simply by perusing the appendices to

Prison Department annual reports during the 1970s we note that other Victorian establishments with similar modern additions include Gloucester, Norwich, Portland, Dover and Rochester. In the same way it might, when referring to 'future potential', have been more informative had the Home Office indicated whether 'replacement' — of sub-standard accommodation on old camp sites — was partially completed, in progress or merely planned. We rather doubt, in view of work already completed, whether establishments such as Acklington and Erlestoke can any longer be accurately described as camps.

In only one respect did the Home Office evidence to the May Committee add to our own knowledge of the condition of the penal estate. Though the addition was modest enough it served to expose at least part of the distortion described above. The physical condition of each complex was given a general rating, presumably of the largest accommodation unit in each complex. In nearly all cases, this meant the oldest unit in the worst condition, and therefore constituted the most negative appraisal. On this basis 38 (33 per cent) of establishments were described as in good condition, 53 (45 per cent) in fair condition and 26 (22 per cent) in poor condition. In passing, it should be noted that these figures accord neither with those summarised in the Home Office evidence nor with the May Committee's reportage of that evidence. In the original Home Office list of establishments, 26 are described as in poor condition, in their summary table this becomes 27 and, incomprehensibly, 24 in the May Report (May, 1979, para 6.37).

Given the May Committee's conclusion that 'there can be no doubt that the main problem is obsolescence' with 'most of the Victorian local prisons . . . at the bottom' (para 6.41), one might have expected most of the 'poor' condition establishments to be from this sector. It is not the case. Only 7 of the 56 pre-1930 establishments, providing 16 per cent of the certified accommodation in this sector, were said to be in poor condition. All of the remaining poor accommodation was in the camps which, as we shall argue, are the least important, most under-utilised and most readily expendable institutions in the prison system.

The Committee appears to have been influenced less by the technical evidence, however, ambiguous, from the Directorate of Works and more by the staff chorus and the squalor largely the consequences of over-crowding, which they witnessed on their visits to prisons. How else could the Committee describe Wakefield as requiring 'a great deal of attention if (it was) not literally, to fall down', when even the Department described that prison as in fair condition and capable of improvement? (para 6.41). Or how, if the obsolescence and condition of buildings were the central issue, was it possible for the Committee to single out Bristol, almost half of whose certified accommodation is in two modern buildings as one of the worst of the Victorian local prisons? (para 6.41). In fact only two pre-1930 prisons, Lancaster and Oxford are described as in both poor condition and as having poor potential and we would quarrel with part of even this assessment. For the rest there is no reason why, with less intensive use and after a general upgrading programme, they should not provide the humane custody which we seek. The old local prisons, like Winchester, are ideally located for maintaining prisoners' links with the community. And their design, despite Prison Department's architectural policy ever since the construction of Everthorpe, in 1958, is now recognised as far from being outmoded. Given the physical soundness of the Victorian penal estate it is quite incomprehensible that the May Committee should have argued that no buildings programme could be regarded as credible if it did not involve either the replacement or rebuilding of the local prisons *'for whose galleried construction there was universal — and we think sound — preference'* (para 6.105, emphasis added). If the reluctance of Prison Department and the May Committee to contemplate a future for the Victorian prisons is not explained by their poor condition then it must presumably rest on the assertion that so many of them are said to have poor development potential. Some 19 out of the 56 pre-1930 establishments are said to be in this category, though it should be noted that only 12 of these are Victorian purpose-built prisons: the remainder are conversions, usually of the small country house type. The Home Office evidence on accommodation gives absolutely no indication as to how development potential was assessed. As we have demonstrated, it could not have been dictated by the physical condition of the buildings. Nor, we think, can it have been dictated by architectural considerations for, as far as we are aware, the design of those establishments said to have 'excellent' or 'moderate' potential, as well as those for which improvement is already planned or in progress is often very similar.

We suspect that size and space have been important criteria. The twelve poor potential Victorian prisons include most, though not all, of the smaller prisons in our system — Swansea, Bedford, Canterbury, Gloucester, Leicester, Northallerton, Usk, Shrewsbury — often occupying restricted urban sites with little or no scope for expansion. The two also described as in poor condition, Oxford and Lancaster, have the additional complication that they are, in their own right, important historical sites with perhaps limited scope for redevelopment. We fully recognise that these prisons are restricted in the space available for recreational, occupational and other communal activities. Furthermore, they presumably lack benefits of scale in terms of staffing. But we suggest that their advantages in locality and morale more than compensate for these difficulties. The cost of their closure and capital replacement would greatly exceed the higher running costs, or redevelopment costs, incurred in keeping them open. It should be remembered that of the £720 million said by the Home Office to be necessary for the buildings programme, £520 million were required for new prisons and only £200 million, a sum attainable within existing capital expenditure budgets, for the refurbishing and upgrading of existing prisons. Because the Home Office evidence and the May Report discuss none of these vital issues, while nevertheless threatening the life of older institutions, we urge that this topic be the subject of a better informed public debate.

Before concluding this discussion of buildings, mention must be made of Dartmoor. In their evidence regarding accommodation the Home Office described four prisons as so run down that there was no alternative but to close and replace them. The prisons were not named and it is worth recording that when Mr Trevelyan, the Director General of the Prison Service, was recently asked to identify them, he failed to do so (NACRO, 1980). However, from the Directorate of Works buildings assessment it seems certain that Dartmoor was *not* in the Department's list and that the four prisons were Lancaster (with 153 places), Oxford (143), North Sea Camp (166) and Haverigg (520). Together, these would account for the 1,000 places referred to in the Home Office evidence, and are the only establishments said to be in both poor condition and to have poor potential. Thus, in singling out Dartmoor for closure (May, 1979, para 6.41), the May Committee exercised independent judgement in condemning a prison, the condition of which the Works Directorate described as fair, capable of and suitable for improvement and presumably, moor conservationists apart, with great potential.

In fact, of course, Dartmoor is a sort of virility test. Its closure has been recommended, planned and announced so often, over so many years, its legend is so great, its age so frequently exaggerated (none of the present cell blocks is from the Napoleonic era), that we suspect no self respecting Inquiry advocating 'positive custody' could have endorsed its continued existence. Our cynicism is not prompted by disagreement — in our own evidence to the May Committee we recommended that Dartmoor, among other prisons, should be closed — but by the arbitrariness of the Committee's judgement. Dartmoor should be closed not because of its negative mystique, or even its inhospitable weather (is this what 'against nature' means?) (May, 1979, para 6.41). It should be closed, together with several other establishments, because it has no advantages of high security, no special facilities, and it is in the wrong place. Be that as it may, by endorsing the broader Home Office population and building projections, the May Committee has not only ensured that Dartmoor will remain open, but that it will, in the future, be joined by the new and similarly isolated establishments, the Dartmoors of the twenty-second century.

In conclusion we think it right that prison buildings, and the overall prisons budget, should be put into some sort of context. In our own evidence to the May Committee we challenged the view which seems to be so generally held as to be orthodox, that the prison service, and particularly its capital programme, had been starved of resources to a degree that it was the Cinderella of the social and law and order services. Having acknowledged that there are undeniably many old buildings in the system (which turned out from Home Office evidence on condition, and the May Committee's conclusions on design, to be nevertheless suitable for their present purpose) we demonstrated that the prison system has a high proportion of modern or modernised buildings. We argued that in this respect our system almost certainly compares quite favourably with other prison systems of similar size and complexity; that the building programme since the 1950s has been one of the largest, if not the largest, in any country; and that, in spite of recent cut-backs, the building programme continues with considerable and, in our view, unjustified momentum. We also provided evidence suggesting that the proportion of postwar accommodation in prisons was lower than that in schools, though not dramatically lower, but higher than in hospitals (King and Morgan, 1979, para 25).

In presenting that case we recognised the limitations of our data. At that stage we had no time to gather other comparative materials and there was no published Prison Department information as to the condition of particular prisons. However, from evidence presented to the May Committee it is clear that our arguments were valid. The May Report was forced to concede 'that at least in England and Wales prisons' *current expenditure has done better than any of the other services including public expenditure as a whole and compares favourably on capital expenditure*' (May, 1979, para 6.95, emphasis added). In spite of this, the May Committee took the view that law and order is in some sense more fundamental than other social services; and that the requirements of the prison service ought to be given special priority since 'in a period when crime, including terrorism, has been an increasing threat to society, it would have been irresponsible and dangerous not to have increased the level of protection' (paras 6.93 and 6.97). Apart from the fact that we rather doubt whether increased expenditure on prisons offers the *best* defence against crime — a question we cannot debate here — we wish to reiterate two points. First, it is unreasonable to argue that prisons should be a special case for additional expenditure when many prisoners need not be in prison at all to protect the public. There are, after all, fewer than 100 terrorists in custody. Secondly, there can be little case for more expenditure unless it can be shown that existing resources are used wisely. Our evidence suggested that there was a waste or mis-use of resources — and as we have seen, the Central Departments were sufficiently concerned about the use of manpower and security costs to ask some probing questions. The most telling arguments for more resources have been based on the level of overcrowding — but even here the statistics are not always what they seem.

2   Overcrowding

A major part of the May Report's recommended building programme stemmed from the Committee's desire to eradicate overcrowding: 20 new prisons were said to be required in order to eliminate cell-sharing.

All discussions of overcrowding in our system must begin with the term 'certified normal accommodation'. The May Report records that on 1 July 1979 the CNA of the prison system in England and Wales was 37,881 and the number of prisoners 40,885 (para 3.2). Nowhere in the May Report is there any discussion of the meaning of CNA but the initial assumption is that the system is at least 12 per cent over-crowded. We say at least 12 per cent because the need to keep a proportion of places vacant for receptions and transfers and other operational purposes may mean that the real level of overcrowding, as experienced by prisoners, is very much higher.

The central aim of Prison Department policy on CNA and living standards over the years has been one man one cell. The alleged short-fall in places has been remarkably constant. In 1962, in the last annual report of the Prison Commissioners, it was reported that the shortfall was 3,245 or 12 per cent of places, in a system with a CNA of 27,818. Each year since 1963 Prison Department has published the number of prisoners sharing cells, a perpetual reminder of the standards to which they aspire and which a massive building programme has failed to achieve. The May Committee has reaffirmed that standard and supported it with a yet larger capital programme.

The use of one cell by one prisoner might seem to be a stable element in CNA assessment. But when is a cell not a cell? And when is it a 'specially enlarged cell' or 'regular dormitory' the communal use of which the May Report approved (paras 6.57 and 6.105) and which makes up a significant proportion of the overall CNA? More than a quarter (10,408 places out of 36,479) of the present CNA for males

114

and over half of that provided for females (630 places out of 1,256), is communal. Our questions regarding CNA are not prompted by mere academic curiosity, but real doubts as to the validity of CNA for assessing overcrowding and, by implication, the gap between accommodation provision and needs within the system. A few years ago, when collecting data for a study of trial and remand prisoners in Winchester remand centre, we noted very considerable fluctuations in the CNA — from 43 in 1965 to 78 in 1972 and down to 64 in 1978 — without there having been any discernible addition or structural alteration to the buildings (King and Morgan, 1976). Similar unexplained changes emerge from an examination of published CNA figures for almost any institution over a period of years. A second doubt was prompted by the fact that the size of cells and rooms, and thus the amount of space available to prisoners occupying them, varied considerably from one prison to another. In our evidence to the May Committee, drawing on measurements and observations made over years of research in several prisons, we demonstrated that some prisoners occupying single cells and thus technically not overcrowded in CNA terms had less space than those officially defined as overcrowded (King and Morgan, 1979, paras 44-53). Without wishing to suggest that floor space *was* or *should* be used as the sole criterion of overcrowding it seemed, in the absence of other objective standards, to serve as a useful starting point. It is enough to destroy any confidence in the concept of CNA.

All sleeping accommodation has to be certified as suitable for a stated number of prisoners according to section 14 of the Prison Act 1952. A copy of a certificate, for a single wing at Brixton, by way of example, was attached to the Home Office paper on accommodation (Home Office, Evidence, vol.I, paper IIC(2), Annex E). The document shows that for each room the number of inmates normally accommodated (which is not the same thing as ideally accommodated), and the maximum number of prisoners that could be accommodated, are recorded together with the room's current use (which is not necessarily accommodation). To this is attached the not very explicit explanation that:

> there are no objective criteria for deciding the extent to which a cell can be overcrowded. The governor decides this on a common-sense basis, consulting the medical officer if necessary. The certification of the accommodation is given normally by the regional directors (para 32).

Such an explanation seems to confirm our fears that Prison Department have no agreed criteria for deciding either normal or maximum accommodation figures. We expect that where cells were originally intended for one prisoner, no matter whether they comprise 130 sq.ft as at Pentonville, constructed in 1842, or 59 sq.ft as at Albany, opened in 1967, this is stated to be their CNA, though we cannot be certain even of that. No doubt there are established CNA precedents for the various arrangements whereby two or three Victorian cells are, by removing side walls, converted to a single room. However, it seems almost certain that as far as larger dormitories are concerned, the absence of criteria produces CNA's of increasing arbitrariness. We accept that, as the Home Office point out, overcrowding is not simply a matter of how many prisoners should occupy a room used for sleeping but whether other services such as kitchens and drains, can cope with a population which they were not originally designed to serve (para 31). But these problems do not mean that agreed and objective criteria cannot be established for certifying accommodation. On the contrary, in a prison system which includes buildings and facilities of great age and diversity, agreed criteria become all the more necessary so that the gap between what is and what ought to be can be readily determined and accusations of inequity avoided. If CNA figures indeed reflected known and accepted standards, claims for more resources could be easily assessed.

Unaware of, or unconcerned by, the ambiguities of CNA the May Committee pressed on to recommend accommodation standards: as a consequence what might have been an important step in the right direction may prove counter-productive. Having perused the European Convention on Human Rights, the UN Rules and the Home Office statement of long-standing aspirations, the May Committee concluded that there must be no enforced cell sharing except in 'regular dormitories' (May, 1979, para 6.57). At a later stage 'specially enlarged cells' were added to the undefined dormitories (para 6.105). Furthermore the Committee recommended that all single cells should have integral or continuous access sanitation and no room, of whatever size, should be shared unless this sanitary standard was met. Because these standards form a major part of the justification for a huge building programme, and have become confused with other accommodation propositions in the May Report, they require close scrutiny.

The Committee made it clear, somewhat to its surprise, that none of its witnesses had 'argued that cell sharing was of itself abhorrent' — indeed 'especially in the local prisons where the opportunities for association are severely restricted and where inmates may be locked up for long periods' the evidence suggested 'that many men would prefer to have a companion than be entirely alone' (para 6.55). Nevertheless by the time the chapter on resources came to be summed up the Committee had accepted, without critical comment, a Home Office

116

assessment that the elimination of cell sharing required the provision of 8,500 new cells (para 6.84); and treating elimination of cell sharing as the same as the elimination of overcrowding, they argued for a building programme which would ensure 'that there shall in no circumstances . . . be more than one inmate in any one cell' (para 6.105). The shift from a desire to eliminate 'enforced' cell sharing, by which we take the Committee to mean that voluntary sharing is acceptable, to no sharing under any circumstances can only be explained by the sanitation standard. We must presume, because it is nowhere stated, that the Committee took the view that no cell ever constructed for one prisoner could have either integral or continuous access sanitation and leave space for sharing. We do not think this is self-evident. If a large Victorian cell shared by two prisoners provides each with as much space as that offered in a small modern cell — a position which the Committee appears to have recognised (para 6.55) — why should it not continue to be shared voluntarily when both the single and shared cell have been fitted with an integral toilet? Or to take the exception permitted by the Committee, how large does a cell have to be before it can be described as a specially enlarged cell?

A further confusion concerns the equation of cell sharing with overcrowding not at an individual level but at prison system level. In 1978 the highest number of prisoners sharing cells was 16,098; of these 11,016 were two in a cell and 5,082 three in a cell. Thus, at the very most in 1978, 7,207 single cells were in multiple use, and 8,896 new cells were required to eliminate overcrowding as defined by May. By accepting the Home Office estimates of 8,500 new cells required the Committee appears to have accepted that other accommodation in the system is being used effectively and that there is little or no slack to be taken up. In fact the Committee did express some dissatisfaction with the under-occupation of certain closed training and open prisons while the local prisons were subject to what was, by any standards, considerable crowding. But in the event, having opted for the continuation of treatment and training, clothed now in the new garb of positive custody, it accepted the Home Office explanations of the phenomenon. In the end all that remained of the dissatisfaction was the suggestion that the Home Office 'actively commence a programme of reaching new local understandings' with local communities so that more prisoners, with more varied offending backgrounds, could fill up these under-occupied establishments (paras 6.58-61).

Before examining the Home Office explanation for under-occupation we should remind ourselves that the 12 per cent overcrowding of the system as a whole involved, on average, 4,438 prisoners surplus to CNA in 1978. Some margin must obviously be left to cope with receptions

117

and transfers, repairs and decoration and other operational needs. The more specialised the use of institutions becomes — sex, age, sentence, security and training differentiation — the larger this margin will have to be. In our own evidence to the May Committee we suggested that a 5 per cent margin should, as a rule of thumb, be a sufficient allowance for efficient administration and prison and Borstal governors agreed with us (SCPS, Evidence, para 13). A 5 per cent margin suggests that in 1978 it would have been reasonable for an average of 1,831 places to be empty, which would have meant that there were 6,269 prisoners surplus to CNA. But this is still some 2,500 prisoners short of the number typically held two or three to a cell because of alleged over-crowding.

The explanations given by Prison Department to account for this discrepancy took four forms. First, pockets of under-occupation occur in overcrowded prisons because 'some cells have to be used as store-rooms and offices and for purposes other than holding inmates' (Home Office, Evidence, vol.I, paper IIC(2), para 35). Corroborating evidence for this explanation was contained in the sample certificate from Brixton appended to the Home Office paper on accommodation. Of accommodation which *might* be used for 127 prisoners in Brixton 'A' Wing the certificate indicated that 12 places were in fact in use as offices, classrooms and store-rooms. If this pattern were duplicated in the other wings at Brixton then it means that some 60-80 accom-modation places were being used for other purposes. What the Home Office appears to be saying is that these places are *included* in pub-lished CNAs but cannot, by definition, be used: overcrowding is the consequence. We find this an extraordinary claim. If it is true, then CNAs are even more meaningless than we have ever suggested. But if published CNAs *exclude* these offices, and we have always understood that to be the case, then this explanation is misleading and irrelevant.

Secondly, there was reference to the under-use of accommodation in open prisons because not enough prisoners are available who can be trusted in open conditions or whose pattern of offences fits with local agreements reached with communities near open prisons. In 1978 the number of places in open prisons and Borstals was 5,804 and the average number of prisoners 5,205, some 10 per cent under-occupation. Of the places unfilled some 200, or one third, were accounted for by a single establishment, Kirkham, because of a local agreement not to exceed a given population. If it is the case that Prison Department regards this agreement as binding then it might be better not to confuse the issue and, like the offices discussed above, omit the surplus accom-modation from the published CNA. If it is the case that prisoners cannot be found to meet the criteria laid down in local agreements then like the May Committee we think that the agreements should be re-negotiated. However, we are not convinced that the open prisons are under-occupied for this reason alone. The Home Office evidence tentatively suggested that there has been a decline in the number of prisoners suitable for open conditions; by this we take them to mean persons who could be trusted not to abscond. We can find no evidence to support the case that this proposition has ever been put to the test; the number of prisoners absconding from open prisons has remained remarkably stable over the past ten years. We think it more likely that the under-occupation of open prisons reflects a lack of flexibility within Prison Department and there can be no doubt that the holding of some 600 places empty in the open prisons has contributed to over-crowding in the locals.

Thirdly, the Home Office pointed to the under-occupation of closed prisons as a policy decision not to prejudice a treatment or training regime, or as consequence of accident or adaptation of the structure or industrial action or some other dispute. Of course it is true that the decision to protect the training prisons from overcrowding, while simultaneously allowing very high overcrowding in the local prisons, is a policy decision. But the protection policy includes more than that. In 1978, there were, on average, 1,431 empty spaces in 27 of the 38 closed training prisons for males and females. Most of the prisons had only a few empty places: were there no overcrowding in any training prison the total population in the closed training prisons would be within a margin of 5 per cent. However, ten training prisons contained 1,119 empty places, and thus contributed almost twice the number of empty places as *all* the open prisons.

We do not know why some of these prisons were so under-occupied. The Home Office provides explanations for particular prisons (para 34). We accept that damage arising from the fire at Chelmsford and the riot at Hull, or adaptation as at Reading, is unavoidable from time to time. However, we deplore the fact that prisoner minorities occupy under-utilised accommodation in the name of treatment and training, or positive custody, while other prisoners said to be ineligible (by reason of their shorter sentences) suffer, as a direct consequence, overcrowded conditions in the local prisons. Thus Grendon is said to have had 114 empty places in 1978 because it has been found that it cannot fulfil its psychiatric role satisfactorily with a population exceeding 200 prisoners. Featherstone had 110 places empty because the prison had too little work and the governor feared that 'idle hands make mischief' in an associated regime. Similarly the 105 empty places at the Verne were attributed to too little work and staff. This policy simply cannot be justified, as we argued in chapter 1, by the results of treatment and training.

119

Prison staff repeatedly claim that their problems stem from the fact that they cannot hang a 'house full' notice on their front gate. Yet this is manifestly not the case in training prisons: it is done as a matter of policy when they are *not* full. Cells in Featherstone stand empty while three men are confined to a cell for most of the day in Manchester or Liverpool and in both cases the reason given is that there is no work. These under-occupied training prisons quite unjustifiably generate overcrowding elsewhere and in turn fuel an argument for more resources. A good part of the total cell-sharing statistics, we would estimate one quarter, is created as a matter of deliberate policy and constitutes a fraudulent claim for additional cells.

Finally, lurking in the background of the cell-sharing issue lies the question of staff disputes. We do not know how many prisons have been or are affected but we suspect that there are more than those mentioned in the Home Office evidence. Certainly the fact that Parkhurst officers refused to take receptions for many months accounts for the fact that the prison had, on average, 147 empty places in 1978. But we believe that other establishments may also have been affected in ways not fully made known. We understand that the new cell block for 192 Category B men at Bristol, completed in July 1975, is not yet operational because of disputed staffing arrangements. Is that also the explanation for the fact that Camp Hill, where a new block for 160 prisoners was opened in July 1976, had 135 empty places throughout 1978? We know nothing about such disputes and have no wish to judge their merits. We wish simply to argue that while such disputes continue, and indeed until the various other anomalies we have cited have been resolved, it is quite wrong for the Home Office to suggest that cell-sharing could be equated with overcrowding and that the elimination of one requires the elimination of the other. It does not.

In our view, under a policy of humane containment, the extra population could be distributed much more widely than at present. For example, we can see no reason why *any* prisoners need to be held three in a cell designed for one even with existing accommodation. Given a 5 per cent margin of empty accommodation and present population levels we think it would be perfectly possible for the 6,269 excess prisoners to be so distributed that a proportion be held in specially enlarged cells and the remainder two each in the larger single cells. In the older Victorian prisons this would simply mean that where two or three cells had been made into one by removing walls and integral sanitation provided, four or seven prisoners would be housed in accommodation certified for three or six. The remainder, perhaps some 5,000, would have to share single cells. But were even this modest adjustment made, the number of prisoners sharing single cells would be reduced from 16,000 to 10,000 and triple sharing, an indefensible arrangement given present accommodation capacity, eliminated altogether. We would also argue for overcrowding to be distributed throughout a greater number of establishments so as to reduce the burden falling on any particular one. But this question needs to be related to the broader issues of living standards.

Manifesto for the normalisation of the prison

In chapter 1 we argued that the question of what living standards are appropriate in prison must be related to the purposes which imprisonment can realistically serve. We maintain that the doctrine of humane containment acts as a double reminder. On the one hand it suggests that the use of imprisonment is never to be justified by aspirations set higher than punishment through loss of liberty and the protection of the public. On the other it acknowledges evidence that the deterrent effect of imprisonment is not increased by humiliating or depriving prisoners. Though subject to punishment, prisoners remain citizens and, in all but a few cases, will soon be released. It makes sound financial, as well as penological, sense to ensure that the standard of life in prison bears some comparison with that in the community so that prisoners are able to make a smooth transition from one to the other.

It is apparent from our discussion of resources in this chapter that their distribution within the prison system is a product of history. Over the years our prisons have become specialised according to supposed differences in the type and quality of treatment and training they provide, and more recently their level of security. Some establishments have taken on functions in respect of particular types of offenders — 'dangerous' prisoners, lifers, long-termers, short-termers, trials and remands and so on. In the case of young offenders, institutions have been differentiated according to sentence — imprisonment, Borstal training and detention. Specialisation of establishments has three consequences. First, prisoners cannot be so easily transferred to where the vacancies are, thus making it more difficult to use resources efficiently. Secondly, it tends to produce inequality in the distribution of resources. The Home Office evidence did not seek to disguise this fact. The squalor and overcrowding in the local prisons is the consequence of protecting the closed training prisons and young offender establishments which get the lion's share of the resources. Thirdly, it increases the distance between the average prisoner and the community from which he or she comes.

If resources are to be used more efficiently, if *all* prisoners are to have the benefit of humane conditions, and if the community ties of prisoners are to be effectively maintained, then the variety of institutions within the system must be reduced. Instead of specialised institutions we need more comprehensive, general purpose establishments — in short more local prisons. We do not wish to rule out the use of some specialist prisons and we accept the need for distinguishing between certain types of prisoner. But we do not think that the present variety of provision can be justified either on security grounds or on grounds of treatment and training or positive custody. Our advocacy of comprehensive local prisons as the main institutions of a reorganised prison system is not simply based on expediency. It is entirely consistent with our principle of normalising prison life.

Finally, before we develop our proposals in detail, we should make it clear that their feasibility does *not* depend on the major reduction in the use of imprisonment for which we argued in chapter 2. The immediate adoption of our proposals would make for greater equity in the distribution of resources — thereby ameliorating the worst deprivations suffered by most prisoners. A general improvement of standards in prisons, however, would be dependent upon either population reduction or the allocation of extra resources. For the reasons outlined earlier we reject the resources solution adopted by the May Committee.

1   The localisation of prison accommodation

We believe that most prisoners should be housed in the establishments closest to their community base. We see no reason why reorganised and less crowded local prisons should not provide adequate health, welfare, educational, recreational, occupational and security facilities. We reject Prison Department's view that most sentenced prisoners should be housed in specialised, and often geographically isolated, training prisons. By localisation of custody we mean simply that sentenced prisoners should generally be held in the prison which minimises the travelling time and expense of their most regular and important visitors. Obviously the need to minimise escort duties dictates that trial and remand prisoners will be held in the establishments which service their court of appearance.

In order to achieve greater localisation *we recommend that the distinction between local and training prisons be abolished and most of the existing training prisons be recommissioned as local prisons*. In our evidence to the May Committee we made detailed proposals, based on the most recent population and accommodation data, stating which training prisons should be recommissioned and the categories of prisoners they should house. Excluding young prisoners and females, we suggested that all untried, unsentenced, civil, short and medium term prisoners (4 years or less) be housed in an expanded local prison system comprising 45 rather than the present 24 establishments (King and Morgan, 1979, paras 182-7).

Though it described our proposals as 'interesting and challenging' the May Committee nevertheless rejected them. It argued that:

> we could not support increased localisation, with the consequent damage to some well-resourced and imaginatively run regimes in the training prisons, unless we could see some substantial counter-balancing advantage (May, 1979, para 6.54).

It accepted the Home Office view, presumably expressed in oral evidence, that 'there was nothing to be gained by making conditions worse for many throughout the system merely to improve slightly the lot of some prisoners in some local prisons' (para 6.53). The over-crowded remand centres and local prisons contain almost twice the number of prisoners as the closed training prisons, and half of *all* prisoners serve the *whole* of their sentences in local prisons. We do not see why the Home Office should dismiss these lightly as 'some prisoners'. But in any case their arguments against localisation do not bear examination. It was said that most training prisons could not be converted without considerable expenditure because local prisons require larger reception and visiting facilities; that a restricted regime, necessary in a prison housing prisoners of different legal statuses, 'could not be operated in establishments designed for fully associated regimes'; that cell sharing was 'physically impossible in at least the newer training prisons'; and that since 'work facilities were geared to a certain population . . . there would be a shortage of employment if that population were exceeded' (para 6.53).

After informal discussions with prison governors we concede that in a few prisons on our original shopping list — Haverigg, Northeye and Highpoint — some of these Home Office objections would be valid. Without modification they would not be suitable as local prisons. However, this hardly substantiates the argument that no advantage attends recommissioning the others. The May Committee's acceptance of the Home Office view perhaps reflects its ignorance of the prison system and its history. No fewer than 13 of the 21 establishments we wished to redesignate local prisons are of precisely the same layout and vintage as the existing local prisons: indeed several of them *were*, until relatively recently, local prisons. The design and location of the prisons at Aylesbury, Chelmsford, Hull, Lancaster, Maidstone, Northallerton, Nottingham, Portsmouth, Preston, Reading, Shepton Mallet, Stafford and Wakefield make them eminently suitable as local prisons.

We have yet to be provided with convincing reasons why the newer prisons at Blundeston, Coldingley, Featherstone, Onley, and Ranby should not become local prisons. Each comprises a number of accommodation blocks that would facilitate the separation of different categories of prisoners, and their communal dining and other facilities are not dissimilar from those in the new remand centres. And we cannot resist pointing out that the provision of small cells in remand centres has proved no bar to the very considerable overcrowding in some of those institutions.

In rejecting the idea of localisation we find it surprising that the May Committee seemed so quickly to have forgotten the scandalous conditions in some local prisons where prisoners are locked in their cells for up to 23 hours a day with little or no opportunity to engage in *any* form of work. These are the proper reference points for our recommendations not the modest reduction in a 30 or 40 hour working week which might occur in a few training prisons. We still think it would be a better use of expenditure, and certainly more likely to ameliorate conditions in the overcrowded locals, if prisons like Highpoint and Northeye were converted to serve as local prisons, than it would be to proceed with the twenty-five year building programme recommended by May.

2   Specialist establishments

There is no justification for drawing a hard and fast line between accommodation provided for short, medium and long-term prisoners. We have argued that short and medium term prisoners should generally be housed in local prisons merely because, given existing parole and remission rules, this would make the best use of the accommodation available. The local prisons, however, would also provide hostel and day release schemes for long-term prisoners coming to the end of their sentences. Nevertheless, we recognise that there will always be a minority of prisoners whose needs cannot be provided for within local prisons. In this we have come to very similar conclusions with regard to adults as did the Advisory Council on the Penal System when considering *Young Adult Offenders* (1974).

If our proposals that 21 training prisons should be redesignated as local prisons were adopted, a further 21 training establishments would remain. In our evidence to the May Committee we recommended that several prisons should retain their existing specialist role — Albany and Long Lartin and subsequently Frankland for Category A prisoners (see chapter 3), Grendon Underwood as a psychiatric prison and Leyhill as an open prison for lifers. Others should develop specialist educational and occupational facilities beyond the scope of most local prisons (King and Morgan, 1979, paras 188-191). But we also recommended, assuming more efficient use of accommodation than is presently the case, that several prisons — six open prisons and Dartmoor — be closed. In view of the Directorate of Works description of the poor condition of those camps this proposal appears to have even greater merit than we knew at the time (May, 1979, Appendix 6). As we made clear in chapter 1, the adoption of humane containment in no sense implies the destruction of specialist facilities for some prisoners: but it does imply that their provision should be carefully justified and should never be at the expense of decent conditions for other prisoners.

3   Untried and unsentenced prisoners

At several points in their Report the May Committee expressed concern over the fate of trial and remand prisoners — the fact that 40 per cent of them subsequently receive non-custodial sentences, the ever-increasing duration of their custody and, not least, the conditions in which they are held. As the Committee put it, 'what we are saying . . . is that remand prisoners . . . suffer the worst accommodation when, arguably, they should have the best' (para 6.41). It is not simply their accommodation which is worst. In a study which we conducted at Winchester nearly ten years ago we found that the conditions for untried prisoners were a good deal more restrictive than for convicted and sentenced prisoners (King and Morgan, 1976). These observations are now commonplace. Indeed it is clear from published reports, from recent visits, and from the experience of one of us (REM) as a member of a Board of Visitors at a remand centre that in some respects conditions for trial and remand prisoners have deteriorated still further. Evidence submitted by the Home Office to the Expenditure Committee and to the May Committee showed that the worst effects of recent economies, overtime restrictions and other industrial actions have been felt in the local prisons and remand centres (Expenditure Committee, 15th Report, 1978, para 14; Home Office, Evidence, vol.II, paper IIE(2) paras 18-20).

Our recommendations for the reorganisation of institutions should ease the pressure on the local prisons from which untried and unsentenced prisoners have particularly suffered. However, these measures would not, of course, ensure that Prison Department created a regime for these prisoners which is consistent with their legal status. In the past Prison Department appears to have taken the view that since untried prisoners have certain special rights under the Prison Rules there is no need to offer them the same facilities that are given to sentenced prisoners. As we have documented elsewhere, however, untried prisoners seldom actually benefit from their rights under the Prison Rules, and so they tend to be doubly deprived (King and Morgan, 1976).

Though Prison Department officially concurs with our view that the rules and conditions for the untried should be such that they suffer no greater loss of liberty than that *necessarily* arising out of their confinement, at present this is manifestly not the case. In the same way that the Bail Act 1976 introduced a presumption of bail so, in our view, conditions for the untried prisoner should presume the retention of all rights except those conflicting with safe custody. The onus should be upon Prison Department to justify any deprivations of such rights and not, as is currently the case, provide modest increments by discretionary provision, to those rules and conditions applying to sentenced prisoners.

Establishing an appropriate custodial regime for the untried requires both amendment of the Prison Rules and more generous facilities and standards of accommodation. We have made detailed recommendations under both headings (King and Morgan, 1976, chapter 6; King and Morgan, 1979, para 199). Though the May Committee shared our concern for the untried their proposals are not likely to ameliorate the conditions which we have jointly deplored. Not only does the May Report contain no detailed regime recommendations but its suggestion that priority be given 'in the initial years (to) a programme of building adult remand accommodation' (May, 1979, para 6.108) would produce little relief for at least a decade and then only in establishments almost certainly at some distance from where they are needed.

4   Prisoners under 21 years

We see no reason why the principles we have enunciated for adults should not equally be applied to prisoners under 21 years. Indeed our proposal for more comprehensive local institutions is entirely consistent with the recommendations of the Advisory Council on the Penal System in *Young Adult Offenders* (1974) for a generic sentence — to replace detention, Borstal training and imprisonment — and for 'neighbourhood' establishments. We hope that these ideas insofar as they were developed by the Labour administration in the 1978 Green Paper *Youth, Custody and Supervision: A New Sentence* will be revived. It goes without saying that, consistent with our discussion of population in chapter 2, we deplore the complacency exhibited in the Green Paper regarding the *size* of the juvenile and young adult custodial population. Furthermore, we support the original intention of the Children and Young Persons Act 1969 that persons under 17 years should no longer be held in Prison Department establishments on either a remand or sentenced basis.

It has to be admitted that the reorganisation of young offender establishments presents difficulties far greater than those to be overcome in the adult sector. Existing establishments are unevenly spread throughout the country and the quality and range of facilities they provide varies enormously. The Advisory Council envisaged neighbourhood complexes with open and closed facilities which would have required the construction of many new buildings, often on new sites. The Green Paper (Home Office, 1978a, p.22) made it clear that such resources would not be made available nor do we think the expenditure would be justified. Much as we support localisation we believe that a major capital programme is too high a price to pay for it. In our view localisation should be achieved to the greatest extent possible within the available stock of young offender establishments. Most young offenders, apart from those with special psychiatric, security or educational difficulties, could be housed in comprehensive local establishments. We recommend, therefore, that all the existing Borstals, detention and remand centres, together with the training prisons currently used for young prisoners at Erlesloke and Swinfen Hall, be drawn into a single unified system of young offender institutions.

Given an unchanged population this would still leave a shortfall of approximately 1,400 places. However, we suppose that a significant proportion of young prisoners — perhaps 400 to 500 — would continue to be re-classified as adults and housed in adult prisons. If so, then the completion of young offender building projects already announced by Prison Department would eliminate overcrowding in this sector (King and Morgan, 1979, para 205).

Because so many young offender establishments are distant from major centres of population we see no alternative but to continue the use of specialised trial and remand establishments. However we hope the Secretary of State will, as was originally intended, devise separate Rules for the operation of Remand Centres under s.47 of the Prison Act 1952. And we recommend that, when population levels permit, Prison Department adopt a flexible approach which will allow the development of young offender trial and remand units in adult local prisons.

5 Women and girls

A highly specialised prison system most conflicts with the goal of localised custody when the number of prisoners eligible for each subgroup is small. In terms of geography it is women and girls who have suffered most from the policy of institutional specialisation, though it is frequently argued that their being housed in separate establishments has brought them other regime benefits. Whereas for males there are 31 prisons (including the geographically separate remand centres) to receive prisoners from the courts, for females the whole of England and Wales is served by just four institutions — Holloway and three remand centres. None of the remand centres is in an urban location. Pucklechurch, to take one example, serves the whole of Central, Southern and South Western England and South Wales. It is six miles from Bristol in a small Gloucestershire village: there is no train service, a poor bus service and Prison Department provides no overnight accommodation, transport or special visiting facilities.

Fortunately Prison Department has not created specialised institutions for females of the kind which characterise the male system. Both women and girls are housed in the remand prisons and two training prisons, one open and one closed, serve also as Borstals: detention is no longer available for girls. Nevertheless, with so few prisons for women and girls it follows that most female prisoners are not easily visited; and the introduction of a generic youth custody sentence will only marginally alleviate the problem. This pattern is the more disturbing when the short-term nature of the female prison population is taken into account. Compared to males, a considerably higher proportion of the female prison population consists of untried, unsentenced and civil prisoners; many more of the untried subsequently receive a non-custodial sentence; and of those sentenced to prison two thirds receive short-term sentences. Though their custody is more temporary the distribution of female prisoners within the system is such as to maximise the disruption of their community ties.

In most other respects the conditions for females within prison are more humane than those for males. However, we have grave doubts whether, given the current population explosion (at the time of writing, March 1980, it was over 1,600, not far short of the total predicted by the Home Office for 1982) these standards will be maintained. In 1978, at the eleventh hour, Prison Department opened Cookham Wood, a new purpose built remand centre for boys, as a closed training prison for women. Even so the new Holloway currently houses almost twice as many prisoners as it was designed for. Female prisoners are beginning to suffer the consequences of overcrowding and resources maldistribution which have long plagued the male system.

In our judgement the solution to this problem lies in the gradual reabsorption of female prisoners into a system of comprehensive local prisons. Before the turn of the century all local prisons housed males and females and we do not see why female units should not be created within several male establishments. Indeed the recent creation of such units for women at Durham and Brixton shows that it is feasible. Though our proposal would undoubtedly involve costs of adaptation we believe they would be offset by savings: localised custody could reduce the enormous escort costs which currently apply at female establishments. Finally we think Prison Department might experiment with mixed groups for some educational and recreational activities, as well as attendance at religious services. Some prisoners may well be unsuitable for such experiments. But when the brief custody of a high proportion of males and females is taken into account, the strict sexual segregation operating in the three remand centres which have male and female wings smacks more of superstition than rational administration.

6   Prison regimes

In chapter 1 we made it clear that our critique of treatment and training, and the suggestion that Rule One be replaced by a statement of humane containment, in no way implied that we consider those activities normally referred to under the treatment and training heading to be of secondary importance. On the contrary we attach great weight to the provision of welfare, medical, occupational and educational facilities. What we are opposed to is the idea that one of the objectives of imprisonment is to provide access to these services and that the internal organisation of the prison service should be geared to that objective. When offenders are sentenced to imprisonment, however, they do not cease to be citizens. Basic services within prison should, whenever possible, be similar to those considered necessary or desirable in the community because prisoners, despite their temporary loss of liberty, continue to be members of the community.

We have argued that the first task of the prison service is to ensure that prisoners serve their sentences in humane conditions and that, particularly in the local prisons, this is clearly not the case at present. The gulf between standards in prison and those prevailing in the rest of the community stems from three factors. First is the view that part of the punishment of imprisonment lies in subjecting prisoners to lower standards: what is often referred to as the 'less eligibility' principle, that standards *should* be lower. To some extent this is a matter decided by personal values. We reject the idea that standards should deliberately be made lower on humanitarian grounds. But we reject it also because, in our judgement, such a policy has no penological value: there is no evidence that prisoners are better deterred by harsher conditions. We consider that prisoners should be constrained only to the extent that such constraint is necessary to achieve the secure management of the prison.

Secondly, is the question of interpreting the Prison Rules. To some extent the personal responsibility, choice and autonomy normally expected of adults in the community is necessarily reduced in prison for security and management reasons. We acknowledge this and the need for staff discretion in applying the rules in the interests of security. But we suppose that *every* activity within the prison has *some* implication for security and we doubt that the considerable discretion which is built into most of the 1964 Prison Rules can really be justified on security grounds (see also Cohen and Taylor, 1978). As things stand the best regimes in our prisons have been achieved not because staff have enforced the 1964 Prison Rules, but because staff have interpreted the Rules generously. One of the more disturbing aspects of the staff disputes in recent years has been the amount of tightening-up which is possible *within* the Rules and which creates intolerable conditions. A strict and minimum interpretation of the 1964 Rules no longer affords a standard of life acceptable in the 1980s. New Rules are required which place the onus on Prison Department to justify any departure from agreed standards.

Thirdly, incongruity between standards in prison and the wider community arises out of the fact that historically the prison has been such an administrative, social and cultural, as well as a physical enclave. As a result persons living and working in prisons lose touch with the world beyond the wall and too easily accept peculiar conditions. There can be little doubt that prison officers have suffered as much as prisoners from this separation. The May Committee 'found members of the service (including governors) a somewhat inward-looking group . . . unrealistic as well as restricted' in their beliefs about conditions outside the prison system (May, 1979, para 8.3). They also described conditions of service which would not be tolerated in most other occupations (May, 1979, chapter 11).

In our evidence to the May Committee we made detailed recommendations for the normalisation of the prison designed to offset these influences (King and Morgan, 1979, paras 212-35). We advocated the systematic revision of the Prison Rules and Standing Orders to include new standards of prisoner accommodation and equipment, access to facilities and regime characteristics, and that these should be published. We also argued that the best way of improving the level of provision within the prison would be to integrate prison and community facilities. The provision of specific prison services tends to promote the belief, and perhaps the reality, that they are subordinated to, or manipulated for, the maintenance of good order and discipline. No good purpose is served by an organisational framework which breeds accusation and mistrust. In our judgement several services — medical, educational, library and chaplaincy — could be wholly integrated with those in the community; and we think that experimental efforts to integrate some recreational and occupational provisions could also be made.

The May Committee had little or nothing to say on these issues. The Home Office, responding to the controversy over the alleged medical mis-use of drugs to control prisoners (McCleery, 1978; Fitzgerald and Sim, 1979), and anticipating calls for the absorption of the Prison Medical Service into the National Health Service, devoted part of their evidence to this topic (Home Office, Evidence, vol.II, paper III(12), paras 16-46). We are not unmindful of the problems which would have to be overcome in integrating the medical, or any other prison services, into community programmes. As the Home Office assert, having their own services does enable them to ensure uniform practices throughout the prison system, to issue practice directions and to transfer personnel in order to provide adequate cover (para 16). Nevertheless it still seems indefensible that prison nursing staff, concerned with the administration of drugs and the supervision of prison hospital units, are not currently required to have the same nursing qualifications demanded of persons undertaking similar duties in an outside hospital (King and Morgan, 1979, para 218). The Home Office evidence corroborated the substance of our claim: only 15 of the 783 prison hospital officers hold formal nursing qualifications and staff resources do not allow the most basic form of in-service training which, with respect to the case of mentally disordered offenders, the Department considers desirable (Home Office, Evidence, para 4). There is actually some evidence to suggest that integration might improve the degree to which prisoners in need of psychiatric care are removed from the prison population altogether. Recent research indicates that improved co-operation between prison and hospital practitioners, best achieved when the same personnel are involved, increases the likelihood that persons remanded for medical reports will be found community facilities which will lead to their receiving a non-custodial sentence (Gibbens, Soothill and Pope, 1977). Nothing presented in evidence to the May Committee has led us to alter our conviction that our recommendations were both sound and practicable.

In concluding this discussion of regimes we would also argue for a more vigorous promotion of contacts between prisoners and their relatives and friends in the community, by visits, letters and the use of pay-phones. Once again we acknowledge that very much more than the minimum contact specified in the Prison Rules is allowed in many establishments. We recommend that these best practices be formally recognised when redrafting the Prison Rules: in our evidence to the May Committee we made detailed proposals for the standards which might be adopted (King and Morgan, 1979, paras 222-3). There is no better method for breaking down the prison enclave, than freeing the flow of information between prisoners and the community. A parallel development would be to free staff from the fetters of the Official Secrets Act.

A Building moratorium

Our discussion of resources would be incomplete were we to flinch from the recommendation to which the whole logic of our argument in this book has pointed. We propose that the Government announce a prison building moratorium. It would be wasteful not to complete buildings at the construction stage and in any case our proposals for the reorganisation of establishments and the more equitable distribution of the adult and young offenders population among them, has rested on the assumption that capital projects started will be realised. But if our population and resources proposals were adopted we can see no reason why all plans to construct new establishments should not be halted. This would in no way preclude much needed on-site redevelopment of existing establishments, including the construction of new buildings, so long as these were *replacements* and not *additions* to the penal estate. Indeed we propose that plans to construct new buildings should always be announced in conjunction with notices of closure.

Despite the fact that we outlined these propositions in our evidence to the May Committee (King and Morgan, 1979, para 191) the Report claimed that 'no one pressed the case for a moratorium' (May, 1979, para 6.74). The Committee seems to have taken the view that advocacy of a building moratorium would involve 'limiting the ability of the courts to send offenders to prison on grounds of space insufficiency'. This, it felt, 'would represent a serious interference by government with the independence of the judiciary' and would be 'entirely arbitrary and capricious in effect' (para 6.75). Apart from the fact that certain sentences — attendance centres, detention centres and community service — have always been rationed by provision, it should be clear that, since prison catchment areas can be and frequently are adjusted, the posting of 'full-up' notices need not have the consequence described. In any case our own proposal is not that the courts should be constrained by means of a building moratorium but that a moratorium

132

should accompany a much more systematic interference by government with the sentencing powers of the courts. The May Committee concluded that discussion of a building moratorium was 'not wholly worthless if it served to remind sentencers that their decisions have consequences upon resources' (para 6.76). We agree, but we can find no great evidence in the Committee's Report that it took that lesson to heart.

5   Managing the prison service
(J. E. Thomas)

Of the eight specific issues which the May Committee was required to examine and make recommendations upon, seven concerned staff, their management, conditions of service or pay. However much the grievances of prison staff are symptomatic of more deep-seated troubles, the May Inquiry was created to solve a crisis of staff and not prisoner control. Over half of the Committee's Report is taken up with administrative and personnel questions, many complex and technical in nature, several the cause of industrial action. By definition, none of these questions is unimportant: but some — the POA claim, super-annuation and allowances, staff quarters, and the dispute over 'continuous duty credits' — are of relatively transitory significance and outside the interest of both the general reader and most well-informed penal observers. Aspects of these problems — overtime, the improved staff-prisoner ratio, the relative insularity of prison staff — have been touched on in chapter 4. My purpose in this chapter is to consider the underlying management issues: the sores which have been festering for years and for which the Minister looked to the May Committee for long-term cures.

The plain, and generally agreed, truth about the management and administration of the English prison system is that it simply does not work. The May Report, in discussing its defects, is not, as novitiates might suppose, being especially incisive or insightful. The Report merely repeats what has been said in earlier reports. Not that the May Committee should be criticised on that account. The reason for its repetition of historic problems is that the weaknesses persist. The last commentator to observe these defects was Lord Mountbatten, when he noted of the organisation, that he was: 'convinced that matters cannot be left as they stand' (Mountbatten, 1966, para 244).

Evidence to the May Committee confirmed that since 1966, when Mountbatten carried out his Inquiry, very little has changed. Indeed, according to the evidence of those best qualified to know, the governor grades of the service, the situation may have deteriorated in recent years. Certainly their choice of language to the Committee is a good deal more forceful than it has been on previous occasions:

> In the evidence received from our members the universal condem-
> nation of the present organisational structure of the prison service

was striking in its anguish and virulence . . . . We are now in a permanent state of crisis management (SCPS, Evidence, para 21).

Nor were the governors the only staff to make such categorical and condemnatory statements. The Institution of Professional Civil Servants, hardly one might suppose an extreme or unreasonable body, employed most uncivil-service-like words to make their point. May describes how:

> they went on to say that what they were really doing was in effect making an impassioned plea that something must be done about the top of what they described as 'this confounded department' (May, 1979, para 5.16).

The IPCS went on to make what has become, in the last thirty years, the most persistent set of complaints about the management of the service. Complaints which, despite May, are likely to continue to persist:

> They, too, told us that they had seemed never to be able to get face to face with the representative of the department to whom they wished to speak: that they never knew who it was who was making or failing to make, the decisions on the points which they were raising; and in any event that the time which was being taken to answer their enquiries was excessive (para 5.16).

It is clear from such remarks by people who work in the system that the defects of management, and the need for effective administration, is the matter of most concern. It is also a matter of great urgency, since the highly centralised administration of the prison service ultimately provides the context within which things do, or do not, happen to prisoners. Yet it is too big an area to discuss in a single chapter. For present purposes the discussion of 'administration' will be limited to three issues: the overall structure of the service; regionalisation; and the vexed question of industrial relations.

The centralisation of the prison system in England and Wales

Prior to 1877, the English prison system was administered, in the main, by justices of the peace. There were some central government prisons: they were originally provided for prisoners awaiting transportation and later those serving long sentences. It was upon this nucleus that the modern prison service was established. In 1877 an Act was passed which brought every prison in the country under central control with the Home Secretary being made accountable to Parliament. This is still the situation, and the prison service remains unique amongst our public bodies (excepting the armed forces) in the absence of any but a purely nominal *local* connection. By this is meant the contrast between the service and, say, the school system which is substantially a matter of local concern, with local management and interests being vital. The lack of a local connection has become a major administrative problem which, in turn, has created a good deal of frustration, as must be clear from the quotations above.

There was a good deal of opposition to centralisation, both in and out of Parliament. The local justices' objections were moderated by their involvement as Visiting Justices (Boards of Visitors in effect). This vestigial relic of local influence, far from being a quaint and rather harmless example of English amateurism, is currently the focus of a good deal of anxiety and concern. This is because it is clear both that the Boards have a duty to monitor what is done in prisons and that, for the most part, they are failing to do so. This issue is discussed in greater detail in chapter 6.

The Prison Commission established in 1877 (it survived until 1963) set out to reorganise the system. A pattern was set for central control which soon became absolute. Edmund Du Cane, the first Chairman of the Commission, has been much maligned. There is no doubt that centralisation resulted in a good deal of advantage for prisoners and staff. But it is also true that Du Cane's Commission set a standard of authoritarianism which, in more recent years, has apparently been consonant with the general tone of the Home Office in its dealings with outsiders.

This style developed in part because of Du Cane's background and personality; in part because people in authority in Victorian England seem to have demanded unequivocal obedience; and in part because, from the moment of its inception, the prison service was seen as analogous to the armed services. This parallel with the armed services has provided a fertile and constant source of confusion about how staff should be treated. For a long time, until 1938, officers were not allowed to have a union, because it was argued that they were para-military. In one of the shabbiest episodes in the history of trade unionism, seventy-four prison officers who joined the police strike of 1919 were all dismissed from the service. The subsequent transition from militarism to 'reformism' contributed to the breakdown of industrial relations in the prison service. This is a theme to which I shall return.

The prison service, after 1877, had its fair share of crises. But it was a small service and easily administered. The advent of modern communications — telephones, motor cars, and so on — meant that those administering the service were able to keep in touch with those in the field. It is difficult to imagine, or indeed to believe, that Alexander Paterson, the remarkable Prison Commissioner of the inter-war period, used to interview *every* prison officer who was appointed. This did not make him universally popular — indeed some critics described his disciples as Paterson's Light Horse — but at least he was recognisable, available and powerful.

There is plenty of evidence that the prison system was in trouble before the abolition of the Prison Commission, which is a matter widely discussed in the evidence to the May Committee. From the 1920s onwards the Prison Officers' Magazine — published unofficially — catalogued the causes of staff dissatisfaction. They complained about reformative policies which made life more comfortable for prisoners at the expense of staff. They attacked autocratic governors, and the 'parasites' running the prison service. (For a discussion of the early years of the service see Thomas, 1972).

After the Second World War, the situation continued to deteriorate. The service was increasing in size; there was talk of the breakdown of discipline; and rumblings were heard about 'mollycoddling' prisoners. Sir Lionel Fox, the penultimate Chairman of the Prison Commission, had a good international reputation, and a sympathetic audience in key places. But it was becoming clear that a critical situation was arising. Many of the tensions were attributed to prisoner overcrowding, a tendency which has not diminished with the years and which, as the discussion in chapter 4 demonstrates, was a dominant theme in both the evidence to the May Committee and its Report. There is overcrowding and it is a problem: it is not only distasteful but also a reflection on the morality of a society which allows it. But though it *is* a problem, it cannot account for every area of malaise in prisons. To take a simple example: many of the most serious disturbances since 1972, have occurred in prisons which are not overcrowded. Similarly all the discussions about officers having to do long court duty, and so on, are irrelevant to central prisons, which are adequately staffed. The causes are a good deal more complex than that.

The abolition of the Prison Commission in 1963, and the absorption of the prison service into the Home Office has been blamed for much of the trouble in the system. The Outstations Branch of the Society of Civil and Public Servants stated to the May Committee that: '. . . the amalgamation of the Prison Commission with the Home Office in 1963 had been an ill-considered and ill-advised measure undertaken for political expedience' (May, 1979, para 5.18). Not everyone agrees with this assessment. One witness:

expressed himself as strongly against the Prison Commission both at the time that it was wound up and any re-creation of it now. It had, he thought, become very inward looking and not at all efficient (para 5.25).

The reason why this discussion about the Commission persists, seventeen years after its abolition, is not because of concern about efficiency. It is because, at the time when the service was reaching a size which could barely be managed from London, an easily identifiable unit was taken into what staff saw as a vast, anonymous bureaucracy. There was a good deal of 'public relations' talk at the time, about how insignificant the change would be, and how this would merely 'regularise' the situation. Despite widespread opposition, the change was made — a procedure which, because of the way it was done, ought to be of as much concern as the change itself (Thomas, 1975). There is no doubt that the instinctive reaction of prison staff to the change was well-founded. After the abolition, those directing the prison service *were* less well known, in part because some key people seemed to have other Home Office responsibilities. The leaders were *not* as identifiable to staff in the field. Staff have complained at this ever since.

The May Committee took the view that a resurrection of the Prison Commission is not desirable (May, 1979, paras 5.6-5.10). Although this must remain questionable it is vital to acknowledge what it was about the Commission which prison staff seem to miss, namely the ability to associate decision and action with personality: to know precisely who is making a decision which affects people. This is, no doubt, a problem outside the scale of any Inquiry. For to have a service with such a degree of intimacy would mean reversing a trend which has been in evidence for some time in the prison service — the evolution of a classic Weberian bureaucracy. Put simply, this means that figures who border on the charismatic or eccentric, cannot be tolerated. The prison service has a history of people who became well-known *because* they were exceptional. A random list might include Du Cane, Paterson, Llewellin, who established the first open Borstal, and Fox. To be recognisable means displaying characteristics which are extraordinary, and it is precisely the presence of such characteristics which in a modern bureaucracy is unacceptable. No one yet has devised a structure to combat such a massive tradition — even if it is assumed that it is desirable. Lord Mountbatten tried, but the fate of his suggestions is the most instructive episode in recent British prison history.

The Mountbatten Report recognised all these problems of identity. Indeed, this Report, as time goes on, is gaining a place as one of the shrewdest, and quickest, sets of observations on the prison service. One of these concerned the virtual absence of leadership. It was to this end that Mountbatten proposed the creation of a new post called the Inspector General who was to be the 'professional head' of the prison service, and who would, *inter alia*, have direct access to the Home Secretary (Mountbatten, 1966, para 251). The recommendation was accepted, and Brigadier M.S.K. Maunsell was appointed from industry to take up the post. The idea was widely acclaimed, and very soon Maunsell began to achieve a reputation as an active, and concerned individual. Standing ovations from uniformed staff greeted him at several prisons, because staff had heard that he was insisting, for example, that correspondence with the institutions should be speeded up.

One has to observe the Home Office at close hand, to understand the effects of demands for speed — unless of course the action is directed at political masters. Pressure for speedy action sits uneasily with the Home Office emphasis on caution, and the truth is that most matters are dealt with in a fairly languid fashion. The Maunsell episode is summarised by the Prison Officers' Association in its evidence to the May Inquiry:

> Brigadier Maunsell was a popular figure in the Prison Service throughout his time in office. However, the Civil Service is not prone to accepting individualism and it became clear at a relatively early stage that the Inspector General was being reduced to a titular rather than realistic head of the Prison Service. This is a lesson of history which is regretted by the Association which believes that many of the problems now being faced are attributable to the very bureaucracy which effectively neutralised the status of the Inspector General (POA, Evidence, p.135).

The 'problem' of the Inspector General was solved by the establishment of a Management Review. This review, which took several years to complete, restructured the Department and put him firmly down the line and, in some ways, out on a limb. He was 'separated from executive functions' (Home Office, 1971). Maunsell resigned, a career governor was appointed to replace him, and the post was retitled Chief Inspector. Thus Mountbatten's attempt to create a recognisable head was subverted, an outcome which, as the POA quotation suggests, made large numbers of staff annoyed and added to their stock of cynicism about the administration of the service.

Regionalisation

During this same period (the late 1960s) Prison Department decided upon another possible way of reducing the 'remoteness' of the administration to which Mountbatten had referred. This was to develop a regional structure. Four regions were established — South East, South West, North and Midlands. These were, and are, staffed for the most part by experienced personnel drawn from the governor, uniformed, and specialist grades. The object was to enable staff and prisoners to feel that authority was nearer and more accessible:

> The aim of regionalisation is to enable the work of the Prison Department to be facilitated at all levels and to help establishments carry out their full share of this work. With this aim in mind, the objectives of the regional organisation are to establish an intermediate tier of support and control near to and more intimately linked with establishments than headquarters can provide, and to delegate to the regions as much operational and administrative responsibility as practicable (Circular Instruction cited in Home Office, Evidence, vol.I, paper IIB(8), Annex A, para 2).

Since there is so much investment in this arrangement, it figures in a good deal of the evidence given to the May Committee. It is, no doubt, a disappointment to the Home Office to learn that there is almost nothing hopeful in that evidence about the possibility of making regionalisation work. Strangely, the Prison Officers' Association had 'nothing specifically to say about regions' (May, 1979, 5.69). But others did, and most of it was critical. The governors, including the regional directors themselves, as has always happened in evidence to such inquiries in recent years, were the best informed, most articulate, and most courageous, of the personnel witnesses. The regional directors were 'unanimous in their evidence that the regional structure as at present constituted did not work efficiently' (May, 1979, para 5.65). As to solutions, it was said by various groups that regions should have greater authority in the operational sense, especially in respect of personnel management and industrial relations. It was also suggested that casework (paperwork relating to problems submitted by prisoners) should go back to London headquarters — which May went on to recommend (para 5.66-5.76). It is worth dwelling upon this, because it explains a good deal of the philosophy which has developed in the prison system.

A cardinal reason for the centralisation of prisons was that it would lead to greater 'uniformity', one of two key words (the other was 'economy') much used at the time. The desire to establish uniformity arose from the fact that a uniform central system could ensure *minimum* standards for prisoners. The lesson of penal history is that the administrators of a system have to restrain the laziness, cruelty, or indifference of people who work in prisons. This is not to allege that people who work in prisons are constitutionally lazy, cruel, or indifferent; or that their propensity for such behaviour is greater than that of persons in other organisations. It is to say that dealing with difficult and powerless people tempts such behaviour, and that when it occurs it has more dire consequences than in most other organisations. Furthermore, in a sophisticated system there is considerable pressure from both staff and inmates to maintain uniformity. Any deviation from it tends to create a furore, not only amongst those groups, but amongst outsiders who deplore what can be construed, or misconstrued, as discrimination, which may be the exercise of discretion. Thus, one of the problems about Hull prison in the early 1970s, when it was a liberal establishment, was that prisoners arriving at other prisons from Hull complained bitterly about the fact that the privileges they had earned at Hull were not allowed at their new prison. The upset caused by this led in turn to staff complaining about there being no hard and fast rules.

The relevance of this for the question of English prison management lies in the fact that discretion cannot be given to regions *and* conformity assured. This has led headquarters to be cautious about how much autonomy it gives to regions, and in turn has led to regions complaining about lack of power. This caution is evident in the papers submitted to the May Inquiry by the Home Office. One of these discusses the pressure to transfer more authority and responsibility from headquarters to regions. It is worth quoting at some length because it sets out very real problems which, if they are followed to their conclusion, may provide effective evidence that the regional system cannot work:

> This view, however, overlooks the problems of developing closer operational support and of transferring more casework. It also ignores the problems that arise in regard to consistency when the expectations about public accountability are rising, the ineluctable constraints on finance and manpower, and the question of the headquarters relationship with the prison service in the field . . . . Much of the case for more delegation of responsibility to regional commands (as opposed to more effective regions) seems to rest on the misconception that it would in some way relax constraints that are common at any level of the public services and necessarily result in quicker responses (Home Office, Evidence, vol.II, paper III(2), para 2).

What is being emphasised in such remarks is that even if the judgement of regional staff could be trusted, and trained to accord with that of headquarters, there could still be a major problem because of what appeared to be discriminatory action. This is especially important at present since, as May observes, there is more and more casework, a good deal of which, it should be added, finds its way to Europe, that unexpected resort of the English prisoner with no Bill of Rights to challenge (May, 1979, para 5.68).

It now becomes understandable why the Home Office used the occasion of the May Inquiry to try to get casework back from the regions: the political turbulence arising from casework is likely to increase. The Home Office also suggested that the infra-structure of 'specialists' (education officers, psychologists and so on) should be abolished. The May Committee supported this view arguing instead that regional directors 'be given the widest possible operational powers' (May, 1979, para 5.75). The May Report gives a hint, but only a hint, of what this means. Regional directors should visit establishments more frequently, and should carry out the 'detailed management inspections heretofore carried out by the Chief Inspector' (para 5.75). Whether or not this is another erosion of the role and power of the latter is debatable.

On these organisational questions the May Committee's recommendations have been unduly influenced by Home Office advice. This is hardly surprising. Of all witnesses the Home Office was the best informed, its interests were most at stake, and its evidence was well prepared. But, as a consequence of Home Office pressures, the May Committee was a good deal more cautious than it might have been. In the case of regionalisation, even if the Report's recommendations are implemented, certain fundamental problems will almost certainly remain. It is pointless for regional directors, however experienced, to visit establishments if they cannot make decisions. This is their constant complaint, and one echoed by governors. Prison governors all too frequently find themselves in crisis situations where they have first to deal with several divisions of headquarters and then have to involve region. In short, the governors saw themselves as having to: 'resolve conflict between the various parts of the Headquarters organisation' (SCPS, para 22). There is no evidence in the May Report that regions *will* be given more authority. Indeed the Home Office evidence quoted above will make clear that there are very good reasons why this is impossible.

The alternative is to begin again; to identify *why* regionalisation is failing and consider other possibilities. It should be remembered that it is not simply that the regional structure is not *working*, it is a positive *blockage* to effective communication. It is extraordinary too that casework, such as petitions from prisoners which have been speeded up since they were handed over to regions, is to revert to headquarters. Thus, one of the few modest successes of the regional organisation is to be taken away.

The May Report is correct to state that the administrative system cannot revert to that which preceded regional organisation. What needs to be reconsidered is whether a geographical division is the best way to break down the monolith. Geographical divisions seem sensible, but they are part of pre-combustion engine thinking. It is now easy to travel to most parts of England and Wales (the Scottish system is quite separate) in a relatively short time. The problem is not *geographical* therefore. It is one of creating a structure which allows some autonomy to its parts, and yet ensures uniformity. In any geographical area there will be several institutions of any given type, open or dispersal prisons for example. If all of these were placed under what might be called a 'functional' region, that is not a geographical region at all but a specialist group in charge of such institutions, then the problem would be on its way to solution. The problem is not that the prisoners in Leeds, a local prison, compare their conditions with those at Hull, a dispersal prison, but that prisoners in prisons with the same classification compare their treatment. The Category A prisoners happen to be the most brittle in this respect, but they merely highlight a problem.

Until the reorganisation of the 1970s, there was what may be described as an embryonic structure of this kind. There was a Director of Prison Administration, and a Director of Borstal Administration. This led in turn to Borstal assistant governors, for example, developing a collective identity, with conferences focusing on their own problems. This was not Utopia. But the division of Prison Department into smaller units, each with special responsibilities for certain categories of inmates, could lead to development of more coherent and cohesive policies within 'divisions'.

In what is generally very sound evidence, the governor grades miss an important point when they write:

> There must be far more decentralisation and delegation from head-quarters to regions. Whether the regions should be geographical or functional is perhaps of secondary importance. Real authority and operational control must be vested in regions and the necessary resources provided to enable this to be effectively carried through. (SCPS, para 24).

This is followed by a demand for greater resources, which is the familiar and predictable solution offered for any of the failures in an organisation. Not only, at present, is such an injection of resources unlikely, but its effectiveness in the light of what has been said would be dubious. A more likely outcome would be the regional duplication of headquarters bureaucracy, administrative sterility as a consequence, and an early call for a further Inquiry. This was recognised by the Home

Office, in its evidence (Home Office, Evidence, vol.II, paper III(2)).

The May Committee recommended that the regions be slimmed down. It is difficult to guess at the likely success of this proposal, but it is marginally more likely to work than a vastly increased regional structure, uneasy in its relationship with headquarters, and with a sustained sense of frustration at its powerlessness. This chapter does not primarily concern itself with inspection (see chapter 6) but it must be noted that the proposal that regions should inspect their own establishments is totally unsatisfactory. The suggestion ignores both the desperate need for an inspectorate which will take an interest in prisoners' affairs, and the fact that, were it implemented, people would be judging their own cause. This would obviously be true in an organisational sense. But in the prison context they would be expected to be impartial about the work of colleagues and friends, often close friends, and conceivably, relatives. This aspect of the May Report is no solution to the urgent problems of inspection.

Industrial relations

So far, this discussion has been about the way in which the administration of the prison service has evolved, the sources of its generally acknowledged defects and the failure of regionalisation as a remedy. However, the failing which caused most concern nationally, and which most immediately gave rise to the May Inquiry, was one of industrial relations: a failing which was especially manifest in the militant behaviour of the uniformed officers. It was this crucial behaviour which the Committee was expected to analyse, and to offer recommendations upon, that would encourage staff to behave in an orderly fashion consistent with the rights of prisoners.

The process of alienation which now seems characteristic of our prison staff is actually endemic in modern prison systems. Prison officers in many parts of the developed world all express the same frustrations (Thomas, 1978). What has gone wrong? The cause of officer hostility can generally be traced to the decision, in most civilised prison systems, to establish reformative goals. Such goals were defined in England in the famous Gladstone Report of 1895, and culminated in the equally well known dictum in the Prison Rules of 1949 that the purpose of training was to establish the will to live a good and useful life. This development led officers to become very apprehensive for a number of reasons. Some of these concerned the necessarily greater freedom which such a policy allowed to prisoners. Officers argued that such freedom increased the chances of attacks on staff. While assessing this claim is a very complicated matter, being a prison officer remains a job in which the chances of serious injury are slight (Thomas, 1972a).

Officers also noted that large numbers of specialist grades began to be appointed. This had several effects. One was that though opportunities for constructive work were being developed, officers were displaced from engaging in it by the recruitment of specialists — teachers, probation officers and the like. Further, they saw this group of specialists as a *cadre* whose primary interests and sympathies were directed towards the prisoners and against the staff. Finally, they claimed that such resources as were available to the prison service, were allocated to prisoners. Such claims have often been dismissed as paranoid, or infantile, but independent inquiries have tended to agree with the officers. Wynn Parry was the first to do so (Wynn Parry, 1958) and the sentiments in that report were repeated by May:

> Amongst the most vocal complaints made to us during our visits was the one which asserted that the facilities provided for staff are very poor indeed when compared with those provided for inmates. As one POA branch representative put it: 'All that we want is parity with prisoners'. Our own observations have in many cases confirmed the validity of this complaint. We have ourselves seen officers crowded into tiny muster rooms with no adequate locker or other facilities, staff toilets which were a disgrace . . . (May, 1979, para 11.2).

This reformative trend was accompanied by the increase in the size of the system, although the two were not, of course, necessarily related. In the minds of the staff, however, the two were confused, and it was argued that together they led to the breakdown in communications which is the constant theme of all discussion on the prison service in recent years. As far as staff are concerned, the breakdown in communications was in part deliberate, and in part due to incompetence.

When one contemplates the history of the English prison officer, and his treatment by the Home Office, one is left wondering why he was so passive (for a full discussion, see Thomas, 1972). The answer is important. It was because the prison service started life as a paramilitary organisation. It attracted men who subscribed to the ethos of such an organisation, both as governors and officers. This disciplined milieu was reinforced by the wearing of uniform, and the gradations of rank, designed to inculcate respect for authority. Officers were also subject to a Discipline Code, which will be discussed later. It was this tradition which, during the period of the First World War, made the task of recruitment to the embryo union difficult. It remains a source of tension, because Chief Officers and many older uniformed staff privately deplore the extreme behaviour which, they say, undermines the backbone of the service. Until recently, there were enough officers remaining in the prison service to ensure that the discipline, which so many advocate for prisoners, was maintained amongst the staff. So, despite increasing dissatisfaction clearly evidenced in the Prison Officers' Magazine, the para-military tradition kept officers in line.

The problem in the last twenty years, speeded up in the last ten, is that this tradition has gone. There were three contributory factors in its demise. The first of these was outside the province of the Home Office. This was, put simply, an increase in militancy in society at large. The rule of thumb observation, commonly made by Chief Officers during the last ten years (and documented by Jones and Cornes, 1977), is that fewer ex-service men have been hired as officers. Instead, more men with industrial experience have turned to the prison service, above all for the security it offers — a security which now is almost unassailable. Such men not only brought into the prison service an awareness of the effectiveness of organised unionism, but also a tradition of distrust of authority which, in British experience in the last twenty years, it has been difficult to reject. Much of the breakdown in discipline between POA headquarters and local branches is due to the existence of these rival perceptions of authority. This is recognised by May in a succinct statement which indicates just how serious, or the pessimist might say, hopeless, the situation really is. Discussing relationships between the National Executive of the POA and its branches, May observes that 'there can now be no automatic assumption that agreements reached at national level will be honoured down the line' (May, 1979, para 10.10).

It should be noted that prisoners too have shared in the growth of militancy and this has exacerbated the breakdown. There is little need to dwell upon this, except to say that prisoners, in many parts of the world, have given notice, often effectively, that they will not lightly put up with a system which erodes what they construe as their rights. Whether this is right or wrong, it is certainly true that a major consequence has been an undisciplined, sometimes vindictive, and occasionally criminal response from staff.

The second important contribution to the breakdown has been the reformative strategy itself. The rigidity of the para-military organisation runs contrary to the needs of reformative tasks. This became evident almost immediately after the Gladstone Report changed the direction of the service. In the early years of this century, governors, in their annual reports, described how they were now visiting ex-Borstal boys, sitting on various after-care committees, and a host of other things, which demonstrated that there was much more concern for the inmates. This spirit grew quickly and was exemplified by Paterson's view that if an officer found an inmate troublesome, he (Paterson) would want to know what was wrong with the officer (Thomas, 1972). It was such attitudes which disgusted Harley Cronin, the first General Secretary of the POA (Cronin, 1967).

It was very difficult to break with the old traditions: officers were not involved in the new policies, in part because of the structural problem of devising a means of both controlling and reforming prisoners; and in part because it was not clear that officers were competent or trustworthy enough. There was a feeling of antique origin that to allow the development of a private relationship between uniformed officers and prisoners would lead to corruption and a generally bad time for prisoners. This, it will be remembered, was precisely why prisons were centralised, and why regionalisation is such a difficult concept to put into practice.

The need to supervise prison officers, and to monitor their behaviour, is implicit in the existence of the Discipline Code, which often amused officers until recent times, with its ban on 'undue familiarity' with inmates. Such rules were quite out of tune with the pressure for officers to become 'involved' with the training of inmates, which is a familiar theme in every report, and every comment upon them since 1945. The May Report is no exception. This pressure from all sides, including the reform bodies, is in no way disreputable. It set a standard and a goal which to many seemed sane and legitimate, had it been achieved.

The fact that it never has been achieved, apart from isolated occasions which had no lasting effect, is the fault of nobody. The amount of 'training' in which officers can become involved in respect of prisoners is slight, because of the reality of the conflict in a modern prison system between control and reformation. This is not to be confused with a more modest goal which would be that officers should treat prisoners decently and humanely. But the vague aim of making officers quasi-social workers had an especially dysfunctional effect. For the attack on para-militarism led to its demise and there was no effective code of behaviour put in its place.

The third contribution to the breakdown of the classic system came from the Home Office, that is Prison Department headquarters, itself. At some point (certainly dating at least from the troubles of 1972), the Department seems to have adopted a policy of 'keeping a low profile', a piece of jargon for which we are indebted to the conflict in Northern Ireland. Thus, when prisoners demonstrated in that year, the *modus operandi* seems to have been to stand back and let them tire themselves out. Uniformed staff learned two things from these events. The first was that in a time of stress, or near chaos, there is a power vacuum which can be filled by anyone wishing to fill it. The second, and related, lesson was that the Home Office response to disruptive prisoner behaviour might be applied to staff who engaged in such behaviour. This was commented upon in the May Report:

> There is a further point that we have heard in various guises from prison officers, governors, and the Department itself. This is that for whatever reason industrial action has been found to produce results, and that the practice of resorting to such action has developed a momentum of its own. The POA argued that it had been the experience of branches that industrial action produced a response that had not previously been forthcoming, which meant that they would be the more ready to resort to such measures the next time an issue arose (May, 1979, para 10.21).

This amazing state of affairs makes the position of the governor untenable. The point here is that headquarters is shielded from the urgency of situations at institutional level where, it is claimed, governors' autonomy has been seriously eroded. Their evidence to May is unequivocal in this respect:

> The governors are also critical of the policies which management has pursued in the face of industrial troubles. They contend that they have felt isolated in the face of trouble and bereft of the support from headquarters which they regarded as their due . . . they claim to receive inadequate support from headquarters in disciplinary cases, and that recommendations for dismissal are not acted upon (para 10.19).

As if all this were not bad enough, evidence to May quoted

> instances of trades officers having refused work but still being paid at normal rates, and officers called in at overtime rates for escort duty, who had refused the duty but had still been paid (para 10.21).

The cumulative effect of all this is that governors are expected to control a prison population, which is becoming increasingly turbulent, with officers who have moved from a para-military discipline to anarchy. One of the most disappointing aspects of the ending of the reformative era, for its optimistic advocates at least, must be the move from discipline to anarchy without an intervening period of professional behaviour. Since this is the linchpin of the central problem facing the May Inquiry, it must be dwelt upon in detail and the seriousness of the situation understood.

The governors, in their evidence, catalogued some of the daily examples of misbehaviour by staff, with which they had to contend:

Prisoners have not been produced at court;

Prisoners have been refused admission to penal establishments;

Prisoners' legal advisers have been refused admission to prisoners;

Prisoners' relatives have not been allowed to visit;

Prisoners' activities have all been curtailed in one form or another;

Other staff (also members of Trade Unions) have been refused admission to penal establishments;

Contractors have been refused admission to penal establishments, causing penalty clauses to be invoked and essential security work to be delayed;

New or repaired units of accommodation have not been manned so accentuating overcrowding elsewhere

(SCPS, 1979, para 159; for a further catalogue of industrial actions see Home Office, Evidence, 1979, vol.II, paper IIE(2).

This is a very serious state of affairs. What was the substance of the evidence offered to the May Inquiry to put matters right? Naturally enough, a good deal of evidence sought to advance sectional interests. A good example concerned the post of Director General. The London Branch of the Society of Civil and Public Servants:

took substantial issue with the contention of the Governors' Branch of their same Society that the Director General of the prison service should be appointed from within the service . . . the task (of a governor) was essentially a 'fairly parochial one with no requirement to acquire a vision for the wider scene' (May, 1979, para 5.20).

It is hardly surprising that May went on to say that: 'such a sentiment . . . no doubt explains some of the relationships and attitudes we have discovered in the present organisations' (para 5.20).

This is a very much more important matter than it might appear. The people making such contemptuous remarks about the governors, are mainly executive grades in the civil service. They carry the burden of the paperwork of the service but have little or no practical experience with prisoners, and are in the centre of the delays in communication about which May heard so many complaints. Their branches of the SCPS constantly try to elevate their status at the expense of the governor grades, and press, so far unsuccessfully, for promotional transfers to those grades. One suggestion reviving an old ambition, was put to the May Committee:

for the appointment at each establishment of an Administration Officer of equivalent rank to the deputy governor . . . the latter should take all the day to day purely operational matters off the shoulders of the governing governor, whilst the equivalent Administration Officer should become responsible to the latter for all the other services and activities in establishments, including such matters as the discipline office, staff quarters, prison officers' detail and censorship of mail' (para 5.81).

The Committee recognised this both for the blatant ambition and potential for organisational disaster it is: 'we do not think that any sufficient case has been made out for any alteration to their status or position' (para 5.83). One cannot blame a representative body for trying to advance its members' cause, but such suggestions, and there were others of a similar kind, did little to deal with the central issue — staff behaviour.

The groups most closely concerned with the industrial relations crisis are the governors and the uniformed officers. Both gave evidence on these matters. The POA evidence itself gave some indication of the enormity of the problem facing the Inquiry. Not only did the latter have to examine ways of improving structures, but it had to try to moderate the attitudes expressed in the POA evidence. These attitudes are quite extraordinary. In 1977 at their annual conference the POA issued a document entitled 'Industrial Relations'. The question is raised in that document of the legal liability of officers taking industrial action in respect of prisoners' entitlements. The conclusion offered must rank as one of the most cynical made by an officers' union:

> Prison officers have no legal obligation to guarantee the statutory entitlements of inmates in circumstances where these cannot be provided due to the fact that prison officers are engaged in industrial action. Accordingly, the provision of any such entitlement for inmates is a matter which is entirely at the discretion of the local branch, having due regard to the form of industrial action being taken at the time (POA, Evidence, p.177).

At the same time, as the May Committee points out, branches are judicious in their choice of action. They: 'have been careful, for example, except in the most extreme cases, to avoid action which would adversely affect the level of overtime and thus take-home pay' (May, 1979, para 10.9). Perhaps the most notable indication of the reckless behaviour of prison officers is that in the six months after the May Inquiry was set up, industrial action occurred on 31 occasions at 25 different establishments (Home Office, Evidence, vol.II, paper IIE(2).

Much of the POA evidence, naturally, was concerned with the detailed matter of pay which was the ostensible reason for the May

Inquiry. The pay dispute was complex, and the May Committee's settlement of it reasonable. Whilst, of course, pay and related matters are of crucial importance, the more significant value of the POA evidence is that it displays how difficult the whole question of industrial relations has become, not least in its consequences for prisoners. The impression is created that staff actions which make the lot of prisoners harder may be no bad thing. For the POA expressed the general view that:

> Inmates are sent to penal establishments for specified periods of time in order to protect the public and to provide an example to those contemplating criminal acts. Unfortunately this is not made sufficiently clear within the penal system itself (POA, Evidence, p.143).

More serious are the general attitudes (however understandable) which such statements as the following illustrate. The discussion is about the Government cuts in 1976, and the resultant officers' action:

> This gave the outward impression that industrial action was the only effective means of securing commonsense decisions from 'management' and since that time its use has formed part of the fabric of industrial relations in the Prison Service (p.171).

This is no doubt true, but underlying it is a very good example of the enormity of the problem. A constant complaint from officers for many years has been the amount of overtime they have to work. Paradoxically, when the Government ordered that this be cut, as it did in 1976, officers protested. The reason is simple. When officers organise their budgets, they do so taking overtime earnings into account. Furthermore, most people join the prison service partly because of the opportunity for almost unlimited overtime. Therefore, despite the strategy which has been a mainstay of POA agitation for many years — deploring overtime — many officers welcome it and rely heavily on it.

There is a rift between the executive and the rank and file in the POA. The widening of this rift, which is typical enough of modern unions, led the POA to make a decision which was to contribute to the anarchy which the May Committee was called upon to investigate. In 1975, branches were allowed to take their own decisions about industrial action. That decision led to governors in some prisons spending vast amounts of time coping with localised industrial action over which they often had no control or scope for intervention. This localised action isolated the National Executive of the POA even more. The gap can be illustrated from its oral evidence. Though the National Executive 'reiterated . . . that industrial action should not interfere with the workings of the courts' (May, 1979, para 10.12), it was unable to ensure the implementation of the policy. The autonomy of the branches meant that militants were able to, and did, flout the policy, and there is every possibility of similar behaviour in the future.

This phenomenon illustrates again the problems associated with the growth of the prison service. It has become very big, and has lost something of its corporate identity. Between 1965 and 1978 staff increased by 88 per cent and uniformed staff by 188 per cent. Governors who, fifteen years ago, knew where most of their colleagues were working, no longer have any clear idea. Nobody is to blame for this, but it does mean that staff tend to concern themselves with parochial matters a good deal more than used to be the case. Devolution in the POA has served to counterbalance the Home Office monolith: both are a manifestation of the same problem of growth.

The governors have had to shoulder the burden of staff militancy. The evidence which the governors gave to the May Committee made it clear that it was a burden with which they had to cope alone. If their evidence is correct (and there is no reason to suppose it is not), then the situation has been intolerable:

> In the face of industrial action on a growing scale Governors received little advice. The Home Office's main concern was to impress on Governors that the Army and Police would not be called in; that normal disciplinary measures would not be used against staff taking any form of industrial action, and that it was up to Governors to keep their establishments running as best they could (SCPS, Evidence, para 150).

This policy left governors at the mercy of any staff wishing to create havoc. At Cardiff, Risley, Bedford and Dartmoor staff walked out and simply left the governors to cope. It was natural, therefore, for governors in their evidence to suggest that prison staff should not be allowed to take industrial action. In doing so, they draw upon the Edmund-Davies Report (1978) in which it is argued that the police should not have the right to strike for reasons which are obvious enough. The governors believe that it is fair to regard prison staff in the same way. They go on to point out that, in the case of prisons, striking is an especially powerful weapon that must be controlled. Governors asked for more power to discipline staff, including the possibility of dismissing unsuitable members. Security of tenure has become so firmly entrenched that the POA even objected to the possible dismissal of the officers who were convicted of assaulting prisoners after the Hull riot of 1976.

Before discussing the May Committee's solutions to this matter of industrial relations, one new explanation for the problems of the prison service should be recorded. It has become a popular belief amongst some people in the service that 'outsiders' have considerable influence on what goes on. The belief is normally expressed in the vaguest terms. Sometimes the influence seems to be of left wing politicians, sometimes a reform group, but whatever the source it is an influence which is seen as damaging and insidious. Two important bodies, in their evidence, went so far as to protest about the influence of 'politics'. The POA, discussing the control unit in Wakefield (for a full description see Thomas, 1975a), point out that it was closed: 'through what the Association considers to be political pressure' (POA, Evidence, p.142). The British Association of Prison Governors, a new body, in its evidence criticised the Prison Department for being over-sensitive:

> Senior civil servants are perhaps quite correctly in other situations by training, experience and inclination over-sensitive to political considerations. The fact that the prison service is . . . in the eyes of the Service 'run by outsiders' is another factor which should be considered in relation to the confusion of management styles' (BAPG, Evidence, p.9).

There are two points to be made here. One is that these criticisms take no account of the public accountability of the service, and indeed protests about it, which attitude is both remarkable and unrealistic. The second is that the myth about the influence of 'outsiders' now seems to have hardened into a certainty which is worth including in evidence to a major public Inquiry. The traditional body representing the governors (SCPS) on the other hand, recognised that there is a problem which goes beyond the creation of an extra-mural folk devil: they accepted the necessity for increased scrutiny and public accountability. Nevertheless, they were concerned to point out that:

> There is all the difference between scrutiny and accountability on the one hand and the subservience of operational efficiency to the stranglehold of bureaucratic interference and administrative commonsense on the other (SCPS, Evidence, para 103).

The May Committee correctly identified the causes of industrial unrest which have been here described. Nor was it very optimistic about the future. Much rests upon good will, of which there is a considerable deficiency. The section in the May Report headed 'The importance of good industrial relations' merely catalogues a number of hopes, which seem optimistic indeed when some of the evidence is taken into account. On occasion the Committee, new as it was to prison matters, was inclined to suppress the unpleasant facts of prison industrial relations. Thus, for example, in trying to discover some cause for optimism, the Committee pointed to the fact that when a governor

153

has *declared a state of emergency* the staff 'have not hestitated to resume their normal duties' (May, 1979, para 10.32). 'Nothing', the Report goes on, 'must be allowed to jeopardise the underlying loyalty which that implies'. One may fairly ask: what loyalty is being talked about?

The Report explains accurately the working of the Whitley Councils and Committees, which are the standard negotiating procedures in the Civil Service. It goes on to show, again correctly, the main reasons for the failure of this machinery. This is again substantially a problem of local and central communication breakdown. The Committee then considered the possibility of establishing local or regional procedures. The Home Office response, which here, as elsewhere in the Report, seems to have been very influential, was predictable. It was that it is impossible to use local procedures, because this would break the 'uniformity' which is necessary over the entire service (May, 1979, para 10.34). There are few issues which are truly local or regional, it was argued, and to introduce local variations would lead to anomalies. The Home Office is quite right: the problem is not a consequence of any unreasonable reticence on their part, but is one which derives from the highly centralised nature of the organisation; a point which has been a constant theme in this account. Since new formal structures are ruled out, the Committee then puts some faith in local initiatives short of major change (paras 10.43-44). There is one possible advantageous change. This is the proposed, and generally applauded, transfer of personnel matters from the Home Office to the Prison Department. A remarkable curiosity at present is that the Director General of the service has no responsibility for pay or personnel. If the Department had its own establishment division, the Director General would gain a central role in negotiation. There was a good deal of sympathy expressed in the evidence to the Committee for this change, although, as the Report points out, the Civil Service Department would still have the final say. The Committee is thus left with few options and it concluded: 'albeit reluctantly, that we cannot at present identify any further areas over which central management can relinquish ultimate responsibility' (para 10.37). Despite the approval of the governors for some regional negotiating organisation, the pressure of the Home Office and the POA deflected that possibility. The arguments of both 'seemed decisive' (para 10.44). The local 'improvements' suggested by the Committee were to encourage governors to take more initiative, to establish joint local committees representing all staff, and to give a member of the governor grades responsibility for personnel matters.

A constant source of discussion within the prison service concerns the power of governors. The governors consistently complain that their power has been eroded. The Department does not fully agree. Whilst accepting that 'there is a measure of truth' in the claim (Home Office, Evidence, vol.II, paper IID(1), para 10), they asserted 'that governors often do not use the powers they do possess' (May, 1979, para 10.36). Evidence for one view or the other is difficult to uncover for obvious reasons, although it is clear that during the Hull riot of 1976 the crucial decisions were made by the governor (Fowler, 1977). As usual, the May Committee accepted the final assessment of the Home Office and called for 'greater exercise of local initiative' (para 10.36).

The second proposal for 'consultation' is in many ways linked to the first. The history of the prison service since 1945 is littered with the wreckage of Consultative Committees, and May recognised the danger of 'talking shops' (para 10.38). The fact is that such bodies fail because they achieve little. This is a commonplace of organisational experience, but it has been heightened in the prison service by the singular absence of local autonomy. There is much exhortation in the May Report, some of which fails to take account of experience. It had, the Committee reported, been told that some staff hesitate about taking part in such meetings, and 'we would urge them most strongly to think again' (para 10.38). Such hopes are, unfortunately, fore-doomed.

The same applies to the notion of making a member of the governor grades responsible for personnel. It is even suggested that he might be 'a troubleshooter in the event of disputes occurring' (para 10.59). This is utter fantasy. Unless such a person has real power to act, and exercises it, staff will not be interested. It is virtually certain that such a man will recognise the cause of 'trouble', and will know how to solve the problem. He will, however, find himself enmeshed in rules over which he has no control. This is precisely why the regional structure has failed. Prison staff are not looking for friendly chats, they are looking for people with the power to resolve a problem within the foreseeable future. If a personnel officer cannot do that, then he is valueless to the staff. If nothing else emerges from the May Report, it must be clear that such a delegation of authority is out of the question.

The May Committee concludes its discussion of this most vital area with a consideration of the case for limiting industrial action in some way. It points to the governors' argument that prisoners are especially helpless, and that the very system of criminal justice could be damaged. The Committee discusses problems of definition of what would be illegal, the general rights of employees, and the difficulties of enforcement. Such restrictions might, it argued, cause 'resentment and frustration' (para 10.49). Nevertheless the Committee concluded that specific agreements might have restrictions written in, and its optimism convinced it that: 'It is far more important to create a situation in which all within the prison service recognise the need to work at improved industrial relations, knowing the results if they do not' (para 10.49). It reiterates that causing suffering to prisoners is 'positively immoral', and that 'we do not believe the POA dissents from that proposition' (para 10.49). This is all quite valueless. Whether or not the POA dissents is very questionable, to judge from their evidence. Even if they agree with May, it does not seem to make any difference to the way the membership actually behaves. For them it was a signal victory. In their evidence, the POA stated that:

> industrial action is a legitimate means by which pressure can be applied where normal means of consultation and negotiation have failed. The Association views this as an essential trade union freedom, the surrender of which would be unacceptable. In this respect the Association wishes to make it plain beyond any possibility of misunderstanding that it does not intend to surrender the freedom and autonomy of its members to seek justice by the only means available to them where other and more customary means have failed (POA, Evidence, p.172).

A major area of discussion was about the Code of Discipline, which supposedly governs the behaviour of uniformed officers. Naturally the POA took the opportunity to try to undermine it. In recent years, as the governors pointed out, the Department had helped in this process by denying its use to governors in 'an industrial situation'. This, the May Committee believes, reflects 'industrial good sense' and further recommends redrafting 'to exempt action taken in furtherance of a dispute' (May, 1979, para 10.51). The POA was even concerned about the practice of ordering an officer to give a written account of his behaviour, the procedures when an inmate makes an allegation against staff, and the suspension of staff while investigations are being carried out. It is understandable, but very unfortunate for the prison service, that the Committee: 'became convinced that it was not for an outside body to prescribe the detailed changes that might be made' (para 10.56). The governors, chief officers, and many officers must have been bitterly disappointed at this abrogation of responsibility. Apart from a recommendation that the Prison Department Whitley Council should include staff other than prison officers (resisted by the POA), and some suggestions for improvements over arbitration, and a ritual call for more training in industrial relations — a certain sign of bankruptcy — the issue was left.

Concluding remarks

And so, what has the May Committee recommended? It should be stressed that the prison service is a very complex, devious organisation to comprehend, and that the Committee was the victim of indecent haste. In respect of the central organisation, the institution of 'establishment' responsibility within the Prison Department has potential, since the affairs of an establishment section affect staff very deeply. The general advocacy of giving more power, independent of the Home Office, to the head of the service, with concomitant up-grading, also offers some hope. And the Committee was wise to reject pressure and to recommend in effect that anyone should be considered eligible for the post (para 5.46). The expansion and reallocation of roles with regard to the Prisons Board is organisationally neutral. The idea of appointing 'two entirely independent non-executive members' (para 5.47) is a concession to the much vaunted principle of opening up the workings of the system. But it is one which the civil service is likely to prove perfectly able to contain. At present many hundreds of members of Boards of Visitors are theoretically acting as monitors for society with, lamentably, very little effect.

With regard to regionalisation, that continuing hope, the recommendations mean little. Geographical regionalisation cannot work, even if the work of regions is restricted. Nor can exhortation to governors, whether by regions or by headquarters, unless the most important functionaries in the entire system, the governors, have more authority. Despite the articulate arguments put forward by the governors, it is difficult to discover in the entire Report a really valuable concession to their experience. They are, in effect, constantly rejected in favour of either the Home Office or the POA.

This is the kernel of the problem. Prison officers have increasingly been protected from the imposition of disciplinary procedures by POA pressure and by Home Office policy. No standards of professional behaviour replaced the traditional system and, as a result, the May Committee was called upon to examine a system which can only be described as anarchic. There is ample, convincing and commonplace evidence that this is so; indeed some of the statements of the POA can be fairly called upon as evidence. In this respect the situation has deteriorated since Lord Mountbatten's Inquiry. The signal difference between the two Inquiry Reports is that nowhere is there any mention in Mountbatten of staff misbehaviour. One must, of course, except his view that a member of staff had helped in the escape of Charles Wilson, the mail train robber, in 1964.

The odd fact is, that despite the tone of the POA evidence, and the extreme behaviour of some staff in recent times, there is still, amongst many officers in the prison service, a desire to curb excessively disruptive behaviour. Individual officers who felt that this is necessary could not easily have given their evidence, nor could it have competed with the institutional evidence. This is not to excuse or disavow any of the ineptitude alleged against the Home Office. It is to say that, far from colluding in the attack on the Discipline Code, the May Committee should have called for it to be strengthened and used. The problem for the Committee was to decide whether or not to restore order. The Committee should have seriously challenged the rights of prison staff to strike or engage in industrial action — for the many reasons it heard and some of which it reported with evident approval. One is the misery that such action causes to prisoners; another is the crude frustration of the processes of criminal justice. The unfortunate truth is that those, such as governors, who have to work the system can expect no improvements from the Report. Officers who want to do their jobs will continue to be pushed into situations with which they disagree, because this Report gave no lead which might restore order. The pay settlements were fair; but as many people said in evidence — and they were not seeking refuge in quasi-Freudian verbiage — the malaise is not about pay. The issue is about the treatment of prisoners in a civilised society and the establishment of discipline, instead of caprice, in the body of men deputed to carry out the task. If such a goal be unrealistic, then we must resign ourselves to the continuation of the present state of affairs.

6 Maintaining standards: who guards the guards? (J. P. Martin)

The dominant fact about prisons in all societies is that they are closed and secret institutions, to which most members of the public have no access. Their inmates are held by the coercive power of the State; their communications with the outside world are limited, and friends and relatives may only visit them under controlled and restricted conditions. Their community has no natural basis, and may bring together individuals so mutually hostile as to endanger each other's lives.

The staff, too, are constrained. There are codes of discipline and a commitment to security which is liable to envelop all who enter the establishment in even a semi-official capacity. Alternative careers may not be easy to find, and dependency on the system increases with years of service. Prisons, therefore, are a test case for the integrity of public administration; a balance has to be achieved between the needs of the individual and of society; inmates and staff should partake in an ordered but humane regime and, above all, the public must be satisfied that the power exercised in private, on its behalf, has been used justly and without excess.

Because the May Committee was set up primarily to de-fuse a crisis of industrial relations these questions took second place. However, as its terms of reference included 'the treatment of inmates' and 'the organisation of the prison services' those giving evidence took the opportunity of raising such matters because of their intrinsic importance, even if they were tangential to the prison officers' claims. The Committee was caught between the fire of those involved in an intricate industrial dispute, and of those only marginally interested in that dispute but deeply concerned about the way the system was developing. This was not surprising, for the Committee was set up at the end of the most troubled twelve years since the modern prison system was established.

In England and Wales there had been a series of disturbances (including three full-scale riots), prison officers had been convicted of assaulting prisoners, and the United Kingdom government had successfully been taken to the European Commission on Human Rights over matters of prison administration. Heavier sentencing by the courts had gradually built up the prison population in general, and the numbers serving very long terms in particular. In consequence the system faced a

159

whole range of problems relating to security and to establishing regimes appropriate for those incarcerated for longer than had ever been intended by those who designed the system. More and more men faced sentences so long that, it was argued, they felt they had nothing to lose in defying authority, so that management came to be dominated by fears about security and control. These were compounded by the arrival in the system of those who denied its legitimacy on political grounds.

The quest for security and control has led to a whole range of measures, some more expedient than others. England and Wales have seen the Mountbatten security classification adopted, but then applied (in a way which almost totally distorted the original proposal) by developing a system of 'dispersal prisons' for men regarded as high security risks. Violent individuals have been housed in C Wing at Parkhurst, 'control units' for difficult prisoners were set up but then more or less abandoned, special (MUFTI) squads have been trained to deal with disturbances, while some prison medical officers have experimented with calming disruptive prisoners by the use of drugs. Less controversially, prisoners permanently at risk of assault by other inmates have been protected by segregation in special prisons. In Scotland both extremes have been tried in the control of violent individuals — some have been placed in 'cages' (cells within cells), while at Barlinnie prison in Glasgow a special unit appears to have been notably successful in handling the same problem (and indeed individuals) in a constructive regime. Northern Ireland has, of course, been dominated by the presence of prisoners who have committed offences for political reasons. Although the granting of 'political status' has been and is a matter of fierce controversy it seems that the administration at the Maze prison has been unable to prevent a large measure of control from being exercised by para-military groups among the inmates.

Although these have been the issues that have excited public attention in this period they do not loom large in the May Committee's Report. Judging from the result, it would seem that the Committee's deliberations were effectively dominated by the closely argued claim of the Prison Officers' Association, the spirited (though less substantial) contributions of other groups in the service and, above all, by the massive body of evidence submitted by the Home Office itself. Given the impossible timetable initially imposed upon it such a result was almost inevitable. It is to the credit of the Committee that it soon realised that 'the real causes of industrial unrest were much more fundamental and had their origins in, amongst other things, a general dissatisfaction with the way the prison services are organised and run' (May, 1979, para 1.1). However, it does not seem to have been in a position to do much about it. The timetable for the Committee itself was extended by six months, the members worked prodigiously hard (para 1.12), but the emphasis had been set by the terms of reference and by the fact that the POA and the Home Office were already well prepared — rather like mediaeval knights in full armour waiting for their entry into the lists for their ritual joust. Despite widespread invitations to give written evidence the process was ludicrously hurried so that few organisations could prepare fully considered representations, particularly as it was not known how widely the terms of reference would be interpreted. In the event it seems that some impact was made, but the Chairman later stressed that his Committee had not been set up to enquire into any part of the prison system anyone might care to mention (NACRO, 1980). Hence although some very important topics got an airing they were marginal to the Committee's immediate concerns, and possibly relied on rather hurriedly produced evidence.

Because of the Committee's orientation this chapter will range more widely than the Report, and will draw on the evidence and other literature in order to provide as full a discussion as possible of the problem of ensuring that proper standards of care are not only laid down, but achieved in practice. If, in the process, one comes to repeat the famous question 'Who guards the guards?' (*Quis custodiet, ipsos custodies?*) — it is not to assume the worst, but to point to the acid test of those given power to maintain the law. Some failures are inevitable; the task is to see that they remain peripheral.

Setting standards

To talk of safeguards implies the existence of standards. Terms such as 'ill-treatment', 'abuse', 'harm' and so on only have meaning because they relate, often implicitly, to standards that are not being met. Such standards may be devised in a variety of ways, and their authoritativeness and acceptability will be similarly varied. There are international conventions, national laws and rules, plus a range of other statements, many of which have been mentioned earlier in this volume. Rather than attempt a further elaboration of standards it may be helpful to consider what causes the greatest worry to inmates and staff. Staff must be considered because serious anxiety on their part can lead to negative attitudes which will inevitably have repercussions for inmates — a classic description of mounting staff-inmate tension is given in King and Elliott's (1978) account of Albany prison between 1971 and 1973 (in chapter 9, 'The Electronic Coffin'). The list that follows is couched in broad terms and assumes a consensus that might be disputed on points of detail, but has the virtue of starting with consumers' needs rather than abstract principles.

Any list must probably start with the need for order and physical security. Prisoners and staff are always aware of potential threats to their personal safety. For staff this fear may be exaggerated; outside Northern Ireland and its special circumstances only one prison officer has been killed by an inmate in the present century. He was actually working at a Borstal, as was the only other staff member to be killed — a Borstal matron (Thomas, 1972a). There are no statistics of serious injuries as such, but if one uses as an index the offence of using gross personal violence to an officer, then in 1978 only 30 inmates were charged with such offences in the entire system of male institutions. This gives an average rate of 1 per 1,284 inmates (Home Office, 1979a). No doubt more staff have suffered lesser injuries, but even so the risk is far smaller than that faced by the police. Nevertheless the anxiety is there, and is perhaps magnified by the fact that the existence of disorder is a conspicuous demonstration of failure of their most basic task.

For prisoners the fears are real enough. Although by all accounts British prisoners are far safer than their counterparts in the USA, the risk of disputes being settled by force, or the threat of force, is high. It is difficult to quantify because of the inmate code of not informing on one's assailant, which leads to gross under-reporting of violence among inmates. Revenge, moreover, is acceptable, while a whole range of personal 'services' can be provided on a basis which is likely to start with extortionate rates of usury and end with crude physical retribution in the event of non-payment. Money or status may be sought irrespective of even the most flimsy contractual basis as, for example, King and Elliott's (1978) description of an enforced collection on behalf of the widow of a notorious ex-Albany prisoner (p.291). Prison language is full of terms for people who wield violent power, and conversely most prison systems are forced to isolate some prisoners for their own protection if, by their crime or supposed conduct, they have offended sufficiently against inmate values. When this protection breaks down either in failure to protect individuals, or in general disorder, the results may be drastic. During the last decade the most celebrated, and best documented, prison riot was at Attica in New York State in 1971. Out of 32 inmates killed, three died at the hands of their fellows during various disputes (New York, 1972). However, while this chapter was being written an even more extreme example occurred at the New Mexico State Penitentiary at Santa Fé in which, according to early reports, at least 39 inmates (probably nearer

50) were killed by other prisoners. The killings involved torture and all manner of bestial maltreatment (*The Guardian,* 6 February 1980). Nothing remotely comparable has happened in Britain, but it remains the case that, as Sykes (1958) concluded, (using a prisoner's words), 'the worst thing about prison is you have to live with the other prisoners' (p.77).

Most prisoners do not wish to be pressurised by other inmates and an ordered regime which limits this possibility will, despite its disadvantages, generally be seen as preferable to anarchy or the dominance of particular cliques. Equally the possibility of violence by staff against inmates is likely to be lessened when they themselves do not feel threatened, and when they feel there is a secure line of command which has to be obeyed.

Second only to order is a need for a sense of justice. Prisoners, after all, are connoisseurs at the receiving end of the machinery of justice and what they greatly fear and resent is the arbitrary use of power. It is, surely, appropriate that in the ultimate law enforcement institution the rule of law should prevail. The term is used in a wide sense, because what is implied here is the concept of natural justice. In essence this means that in all decision-making situations, in the hearing of applications and in adjudications of disciplinary offences, scrupulous care has to be taken to acquaint prisoners with information being taken into account, to allow them to rebut it if they can, and to make sure that they have a real chance of being listened to. This may well be to extend to prisoners standards which they themselves might not apply to others, but the prison should set an example in this respect.

The underlying point is that the uneven power relationship between the prison and the inmate imposes a continual moral duty on the powerful to act justly, with due deliberation. This is often far from easy. Prisoners have much time for thinking up complaints which are difficult to handle and which may be calculated to embarrass the authorities. This, after all, is one of their means of survival (Cohen and Taylor, 1972), and a good prison administration will understand and show a certain tolerance. A corollary of the duty not to rely on excessive power is to avoid unfair administrative practices. Examples of such might be the use of parole schemes for administrative ends, such as maintaining the size of the prison workforce (Hawkins 1972), or the setting up of 'control units' on the basis of obscure interpretations of the Prison Rules. (The legitimacy of these interpretations was recently the subject of litigation between an ex-prisoner and the Home Office.)

The third area of need concerns what might be termed the 'mental life' of the prisoners. Most prisoners fear what imprisonment is going to do to them mentally and socially. There is a whole range of possible anxieties — being cut off from relationships with family and friends, lack of mental stimulus — particularly for those serving long terms who characteristically fear becoming 'cabbages' — and the risk that compliance and order will be achieved by the excessive use of drugs, possibly with adverse long-term effects (Cohen and Taylor, 1972). This fear of the social consequences of conviction is both real and valid. Martin and Webster (1971) have demonstrated that the effects of imprisonment in these respects are usually bad, and cumulative from sentence to sentence. If the courts do not actually intend to inflict social damage then any civilised regime should take what steps it can to mitigate these sorts of harm.

Finally, there are the physical standards — the provision of food, clothing, light, warmth and medical care. Most can be defined with reasonable objectivity (see chapters 1 and 4), so that it is possible to monitor performance. This is a crucial task of inspection and/or supervision. How it can be carried out is discussed later in this chapter, but it is worth pointing out here that monitoring is at its most difficult where medical care is concerned — a subject on which the May Committee had almost nothing to say.

Missing from this list, however, is any principle that can act as a check on the level of humanity at which the whole system operates. The desire for safety, justice, mental health and measurable standards for physical conditions would, no doubt, have been endorsed by Sir Edmund du Cane and Sir Joshua Jebb — those formidable administrators who left their stamp upon the prisons of England and Wales, and who achieved much order but less humanity. This is the crucial issue, and there is no shortage of aphorisms, statements of principle, and indeed of statements on which administration is said to be founded. But are their implications clear enough, and are they really accepted — either by the public or by prison staffs and administrators?

Despite the statements of official policy, the endorsement of the *Standard Minimum Rules for the Treatment of Prisoners* (Council of Europe, 1973), and the United Kingdom's ratification of the *European Convention on Human Rights* (Council of Europe, 1950), it is difficult to believe that these principles have really been accepted at heart in this country. It seems that many people have considerable reservations about the standard of life that prisoners should be able to enjoy. In the English context it is probably best seen as a manifestation of the old Poor Law principle of 'less eligibility'. Originally applied to the destitute, who were not necessarily criminal at all, how much more relevant is it to those who have offended against the social order. Hence the strong undercurrent of feeling that prisoners should not be entitled to live better than the sick, the aged and the poor (who have harmed no one). Hence, too, part of the resentment of prison officers who have long complained that prisoners have been treated more favourably than they themselves (Thomas, 1972). Less eligibility is unlikely to be a major issue where basic provision is concerned, but is likely to be considered where privileges are involved, particularly perhaps the gaining of long-term qualifications such as Open University degrees. It is also likely to come to the fore in times of confrontation when the system and the status of staff are threatened.

Nevertheless, the principles have a moral force, and the rhetoric should be turned into reality. If this is to be done it is necessary not only to specify standards in as much detail as possible, but to establish adequate machinery to monitor performance. Before discussing the machinery it is necessary to indicate the nature of the Rules and Standing Orders. How far such rules themselves may be challenged will be considered in the section dealing with the European Convention on Human Rights.

1   The Prison Rules and Standing Orders

The legal basis of prison administration in England and Wales is the *Prison Act, 1952*. Under this Act the Secretary of State is empowered to make Rules, in the form of Statutory Instruments, which have to be approved by Parliament. This approval may at times be a pure formality. The effect of the Rules is to give the Secretary of State a great deal of discretion as to how prisons should be run. Sir Lionel Fox, when Chairman of the Prison Commission, pointed to the administrative advantages of the system, which dates from the *Prison Act, 1898*:

> The value of this more elastic procedure, which made it possible for changes to be effected without fresh legislation on each occasion, is indicated by the fact that under it the natural development of fifty years was able to proceed without further intervention by Parliament (Fox, 1952, p.58).

The system is now governed by the principal Rules, dating from 1964 (SI 1964 no.388) and amended several times. The Rules, however, are couched in fairly general terms, and this has led to the gradual development of a set of Standing Orders, issued by Prison Department Headquarters in an attempt to secure a degree of uniformity of administration and, in particular, to indicate which matters are dealt with at each level of the service. Standing Orders are amended or supplemented as required by Circular Instructions. The Prison Rules are published documents, but Standing Orders and Circular Instructions are treated as strictly confidential.

The legal basis of these rules and regulations is somewhat confusing. The Prison Act is, of course, legislation of incontrovertible status. The Prison Rules, however, are delegated legislation, but the courts have held 'that no legal action is possible where a prisoner has suffered inconvenience or detriment as a result of a breach of the Rules' (Zellick, 1974, p.186). Standing Orders and Circulars would appear to gain their authority either as expressions of the Secretary of State's discretion under the Rules, or simply as instructions issued by an employing body to its employees (which they are bound to obey unless actually illegal). They have, therefore, a very real force for the staff of the Department.

The prisoner may have difficulty knowing exactly what his position is. Rule Seven prescribes that every prisoner should be provided with the relevant written information in his cell, and this should be read and explained to him if he cannot read or understand it. It is, however, difficult to know whether the selection of information is adequate (how can the prisoner tell?), and whether it is in fact always available — prisoners have been known to complain that it has been destroyed or is out of date (King and Morgan, 1976).

Anyone seeking to know whether a prisoner is being correctly treated under the Rules starts from a disadvantage. Action may have been taken under a Standing Order to which the prisoner and/or his advisers have no access, and the Rules may not be available to him. Even if they are, they give such a wide measure of discretion to the governor, other officials of the Department, or to the Secretary of State, that it becomes a matter of judgement as to whether the Rules have been obeyed. The problem was clearly stated by the Jellicoe Committee (1975):

> Almost all the crucial points in the various Rules depend on the exercise of judgement. For example,
>
>> 'Order and discipline shall be maintained with firmness, but with no more restriction than is required for safe custody and well ordered community life.' (Prison Rule 2(1))
>
> or 'Nothing in this Rule shall require a prisoner to be deprived unduly of the society of other persons.' (Prison Rule 3(3))
>
> or 'The food provided shall be wholesome, nutritious, well-prepared and served, reasonably varied and sufficient in quantity.' (Prison Rule 21(4))
>
> or 'An officer, in dealing with a prisoner, shall not use force unnecessarily and, when the application of force to a prisoner

is necessary, no more force than is necessary shall be used.'
(Prison Rule 44(1))

A host of other examples could be cited, but it should be obvious that this type of rule means little without knowledge of the spirit in which it is administered. To leave such matters solely to those employed in the Prison Department savours far too much of making them judges in their own cause (p.28).

An approximate indication of the extent of discretion in the Rules can be given simply by counting the proportion of those Rules relating to the regime (some relate to other matters) which include an element of discretion in at least one clause. Slightly over 75 per cent come into this category, so that it was not for nothing that such an experienced administrator as Sir Lionel Fox celebrated the value of this 'elastic procedure'.

Unquestionably conditions and facilities for prisoners have improved immensely during the present century — the contrast between the modern English prison and the conditions described in the historic accounts of Hobhouse and Brockway (1922), or Macartney (1936) is obvious enough. But an examination of the *Prison Rules* (1964) and the various amendments, suggests that their details still owe more to administrative requirements than to a coherent set of principles. At best they represent an evolving paternalism, at worst a bureaucratic retreat in the face of external pressure.

No doubt this evolution would have continued as before, subject only to national pressures, but for the last thirty years the United Kingdom systems have been placed in a context of international standards, those of the European Convention on Human Rights (Council of Europe, 1950). For the first time it has become possible not only for our rules and standards to be compared with others, but for the government to be required to alter them. The application of such international standards, although by no means rapid, has introduced a new factor making for change. The impact of this development of international law must now be considered.

2 The impact of the European Convention on Human Rights

The Convention is an international agreement to which the British Government is a signatory. Its fundamental principle is that every member State is required 'to accept the rule of law and of the enjoyment by all persons within its jurisdiction of human rights and fundamental freedoms'. A government is bound by the Convention and any of its Protocols to which it is a signatory. The United Kingdom government has ratified the Convention, but not the fourth protocol which relates to personal liberty and freedom of movement. Anyone seeking redress on a matter concerning the United Kingdom has to do so by applying to the European Commission on Human Rights under Article 25. As the Convention has not been incorporated into national law it cannot be enforced by taking action in a British court.

It is impossible in a comparatively brief section of this chapter to do more than outline the features of the Convention most relevant to imprisonment. The reader who needs a more authoritative guide should consult F.G. Jacobs, *The European Convention on Human Rights* (1975) from which much of this account is derived. The Convention is expressed in very broad terms: some rights relate directly to prisoners, while others may be infringed as a consequence of imprisonment.

Pride of place must be given to Article 3 — 'No one shall be subject to torture or inhuman or degrading treatment or punishment'. Apart from deliberate torture the Convention also applies to 'physical ill-treatment or brutality by prison officers or police officers, or inadequate conditions of detention, lack of medical treatment, and so forth' (Jacobs 1975, p.28). The most flagrant violation was that of the Greek government following the revolution of April 1967. The Commission examined allegations of the widespread use of a variety of tortures and confirmed them. Negotiations with a view to reaching a friendly settlement broke down, and in 1969 the then Greek government actually denounced the Convention and withdrew from the Council of Europe. The direct enforcement of the Convention therefore failed, but the regime was utterly discredited and in due course was superseded.

The Greek case, however, was extreme in that torture was used as a matter of policy on repeated occasions. It was classed by the Commission as an administrative practice, and therefore more serious than isolated cases of ill-treatment by individual officers acting without official connivance. In the United Kingdom, by contrast, the government could rely on Rule 44 of the English Prison Rules (and analogous ones in Scotland and Northern Ireland) which prohibits the use of force, or unnecessary force, and also the use of provocative behaviour on the part of an officer. Clearly isolated violence by individuals could not be classed as an administrative practice, but the government could still be taken to the Commission once the domestic remedies had been exhausted. Its incompetence, however, might be manifest if it had failed to provide adequate supervision when a violent situation might have been expected, such as during or after a riot.

It would also seem that treatment may be regarded as inhuman when penalties are disproportionate to the offence but, as Jacobs puts it:

> Article 3 must also be regarded as setting an absolute limit, based on respect for the human person, to what treatment is permissible, regardless of its label, and regardless of the victim's own conduct. Article 3 should be considered as imposing an absolute prohibition of certain forms of punishment such as, perhaps, flogging, which are by their very nature inhuman and degrading (p.31).

Since that comment was made Jacobs' interpretation has indeed been borne out by the Court's judgement against the United Kingdom over the birching of a juvenile as a criminal sanction in the Isle of Man: it was held to be a degrading punishment contrary to Article 3 (*Tyrer v UK* (1978) 2 EHRR.1).

Although prison labour is expressly excluded from the prohibition of forced labour, presumably excessive labour such as that developed by our Victorian ancestors in the form of the treadwheel and the crank (Webb, 1922; Ignatieff, 1978) could have been condemned as 'inhuman or degrading' had the Convention existed at that time.

The second area of crucial importance to prisoners relates to access to the courts in civil litigation. Article 6 begins:

> In the determination of his civil rights and obligations or of any criminal charge against him, everyone is entitled to a fair and public hearing within a reasonable time by an independent and impartial tribunal established by law.

This, coupled with Article 8 which protects privacy, family life and correspondence, has had some impact on the United Kingdom and has actually led to an addition to the Prison Rules. Since the *Golder* case in 1976, Rule 37 A(4) of the Rules for England and Wales has allowed prisoners to seek legal advice either if they may become a party to court proceedings or if they wish to institute such proceedings. Although the Rule is qualified by the phrase 'Subject to any directions of the Secretary of State' it unquestionably breaks new ground so far as United Kingdom prisoners are concerned, and it seems doubtful if such an innovation would have occurred but for the existence of the European Convention.

It remains to be seen whether further cases based on Articles 6 and/or 8 can be used to undermine Prison Department's entrenched belief in censorship (however benignly paternalistic). It may be that in future years neither prisoners nor the Department will be so well protected from foolish behaviour — such as prisoners pestering celebrated people with letters, or writing libellous or aggravating letters to people they know outside. It is very likely that the sum total of 'aggravation' will increase but in a free society that may be preferable to a paternalism that may encourage a false view of human relationships.

Article 9, providing for freedom of thought, conscience and religion, is also relevant to prisoners, particularly in multi-racial societies. Although comparatively easy to accept in principle, its application may lead to all manner of practical complications with regard to providing access to Ministers of religion, and to meeting at least some of the dietary requirements of certain groups. Its observance is a relatively personal matter, liable to affect only small numbers of inmates, but to them it may be of vital importance. Provision for such minority groups may well constitute one of the more sensitive tests of the humanity of any penal system. No doubt there are variations from prison to prison but, as a purely personal impression, it seems that the English system tries quite hard to cater for minority groups, particularly in respect of special diets. (Although not a religious matter it is interesting to note that one of the grievances of the Attica prisoners was inadequate provision for the significant minority of Spanish-speaking inmates).

These Articles are the ones most important for prisoners, though others have some relevance. It will be seen from this discussion that, although expressed in very broad terms, the European Convention on Human Rights can relate to very specific aspects of penal administration. It has the advantage of not being bound by the limitations of particular national legal systems. It may be, therefore, that the Convention will apply even where a national legal system does not provide a legal remedy. As Jacobs notes:

> the Commission has frequently said that the term 'civil rights and obligations' employed in Article 6(1) cannot be construed as a mere reference to the domestic law of the State concerned, but relates to an autonomous concept which must be interpreted independently of the rights existing in the domestic law, although the general principles of the domestic law of the Contracting Parties must necessarily be taken into consideration in any such interpretation (1975, p.8).

The appeal to supra-national standards may be salutary for Prison Department because, however paternalistic it may be in practice, its Rules do not always stand comparison with those of other countries. For example, Jacobs comments on the *Knechtl* case (which the United Kingdom government settled out of court) 'the restrictions imposed under the English Prison Rules appear to have had no parallel in the other Contracting States' (1975, p.91). The standard-setting role of the

170

European Convention is clearly of great importance, but the thinking of the Commission has developed one unfortunate tendency, namely it has sometimes taken the view that various restrictions may be treated as 'inherent' features of the mere fact of imprisonment, and as such justify a restriction of what would otherwise be a general right. For example:

> in the De Courcy case, the Commission stated that 'the limitation of the right of a detained person to conduct correspondence is a necessary part of his deprivation of liberty which is inherent in the punishment of imprisonment (Jacobs, 1975, p.199).

Jacobs is in no doubt that 'this doctrine is both incorrect and unnecessary'. It is incorrect because contrary to the whole scheme of the Convention which is intended to apply equally to all people and not to exclude a particular class, while it is unnecessary because the Convention 'does permit limitations in specified cases'. Fortunately the Court seems to have disapproved the Commission's notion of 'inherent feature' and, in the *Golder* case at least, has reaffirmed the right of access to the courts and to legal advice. Only time will show whether the notion of 'inherent feature' retains any credibility, but Jacobs argues strongly that

> the drafters of the Convention had continually before their minds the situation of the convicted prisoner . . . it may be deduced that they have the same rights under these Articles 2, 6 and 7 as persons at liberty . . . Article 18 . . . makes it clear that the only restrictions permitted are express restrictions, prescribed for a particular purpose; and there can be no implied restrictions for which *ex hypothesi* no purpose is prescribed (1975, p.200).

The question then arises, how effective is the procedure of enforcing the standards laid down by the Convention?

The procedure itself is comparatively simple. All prisoners have a right to petition the Commission, although applications may be photocopied by the prison authorities en route. The procedure is described in Jacobs (1975, Part IV), but its essential features are that the complainant must have exhausted any domestic remedies available to him or her, and that the Commission has to decide whether the complaint is admissible according to its rules. If the application is declared admissible the Commission examines the merits of the case and then places 'itself at the disposal of the parties with a view to securing a friendly settlement of the case'. All this may take a considerable time — 'the Commission's examination of the merits usually lasts about two years' (Jacobs, 1975, p.253). This may be due to the complexity of the investigation, the difficulty of reaching a friendly settlement or a combination of the two. Only if a friendly settlement cannot be achieved (as in the Golder case) is the case taken to the European Court of Human Rights. This is done by the Commission itself and, strictly speaking, the original applicant has no part in the proceedings. However, it has become normal practice for the applicant's lawyers to join with the Commission's delegation in arguing the case before the Court. This, in effect, allows the applicant to put his case fully and directly. The findings of the *Court* are legally binding.

The Convention has the immense value of being supra-national, and the breadth of experience of the Commission means that it will not necessarily accept a particular government's narrow interpretation of a part of the Convention. It has in fact been the only body capable of forcing the United Kingdom government to change its Rules. The achievement may not have been spectacular as the new clause (4) in Rule 37 begins with a qualification which appears to begrudge the whole concession: 'Subject to any directions of the Secretary of State, a prisoner may correspond with a solicitor'. However, that may just be a matter of administrative procedure, and it is an advance on the previous situation.

Although appealing through the Commission may have powerful effects they are not rapid, and decisions may not even benefit the original applicant if his sentence ends meanwhile. Nevertheless, as far as British prisoners are concerned, the Commission has done more than any other body to reduce the official stranglehold on communications between prisoners and lawyers. The procedure is still cumbersome as the Secretary of State may not allow contact until the internal procedures have been complied with, and these may include the prisoner having to face the charge of having made a 'false and malicious allegation'. The way is not without obstacles, though outright denial of access is no longer likely. Delays, however, may make it harder for the solicitor to establish a case — see for example a complaint reported in *The Guardian*, 16 January 1980.

At the time of writing, early in 1980, various applications relating to censorship are still pending. Whatever their ultimate outcome the general pressure may lead to some further liberalisation, and might lend some support to those Home Office experiments to reduce censorship which seem to have run into difficulties. Mr Dennis Trevelyan, Director General of the Prison Service, recently told a House of Commons Select Committee on Home Affairs that 'after discussions with the Prison Officers' Association plans had been suspended. Officers thought stopping censorship would undermine security' (*The Times*, 18 December 1979).

The importance of the Commission in the setting of standards at a general level is, therefore, great. It does not, however, deal with many of the details of administration which are troublesome at a practical level where rapid resolution of problems is needed. Its time scale is long, but in setting the practice of one nation against others it has a unique authority.

3 The Council of Europe's Standard Minimum Rules

The Standard Minimum Rules for the Treatment of Prisoners (Council of Europe, 1973) should be mentioned because, although they lack the authority of the European Convention, the May Committee took them seriously and they have been endorsed by the government. The May Committee concluded that:

> Although none of these provisions is mandatory and the requirements give the authorities a good deal of latitude, it is difficult to be confident that our more grossly overcrowded accommodation can be defended in the face of what it is evident the Rules are directed towards. Nor is this mere legalism: the Rules have moral force precisely because they are intended and do properly reflect our perception of what conditions in contemporary society it is reasonable to impose. In all these circumstances our opinion is that the Standard Minimum Rules must be interpreted in the UK as requiring at the least in the available accommodation a target of a minimum of no enforced cell-sharing, except in regular dormitories, incorporating continuous ready access to lavatories or integral sanitation as appropriate . . . these costs . . . are simply an unavoidable part of the current price of having prisons at all (May, 1979, para 6.57).

The endorsement of an international standard, and the reiteration of its moral force is surely to be welcomed, but at the same time doubts are raised. It seems likely that one of the restraints in the use of imprisonment is the knowledge that prisons are overcrowded; many people might fear that if the overcrowding were reduced sentencers might feel freer to use custody and we might, in a few years, simply end up with a larger but still overcrowded prison system. Indeed the British Association of Prison Governors made precisely this point in its evidence — 'whenever additional resources have become available, demand has immediately increased to take up the slack' (BAPG, Evidence, para 14).

In practice there may not be too much cause for anxiety. The May Committee's statement is, as it were, on the political record and Prison Department is likely to use it in support of its claims for resources. But while the government is busy trying to hold down capital expenditure limited funds might be better spent elsewhere in the criminal justice system.

Generally speaking the Standard Minimum Rules are couched in broad terms and give as much scope for administrative discretion as our own *Prison Rules*. Whereas the *European Convention on Human Rights* has been used to reduce censorship, no such achievement could be hoped for from, for example, Rule 37 of the *Standard Minimum Rules*:

> Prisoners shall be allowed to communicate with their family and all persons or representatives of organisations and to receive visits from those persons at regular intervals *subject only to such restrictions and supervision as are necessary in the interests of their treatment, and the security and good order of the institution.* (Emphasis added).

With such guiding principles what has the prison administrator to fear?

The main point that emerges from our discussion of official standards and principles is the extent to which their application involves interpretation and judgement. Few witnesses to the May Inquiry were prepared to go much beyond the kinds of statements enshrined in the European Standard Minimum Rules. The most systematic attempt was by King and Morgan (1979) through their discussion of the minimum use of security principle and what they call the normalisation of the prison (see chapters 3 and 4 of this volume). But as these writers acknowledge this is but a first step towards a more careful re-writing of the Prison Rules, and important though these efforts are, the problem of judgement and discretion in the application of the Rules will not go away. The supervision of penal administration in the interests of the community entails a similar degree of judgement and with this in mind we can now turn to consider the machinery available to ensure that standards are maintained.

The machinery of supervision

The machinery developed to ensure that standards of care are satisfactory is elaborate. This discussion is based on that established in England and Wales, though some differences in Scotland will also be referred to. It will be described only briefly, but its limitations will be discussed at the end of this chapter. There are four main constituents.

1   Internal review by Prison Department

This is undertaken periodically by inspections and more or less continually by the procedure of petitioning the Secretary of State. Inspections may be made by the Department's own inspectorate, headed by the Chief Inspector, working on a quinquennial programme, or by the Regional Directors and their staffs who visit prisons more frequently but inevitably exercise a less systematic supervision. In addition the Chief Inspector may be called upon to examine particular events, such as the riot at Hull Prison in 1976 (Fowler, 1977). In a somewhat similar way this function can also be undertaken by Regional Directors (at the time of writing the Director of the SE Region is examining the handling of a demonstration at Wormwood Scrubs on 31 August 1979). The results of such internal reviews are rarely published. The Prison Department's Annual Reports usually include about a page on the work of the inspectorate, with a list of establishments inspected, but the only report as such to have been published, no doubt in condensed form, was that relating to Hull. The Board of Visitors at Wormwood Scrubs is reported to have asked the Department to publish the report on the disturbance in that prison, but it is not yet clear whether this will be done.

Petitions are requests by inmates to the Secretary of State, and are used to raise any matter where an inmate thinks he has been unreasonably treated. Very little is known about how the system works, although part of the Home Office evidence to the May Inquiry refers to petitions against the outcome of disciplinary proceedings (Home Office, Evidence, vol.II, paper III(16), pp 243-50). At Headquarters level about a third of petitions dealt with related to adjudications. Obviously, therefore, the great bulk of petitions relate to other matters.

2   The Board of Visitors

Each Prison Department establishment has such a Board, consisting usually of about twelve members. About half of them are Justices of Peace, and half are lay members with an interest in the work. The Board of Visitors carries out a multiplicity of functions. It is supposed to supervise the quality of administration and care of the inmates, to investigate the handling of grievances, and to act as the tribunal for hearing the more serious disciplinary charges. The official account is given in the Home Office evidence to the May Committee (Home Office, Evidence, vol.II, paper III(13), pp 223-31), and an extended discussion of the functions was given by the Jellicoe Committee (1975). Boards are technically independent, but their members are appointed by the Home Secretary and the range of their functions, and a degree of uncertainty as to where their loyalties lie, mean that it is uncommon for them to take public positions on the more controversial issues of policy. They are required to submit annual reports to the Secretary of State, but these are not published so their work remains almost entirely private. Their legal powers of access, however, are extensive and quite sufficient to enable them to exercise effective supervision.

In Scotland the analogous bodies are known as Visiting Committees, and the method of appointment is similar for Borstals and young offender establishments, but with those for adults appointment is by specified local authorities. Whether this makes any practical difference is uncertain.

3   The Parliamentary Commissioner for Administration

Colloquially known as The Ombudsman, the Parliamentary Commissioner is empowered to investigate cases of alleged maladministration submitted to him by Members of Parliament. Prisoners can raise matters with MPs provided they have first attempted to use the internal machinery for the redress of grievances. Relatives might also raise matters relating to them. During the early years of his office the Commissioner only published reports on a selection of the cases he investigated, so that it is impossible to know how much of his work was generated by prisoners. However, for a number of years all reports were published and this has enabled a simple analysis of prison cases to be made. Unfortunately the present Commissioner is about to revert to selective publication, though offering facilities for *bona fide* research workers.

In 1977 a Committee of Justice drew attention to the small number of prison cases and the limited range of subjects that the Commissioner was able to deal with effectively. Since that time it seems the number of prison cases has increased slightly, so that in the period August 1976-July 1979 a total of twenty cases relating to prison conditions was reported on. Even so in only one of the three years did the number exceed five. Prison cases are always dealt with by the Commissioner's staff working in pairs, and the usual method is to examine all the relevant documents, which are always made available by the Home Office, and to interview the complainant and any staff members who can give information relevant to the complaint. Judging from recently reported cases the complaints are frequently multiple in character; two or three issues at a time are quite common, and one case reported in 1978 actually covered seven different points (Case 2/476/77).

4   The courts

Traditionally the courts have been very reluctant to exercise any form of supervision over the administration of prisons (Zellick, 1974, 1979), but they may become involved with questions of discipline in either of two ways. First, if an offence against prison discipline is also an offence against the criminal law it is possible to bring prosecutions in the criminal courts. The most recent major use of this method in England was probably following the Parkhurst Riot of 1969 when several of the men involved were tried and received further sentences. Since then it has been used less and less in England, but some prosecutions have occurred in Scotland.

Secondly, since the case of *R v Hull Board of Visitors, ex parte St Germain* it has become possible for prisoners to apply to the Divisional Court for judicial review in respect of awards made in disciplinary hearings by Boards of Visitors. However, it is not yet clear how ready the Court will be to entertain such applications. In the Court of Appeal Megaw L.J. took the view that:

> Such interference . . . would only be required, and would only be justified, if there were some failure to act fairly, having regard to all relevant circumstances, and such unfairness could reasonably be regarded as having caused a substantial, as distinct from a trivial or merely technical injustice, which was capable of remedy (1 All ER 713 (1979)).

On this basis provided Boards stick closely to the procedure laid down, it would seem unlikely that such applications will be numerous.

Suggestions for improving supervision

It will be simplest to consider in turn each of the main forms of supervision described above, and to combine in a single discussion the May Committee's conclusions, the suggestions contained in evidence and any comments that now seem relevant.

1 Inspection and internal review

In a system as secretive as prisons in the United Kingdom it is difficult to describe, leave alone evaluate, the internal mechanisms intended to ensure the maintenance of adequate standards. The May Committee found inspection 'the most difficult organisation issue' (May, 1979, para 5.50) and it was also sceptical about petitioning as a way of handling inmate grievances. As it drily observed, 'we have not, for example, been impressed by the length of time taken to answer petitions' (para 5.57); even more severe criticisms were made to the Expenditure Committee (1978, para 177), one experienced witness saying he felt the whole system completely useless. The system is mysterious; Prison Department says nothing about petitions in its annual reports, though the Ombudsman clearly regards them as a careful system of administration, albeit unnecessarily slow at times. In the absence of further information his general support is significant.

The central issue with regard to inspection is that of independence. The scepticism of penal reform organisations was only to be expected, but the governors' comments were most trenchant:

> The inspectorate in our opinion lacks resources and respect for its authority is declining. It should be quite separate from headquarters and report directly to the Director General and the Secretary of State. We believe its findings should be made public, without reference to headquarters staffs or politicians. Enquiries should be carried out independently. The inspectorate was seen to be a significant innovation, welcomed by all, but is now seen as unimportant (BAPG, Evidence, para 35).

Such views are expressed with a fervent simplicity, but coming from the people most directly subject to inspection they are a *cri-de-coeur* which should be respected. Something is wrong. It seems as if a process which should throw light on the system is being muzzled for fear of the administrative and political consequences: more administrative than political one suspects — strong politicians can always ride such things, but administrators are apt to fear the light, for their responsibility is unmistakable. This is not a new phenomenon. It was exposed with the utmost clarity by Richard Crossman (1977). For several weeks in March 1969 he and his Departmental Ministers fought for the publication of the full report on the Ely Hospital scandal (NHS, 1969), and the establishment of an independent inspectorate reporting directly to the Minister (Crossman, 1977, pp 418-36 *passim*). The result was the creation of the Hospital Advisory Service which did much to improve the quality of care in long stay hospitals. The most significant features of the story were that the Department had known about the problem for several years but had simply filed the reports, and that, when forced to face the issue, the officials in fact were constructive and came up with a positive plan.

The Home Office has perhaps not quite got to that stage. It has already been faced with a recommendation from the House of Commons Expenditure Committee (1978) which reported:

> We raised the question of an independent inspectorate of prisons with the Home Office. We accept their assurances that the present system of internal inspection is extremely useful to the Prisons Board, but *we recommend the establishment of a fully indepen-*

dent inspectorate, reporting directly to the Home Secretary, and carrying out some of the duties given in other countries to an ombudsman. Such an office did exist before the nationalisation of the prisons in 1877 and until then played a very significant part in shaping the policy and regulating the administration of our prisons. There is work, we are convinced, for a conspicuously independent official of this kind, whose appointment would do much to allay some of the fears we have heard expressed about the inadequacy of the Prison Department inspection and grievance machinery (para 176).

Nevertheless, in the following year the Home Office submitted evidence to the May Committee which, although it discussed the question at length on a rather constitutional level, was unmistakably negative in tone (Home Office, Evidence, vol.II, paper III(15) paras 237-42). The May Committee, however, while finding the subject difficult, and while agreeing that internal inspection was a necessary feature of administration, ended in a position quite close to that of the Expenditure Committee. It thought that internal inspection should be a responsibility of Regional Directors, but that there should also be:

> within the Home Office an independent department to be called the 'Prisons Inspectorate' headed either by someone independent of the civil service entirely or by a senior ex-governor as the Home Secretary may decide (May, 1979, para 5.62).

This body would essentially operate *ad hoc*, making special enquiries, examining particular features of the system etc as desired by the Home Secretary. It would have a trouble-shooting role, and its reports would be published, subject to security considerations (para 5.62).

Although this Inspectorate would not deal with inmate or staff grievances in the normal course of events, it would have a general impact and supersede those private enquiries which are at present favoured by Prison Department. It is strange that the Department fails to realise that inspections of situations that have gone wrong will not be viewed with confidence when the inspector is intimately concerned with the administration that is being inspected. This applies both at the level of the Chief Inspector, who is a member of the Prisons Board, and at Regional level where Directors are even more directly responsible for establishments in their areas. Thus the Regional Director of the South East Region is investigating the handling of the disturbance at Wormwood Scrubs in August 1979 despite the fact that his immediate deputy has already publicly commended the staff who took part in the operation (*New Statesman*, 23 November 1979). Coupled with the evasive series of statements on the seriousness of the injuries incurred during the incident, the institution of this sort of enquiry is likely to have exactly the opposite effect in terms of public confidence from that which the Department presumably wishes to create. This is an area where the May Committee was surely right.

2   The Board of Visitors

The May Committee spent a mere five pages of its Report on Boards of Visitors and devoted much of its discussion to the question of whether Boards should undertake adjudications. They were slightly apologetic about this:

> We are conscious that concentrating on this one issue is in danger of appearing to put our views on Boards out of balance. In fact we consider their other functions of equal significance and susceptible of greater developments (May, 1979, para 5.104).

In effect it followed the Home Office reaction to the report of the Jellicoe Committee in rejecting the main proposal about adjudications, but broadly supporting many of the others (Martin, 1980). In doing so it disregarded the evidence of most of the penal reform organisations. The POA and the British Association of Prison Governors supported the present system, but dismissed the matter in a sentence or so; clearly neither regarded Boards as of importance except as disciplinary bodies.

The only full survey of Boards and their functions is that made by the Jellicoe Committee in 1975. Developments since then have been described and discussed by Martin (1980) and it may be convenient to summarise them here.

Boards have faced a testing five years. There have been riots at Hull and Gartree, a demonstration at which over fifty prisoners were injured at Wormwood Scrubs, and a ruling by the Court of Appeal that the disciplinary proceedings of Boards are subject to review by the High Court.

Although the Jellicoe recommendations were initially attacked, most of the operational ones were later endorsed by the Home Office, and the Report is said to be discussed at training courses for Board members. All Boards were provided with copies and asked to discuss them, and there seems to be an impression that at a local level it had some effect on working methods.

Three Boards have undergone the severe test of having to cope with major disturbances. The Hull Board faced a riot for the first time and, in spite of some conscientious efforts, did not emerge with much credit. It tried, but failed, to prevent the ill-treatment of inmates after the riot, and it made history by having some of its adjudications over-turned on appeal. It appears to have been old-fashioned in its style, with dominant chairman and acquiescent members, and to have been unaware of, or uninfluenced by, the issues and recommendations dis-cussed by Jellicoe. Cynical prisoners would, no doubt, have said this was exactly what they would have expected from a Board of Visitors.

The Gartree Board, having long-prepared plans for the careful super-vision of their establishment, and enjoying a positive leadership which encouraged all the members to play their part, rose to the occasion. They attended during the riot, in accordance with their principles of operation and, it should be said, at the request of the Governor and the local branch of the Prison Officers' Association; members accom-panied staff into each wing after the surrender, and maintained a presence in the prison for three days thereafter. Subsequently they also assisted in the checking and despatching of property belonging to prisoners transferred elsewhere. As a result prisoners and staff were protected, and the local POA produced an admirably fair account of what had taken place, and acknowledged the help given by the Board.

Under the present system the Board, of course, had to adjudicate on the rioters. Great care was taken, particularly over the calling of witnesses, if desired by inmates, and from the absence of appeals it would seem that the errors of the Hull adjudications were avoided.

The Gartree Board, therefore, showed that, at its best, a Board of Visitors can play a vital part in handling the most difficult situations that face a prison administration. It is only to be hoped that the lessons of Gartree have been learned as well as those of Hull.

The Wormwood Scrubs incident is still the subject of investigation at the time of writing and there is insufficient evidence to know how effectively the Board behaved. It has been criticised by PROP (1979), but its own account has yet to be heard. The crucial questions are whether the Board had a contingency plan, how it was implemented, whether Board members were present when the MUFTI Squads went into action, how soon members visited the prison, whether the Board reported independently to the Secretary of State and, ultimately, whether the adjudications after the event survive the scrutiny of the Home Office, the High Court and, conceivably, the Parliamentary Commissioner and the European Commission on Human Rights.

It would be a mistake, however, to rest the case for Boards of Visitors on their role when major incidents occur. It is argued fully in the Jellicoe report that their overall supervisory role in the public interest is vital (Jellicoe, 1975, chapter 3), and that this depends on paying scrupulous and impartial attention to the welfare of inmates and staff. This has been endorsed by the Expenditure Committee (1978) and the May Report (1979, para 5.104). In any institution there are bound to be conflicts and unsatisfied needs, and this is particularly likely in a closed society where minutiae assume exaggerated importance. Members of groups who spend most of their working and social lives talking to each other can easily lose their sense of proportion and the members of Boards of Visitors, by being around frequently and able to listen carefully and impartially to all concerned, can perform an invaluable balancing function. Far more than the Parliamentary Commissioner are they able to question discretionary decisions, not on grounds of their consistency with Standing Orders, but whether they are wise in that particular human setting.

As Jellicoe emphasised, this interpretation requires a new spirit of semi-professional, but voluntary effort, rather than new powers or rules. If it is generated and sustained, Boards of Visitors will survive; if not, they do not deserve to.

3   The Parliamentary Commissioner for Administration

It has already been mentioned that the British version of the Ombudsman appears to do far less prison work than his counterparts in other countries; some, indeed, have appointed Ombudsmen specifically for correctional systems. Nevertheless, the British Ombudsman does deal with complaints raised by prisoners, and it is important to examine what he is able to achieve in the British context. The following analysis is based on the twenty cases reported in the Commissioner's Reports covering the period August 1976 to July 1979.

Complaints to the Ombudsman can only be submitted by a Member of Parliament, and a prisoner can only write to an MP after he has raised the matter with the Board of Visitors and failed to receive satisfaction from their handling of it. In comparison, therefore, with many other systems complaints received by the Ombudsman have survived a filtering system at both local and national levels. This is not to say they are more, or less, justified as a result, but it does indicate that the complainant is unusually persistent. It is also likely that the matter, or matters, complained of will be complex, and one prisoner may raise a number of issues at the same time — for example the first five cases of the twenty involved at least sixteen items (there is a certain ambiguity because of a tendency to overlap). In most cases there may well have been quite a considerable lapse of time since the incident complained of actually occurred.

The twenty complainants raised a wide range of topics. The difficulty of distinguishing between the nuances of some of the multiple applications makes counting and classification rather rough but, on a conservative basis, the twenty complaints covered twenty-one topics with a total of forty-seven mentions. The most common subject of complaint was access to, or the quality of, medical or dental treatment, (ten mentions). Next came the handling of petitions, particularly the delays involved (six). Problems of gaining access to a solicitor, and transfers between prisons were both investigated on four occasions. There were three complaints of suppression, etc of correspondence. Apart from these a wide range of other topics were raised at least once — treatment of remand prisoners, delays in getting results of parole applications, alleged destruction of property by staff, the use of Rule 43, and the conditions of prisoners held under it, racial discrimination, access to educational courses and so on. Notably, only one of the forty-seven investigations related to an alleged assault. For what it is worth the list and frequencies of mention appear to have been broadly similar to the subjects raised in the form of applications to the Board of Visitors at Albany during the mid 1970s. Obviously they would all have been raised with a Board before getting to the Ombudsman, but it suggests that cases reaching him were reasonably representative of the considerably larger numbers being considered by Boards.

The results of these complaints, apart from the prestige value of having achieved an investigation by the Ombudsman, cannot have been very satisfying to the prisoners concerned. The great majority of complaints were not upheld or, if upheld in part, the results of Home Office action were not regarded as having been harmful. For example a prisoner who complained of a conspiracy to deny him justice got a rather mixed set of results. There was a strong condemnation of the failure to handle petitions with reasonable speed:

I regard the Home Office's failure to reply to his petition of 10 August 1973 before 19 September 1974 as inexcusable . . . Home Office failures in this respect did nothing to enhance the prospects of his appeal being successful, or to convince him of their impartiality

but the general conclusion was:

. . . I have criticised these administrative failures, but I am satisfied they are no more than that. My investigation of the complaints has given me no reason whatever to believe that the Home Office's actions were calculated to deny him justice (Case C 622/V).

Or in another case:

. . . while I regard the Home Office's present policy governing the subsequent posting of a stopped letter as unduly restrictive, I do not consider the complainant suffered any injustice as a result (Case C 167/L).

In another case a prisoner was charged with assaulting an officer and various punishments were imposed by the Board of Visitors. Friends of the prisoner complained to an MP who took the matter up with the Home Office. In turn it found the result of the adjudication was unsatisfactory and the Parliamentary Under-Secretary of State decided to remit the punishment. This took time and the prisoner served fourteen days in cellular confinement, but did not have to forfeit fifty-six days remission. The Parliamentary Commissioner criticised the Home Office for the failure of its internal review of adjudications:

> I criticise them for their failure to recognise and act on these procedural defects more promptly. But the time-scale was such that . . . I therefore cannot say that the Home Office's failure caused them to suffer injustice (Case C 660/V).

One cannot fail to be impressed by the thoroughness of the Ombudsman's enquiries. They deal with issues similar in kind to those brought to Boards of Visitors, but their thoroughness and access to central government, not to mention administrative experience, produce results well beyond the scope of non-professional bodies. On the other hand they suffer from serious limitations. The greatest of these is that the Ombudsman is not in a position to question the Prison Rules, or the Standing Orders issued by Prison Department. From his point of view they are parliamentary, or ministerially approved, acts where the discretion lies with the Minister. He may, indeed, hint that the wisdom of some policy decisions is doubtful, but no more than that, for example:

> At one time a prisoner who was an appellant had a statutory right under the Prison Rules to correspond with his legal advisers and other persons in connection with his appeal. But from 1 January 1973, the right to correspond with persons other than his legal adviser was removed by the Prison (Amendment) Rules 1972 (SI 1972, no.1860). It is not for me to question measures Parliament has approved; that must be for Parliament itself (Case C 662/V, reported in 1976-77, HC 46, p.188).

When Prison Department Standing Orders are closely guarded secrets it is disconcerting to find that the Parliamentary Commissioner's terms of reference oblige him to accept their validity unless they appear to conflict with the Prison Rules.

The *Knechtl* case is particularly instructive on this point. Knechtl wanted to seek 'legal advice or legal aid in order to commence legal proceedings to claim damages for negligence' against the prison medical service. He petitioned four times but was turned down. The case was investigated by the Ombudsman who found that the Home Office had followed the rule without maladministration and therefore he could not question the Department's decision. He suggested to the Home Office that they might review the operation of Rule 34 (8) but, having done so, they reaffirmed their belief in its correctness, and indeed its necessity. In due course the Permanent Under-Secretary of State defended the decision when the Select Committee on the Parliamentary Commissioner for Administration had urged reconsideration. He did so primarily on the grounds that prisoners were litigious people, that it was difficult to run a good prison medical service as it was, and in the interest of discipline medical officers and consultants had to be protected from the risk of frequent legal proceedings. The Department therefore always required prisoners to make out some sort of case before allowing access to legal advice that might result in proceedings (1970-1971, HC 513, p.267).

Knechtl's case was duly submitted to the European Commission on Human Rights and declared admissible. The Home Office then settled the case, making an *ex gratia* payment to Knechtl. It then went on to modify its practice and issued what has been described as a White Paper on *Legal Advice to Prisoners*. However, this was published in a particularly obscure form in which the subject matter is not even mentioned in the title, viz. *Observations by the Government on the Second Report from the Select Committee on the Parliamentary Commissioner for Administration, Session 1970-71* (Session 1971-72, Cmnd 4846). Thus are matters of principle conceded by stealth.

The other major limitation on the capacity of the Ombudsman to handle prison cases derives from the fact that he only receives applications at the end of a fairly lengthy procedure, so that the matter may be somewhat stale by the time his officers arrive on the scene. They must, therefore, rely fairly heavily on records. If an alleged act has not been recorded, and any supposed witnesses still available do not recall or confirm it, then nothing much can be done. Hence the Ombudsman may be forced to conclude on a rather unsatisfactory note, for example, on Case 2/689/78 there was no written record of a prisoner's complaint that, although he had a heart condition, he had been required to scrub floors. Faced with this conflict of evidence the Ombudsman was unable 'to uphold the generality of the complaint made on Mr K's behalf'.

Conflicts of evidence were sometimes resolved by careful investigation, such as the complaint that staff had damaged a prisoner's property after a demonstration when prisoners had barricaded themselves in a dormitory. Evidence was taken from three members of the

Board of Visitors, and from staff, which confirmed that the inmates had destroyed everything except metal bedsteads before the barricade was removed; the complaint was not upheld (Case C 720/K).

More than once the Commissioner had commented that complaints about general conditions are outside his remit, but give cause for concern. For example, in a report about Durham prison (Case C 249/77), he rejected the complaint but said 'the facts which I set out in this report illustrate and justify the concern which has been expressed about conditions in some local prisons'. Similarly a complainant from Liverpool prison received apologies from the Home Office about the delay in fixing an appointment with an optician and a mix-up over a transfer, but was told that the Ombudsman could offer no remedy for a complaint about the general condition in that prison (Case 2/388/77).

From this brief survey we can conclude that, despite the limitations mentioned, the Ombudsman has real achievements to his credit where the problems were of administrative correctness. Details like the calculation of the date of eligibility for parole, detecting inefficiency in handling petitions, are effectively examined in ways which no other existing body could do equally well. Perhaps the outstanding result of recent years was securing compensation on an *ex gratia* basis for occupants of B Wing at Hull, and seven other prisoners, whose property was damaged and lost when 'the staff who were then ordered to strip the vacated cells of their contents carried out this task with an excess of zeal' (Case 2/848/77, para 14).

The Ombudsman can claim to have inspired some changes in the system. But although he has been critical of the Home Office he has also shown understanding of their problems, and has rejected the majority of complaints. Even the fact that prison cases are so rare has value in that the Commissioner's comments are considered at a very high level in the Department, with the Permanent Under-Secretary of State being personally involved. How far prisoners are satisfied is difficult to tell, but to be investigated by the Ombudsman itself is likely to be a source of prestige, while actually to receive an apology from Prison Department must surely be gratifying to any inmate.

4   The courts

The adjudication in private of offences against prison discipline is obviously unattractive in terms of civil liberties. The integrity of the proceedings which, in a criminal court, are open to public view and reporting, has to be taken for granted. The proceedings are inquisitorial and it has to be assumed that the evidence was thoroughly examined, and that the defendant's case was adequately put. The decision, moreover, does not require the strict standards of proof needed in a criminal court to establish guilt beyond reasonable doubt. As the Home Office *Procedure for the Conduct of an Adjudication by a Board of Visitors* (1977) puts it, the 'adjudicating body must establish the facts, evaluate the evidence and then apportion responsibility for an incident in a way which will be seen as just and fair by both sides of the prison community' (p.2).

The ideal of trying at least the major offences against discipline in the criminal courts appealed to several witnesses to the May Inquiry — King and Morgan, the NCCL, NACRO and the Howard League. Some judges were said by the Committee itself to favour 'more cases being put to the ordinary criminal courts where an offence against discipline is also an offence under the criminal law' (May, 1979, para 5.97), and this is probably consistent with the practice in Scotland. The evidence submitted by the Crown Office (kindly made available by the Crown Agent) shows that where assaults on prison officers were concerned, over the period 1975-1978 inclusive almost two thirds of such offences were investigated by the police, and of these almost three quarters resulted in criminal prosecution. A prosecution policy, however, has its disadvantages: there may be delays, there is a great risk of collusion between witnesses and, most important, there may be prejudice against the accused on account of the nature of the offence — 'the credibility attached to the evidence presented by the defence is significantly handicapped before the trial begins once the jury have read the circumstances of the offence narrated in the indictment before them' (Crown Office, Evidence, Part III, p.14).

The May Committee did not really distinguish this point fully in its discussion of whether the adjudication of serious offences should continue to be done by Boards of Visitors. On the whole it took the view, supported by those judges consulted informally, that Boards, if subject to review by the Divisional Court, were quite adequate as adjudicating bodies. An internal hearing has, of course, great advantages in terms of speed and logistics and, from the administration's angle, a desirable absence of publicity. Even if the accused are all convicted the efforts of the defence, in open court, are almost bound to question and/or damage the reputations of the authorities and staff. The lack of a public trial will deprive the accused of the interruption to their sentence provided by weeks in court, and the attendant dramatisation of themselves and their contribution to prison folk lore; on the other hand they may actually get shorter sentences than would have been imposed by a court — even the loss of remission imposed after Hull looks fairly modest compared with some of the sentences after the

Dartmoor mutiny and the Parkhurst riot. Admittedly some Crown Courts have been known to impose concurrent sentences in prison cases, but presumably such exercises in futility would not be repeated if trials became more common.

The disadvantages of internal hearings as now conducted are serious, particularly with the major types of offence known, in the language of the Prison Rules, as 'Graver' and 'Especially Grave Offences'. Most important are the absence of external scrutiny (except in the case of an appeal) and, above all, the lack of defence counsel. Now that the stage has been reached when almost all defendants in the Crown Courts are legally aided it is surely anomalous that serious disciplinary charges, which may have drastic effects on how long offenders actually spend in custody, can be tried with no more cross-examination than can be managed by the accused in person and/or by the Board members who probably want to remain neutral. The role of inquisitorial chairman is not easy (continental judges after all are trained in it), and with the best will in the world a Board chairman is unlikely to test prosecution evidence as carefully as would be done by a defence advocate.

These considerations have been powerfully reinforced by the recommendations of the Royal Commission on Legal Services (1979) which reported shortly before the May Committee. Its report not only advocated the extension of duty solicitor schemes to prisons, but categorically stated that legal representation should be the norm where loss of remission is concerned:

> We regard a loss of remission as equivalent to an extended loss of liberty. In general, we consider that no one should face the risk of loss of liberty without the opportunity of legal advice and representation, though accepting that strict application of this principle in prison should not impede disciplinary arrangements in relatively minor cases. Accordingly we think that there are good reasons against imposing a penalty involving loss of remission on any prisoner unless:
>
> (a) he has been given the opportunity of being legally represented; or
>
> (b) the period of loss of remission awarded is seven days or less; or
>
> (c) in circumstances such as those prevailing in Northern Ireland, the Secretary of State on security grounds prescribes alternative arrangements
>
> (Royal Commission on Legal Services, 1979, vol.1, p.99)

The importance of this statement of principle cannot be overestimated. For the first time the administration of justice in prisons has been considered using the standards applied to the criminal justice system as a whole; the contrast is obvious. There can, too, be little doubt that the Royal Commission is more in tune with the spirit of the European Convention on Human Rights. Up to now the administration of justice in prisons has evolved, having started from something very primitive indeed. The point has now been reached where a qualitative change is needed.

The real trouble is that the principal Prison Rules (those of 1964) derive from a period when disturbances were comparatively rare, and in fact included the possibilities of corporal and dietary punishment. Their historical origins lay in a more brutal age when punishments which are now designated as 'inhuman and degrading' were taken for granted as features of prison discipline — see for example Macartney (1936), or Hobhouse and Brockway (1922). It was perhaps something of an historical accident that the power to impose corporal punishment was retained effectively at magistrate level within the prison system, whereas in the adult courts it was reserved to the high court. It remains anomalous that a body such as the existing Board of Visitors, which is analogous to a bench of magistrates, can wield, in private, powers effectively greater than those of a magistrates' court sitting in public with the guidance of a legally qualified clerk. *Pace* the May Committee and the Court of Appeal a Board *can* for especially grave offences order forfeiture of remission in excess of 180 days, limited only by the length of the original sentence (Rule 51(3) as amended by the Prison (Amendment) Rules 1974, SI 1976/713). Even for the 'graver' offences 180 day periods may be forfeited consecutively, dependent on the number of charges.

Since the passing of the principal Rules in 1964 adaptation has been by way of administrative improvisation, and the time has surely come when it would be better to reconstruct the system in ways which are constitutionally more appropriate and also more realistic about grave offences.

The reconstruction should take a range of questions into account. The first group of these should consider what bodies are appropriate to adjudicate offences of various degrees of seriousness and what penalties they should be empowered to impose. The second group should be based on the question of ensuring that defence and prosecution cases are adequately put. The third problem is that of secrecy.

An appropriate model for this process of re-thinking might be the Streatfeild Committee on the Business of the Criminal Courts (Home Office and Lord Chancellor's Office, 1961). The Committee might be chaired by a senior lawyer and would include representatives of the

Lord Chancellor's Office, Prison Department (including governors and discipline staff) and a few independent members with relevant expertise. In the process it would contribute to a thorough-going revision of the Prison Rules, so that a new set of Principal Rules could replace those introduced nearly twenty years ago.

If such a committee were to act boldly it might consider some of the following suggestions:

i.   Design a procedure for the hearing of *very serious* disciplinary offences within prisons but with the safeguards of

   (a) Adjudication by lawyers of standing. This could be done *either*: by adopting recommendation 33 of the Jellicoe Committee (which envisaged a panel of such adjudicators, to be appointed by the Lord Chancellor with the administration co-ordinated by Governors and Circuit Administrators); *or* by legislation which would enable the Crown Court to sit in prisons.

   (b) Adoption of a fully accusatorial system with representation of prosecution and defence.

   (c) Press reporting to be allowed, subject perhaps to restrictions on reporting of matters relating to security.

This procedure would have to be reserved for the most serious offences, i.e. those relating to mutiny, escapes and assaults involving 'gross personal violence'. There seems, incidentally, no reason why gross personal violence to persons other than officers should be treated more leniently than the same behaviour towards officers. On the other hand it would be necessary to subdivide the offence of assaulting an officer to allow the more technical of such offences to be dealt with in a less elaborate manner.

ii.   There should be an intermediate level of adjudication which would cover the remaining offences currently dealt with by Boards of Visitors, but with more precise limitations on the power of sentencing, such as a maximum forfeiture of remission of 180 days on any one occasion. Anything appearing to merit more than this should be dealt with by the more formal procedure.

At this level adjudication should be undertaken by an independent tribunal as recommended by the Jellicoe Committee. Alternatively the legislation empowering the Crown Court to sit in prison might include a provision allowing the local magistrates' court to do so as well. Very much as a last resort the Board of Visitors' system might be retained, its powers having been reduced, preferably in a form which made it clear that a separate panel of the Board did adjudications while the remaining members did not. It would be difficult to make a division of function like this look convincing to prisoners, but in the last resort it would be better than nothing. The May Committee's approval of Boards of Visitors as adjudicating bodies stemmed from a concentration on the quality of adjudication rather than on the supervisory work of Boards (May, 1979, para 5.103). The Jellicoe Committee saw supervision as the pre-eminent function, which was unavoidably weakened by the crucial role of Boards in the disciplinary machinery; the May Committee disagreed, but gave no clear reason for doing so.

It seems doubtful whether legal representation as such would be necessary, bearing in mind the restrictions on sentencing, but it would be important for defendants to receive advice on presenting their defence. Officers laying complaints can always obtain advice from their seniors, so it would ensure a proper balance if prisoners could be advised as well. This was recommended in a persuasive note of dissent to the *Report of the Working Party on Adjudication Procedure in Prison* (Home Office, 1975). It was argued that the Board should appoint one of its number to be a 'prisoner's friend' to advise the prisoner on his case, and to question witnesses on his behalf. The author of the note, himself Chairman of a Board of Visitors, maintained that:

> if Board members act variously as adjudicators and prisoner's friends, this will provide a continual reminder of this dual role and can only strengthen that unique and most valuable institution, the Board of Visitors (p.43).

Without necessarily accepting the whole of this argument the proposal certainly seemed worth trying, and for a while it appeared that this might happen. *The Report of the Prison Department for 1977* (Home Office, 1978b) indicated that the proposal had been followed up:

> The necessary consultations are nearing completion and, although the representative staff associations do not feel able to take part at the moment, it is hoped to begin an experiment later in the year to examine the provision of assistance, by members of Boards of Visitors, with preparation of an inmate's case (para 68).

Unfortunately this hope was not borne out, and the Report for the following year (Home Office, 1979a) explained:

> It did not prove possible, as had been hoped, to make a start in 1978 with the experiment to test the provision of assis-

tance by members of Boards of Visitors to prisoners facing adjudications by Boards. At the end of the year consultations were continuing with the Boards and staff of the prisons which it is proposed to involve in the experiment (para 77).

It remains to be seen what lay behind this failure; possibly lack of will on the part of the authorities, possibly a reluctance by staffs to accept that prisoners have a right to natural justice; whatever the reason both should reflect that this is not such a revolutionary proposal as all that. In the armed forces, also concerned with discipline, the relevant Acts all prescribe that a defending officer or counsel shall be appointed at all courts martial unless the accused refuses in writing (see for example *Rules of Procedure* (Army) 1956, SI 1956/162). A Rule of this kind has obtained for at least the last 25 years, and probably longer. A discussion of the problems of lay defenders may be found in the *Report of the Army and Air Force Courts Martial Committee, 1946* (War Office, 1949, para 91). The procedure is scrupulous in protecting the rights of the accused.

On the question of publicity it would seem unnecessary to allow press coverage of adjudications on comparatively minor matters where the penalties involved were limited (as with minor cases in magistrates' courts, they might not be regarded as very newsworthy). The interests of the defendant and of justice should be adequately covered by the system of prisoners' friends and review by petition and, ultimately, the Divisional Court. Three other minor safeguards should be possible: first, if (as Jellicoe recommended) Boards of Visitors published a general report on their stewardship each year they could and should discuss the state of discipline in their prison; second, in the event of a petition the prisoner's friend should be consulted about the matter; third, a neutral 'observer' might attend and could be consulted in the event of a petition — an American precedent for this sort of role is the presence of a member of a correctional ombudsman's staff at disciplinary hearings. A proposal on these lines could be quite cheap and simple, using discreet volunteers, as happens with independent members of local review committees.

iii. There would seem to be little case for change at the level of offences dealt with by governors, given that their powers are limited and that some redress may be available by way of petition. It would be possible to conceive a structure which allowed appeals from the governor to the Board of Visitors as discussed in the Home Office Evidence (1979, vol.II, paper III(16) para 19). But the most likely consequence would be to transfer much of the system of adjudication to Boards which would impose an intolerable burden on unpaid part-time volunteers, and would be totally contrary to the Jellicoe principle of separating Boards from the enforcement of discipline. A minor improvement would be to give priority to petitions relating to such adjudications so that they were dealt with before the matter became stale and nothing could be done about it.

None of these suggestions precludes the prosecution of disciplinary offences in the criminal courts if they are also offences under the criminal law. However, despite the Home Office claim (May, 1979, para 5.100) that the most serious offences are referred to the police it seems that this has not been the practice with major incidents such as those at Hull and Gartree, and the IRA demonstration at Albany. It is precisely because of the difficulties of sending such cases to outside courts that new procedures have to be devised.

Finally it should be recognised that the notion of perfect justice in trying offences in prisons is chimerical. For the reasons adduced by the Crown Office, the May Committee, the Prison Department, the author of this chapter (Martin 1974) and, no doubt, many others, such adjudications are bound to rely more on the judgement of the adjudicators than is normal in a court where witnesses are usually much less involved with each other and with the accused. Obviously adjudicating procedures should satisfy the standards of natural justice and, particularly where much is at stake, justice should be seen to be done; nevertheless the Jellicoe Committee was surely right to emphasise prevention. Some disciplinary offences, such as those arising from feuds between inmates, possession of prohibited materials and so on, are unavoidable; but fair, consistent and careful administration can do much to minimise the incidence of offences. Repressive regimes are likely to be marked by numerous offences against discipline, and the right principle is enshrined in Rule 2(i) of the Prison Rules, 1964 — 'Order and discipline shall be maintained with firmness, but with no more restriction than is required for safe custody and well ordered community life'. It is the achievement of this ideal that is at the heart of the matter. Important though adjudications are, they are essentially subsidiary to the well-being of the prison community as a whole. The May Committee showed some appreciation of this, but in the end their somewhat judicial emphasis was probably mistaken.

Additional safeguards

It would be unrealistic to leave the question of safeguards without considering two other major influences. Neither is a matter of formal machinery, but they are crucial to the whole edifice of safeguards. They are staff morale, and publicity.

1   Staff morale

Staff morale is vital to the quality of care. Staffing matters are mainly dealt with elsewhere in this book; here it is sufficient to draw attention to the repercussions of staff morale on the maintenance of discipline and the handling of inmates. Perhaps the greatest tragedy of the English prison system is that, so soon after its reconstruction in 1877, it developed in such a way as to allow the emergence of the generally aggrieved attitude of the discipline staff towards the Home Office that is so fully documented by Thomas (1972). The troubles which led to the setting up of the May Committee merely represented the latest expression of a long resentment at what officers regard as their low status and pay. Such feelings are no doubt exacerbated by the inward looking nature of the staff community of most prisons, rendered almost inevitable by the phenomenally long hours of work and the tendency to live in closed estates or groups of houses occupied only by prison staff. It is a perfect setting for the nourishment of grievances and, to its credit, the Prison Officers' Association has now recognised the undesirability of the traditional arrangements:

> If the Service is to develop as a reflection of society's attitude towards prisoners it is necessary that prison officers, as society's representatives, should be integrated within the community they serve. This also has the added benefit of projecting a favourable service image by demonstrating to the public at large that prison officers are ordinary working people (POA, Evidence, p.31, para 22).

With such a background it is not surprising that officers are not always enthusiastic about inmate rights. Indeed given the difficulties of achieving satisfaction in the job, the failure so far of efforts to enhance the role of the discipline officer, and the ever-present threat of challenges to personal or professional authority, it would require quite a degree of maturity to face increasing demands for 'rights' with equanimity.

If this general feeling of being under threat is intensified by riots or demonstrations then strong reactions are very probable. Not only may they be intense but, it seems, they can be very long lasting. The aftermath of the 1972 disturbances at Albany provides an excellent example. King and Elliott (1978, p.301) have shown how Albany jumped at once to the head of the league for numbers of disciplinary offences having previously 'been in no way exceptional in this respect'. The Annual Reports of the Prison Department show that this position has been retained until the present day (in 1978 one very small prison had a higher figure but this may have been due to chance). In 1978, six years after the troubles, the rate of offences at Albany was two and a half times the average for training prisons, and well above any other dispersal prison. As King and Elliott showed, the staff reaction to indiscipline was to turn to a legalistic style of order maintenance and to report numerous minor offences which, in a more liberal era, might have been overlooked.

The point, therefore, is very simple. A staff that feel threatened will be more legalistic and more restrictive; if conflict is violent, then the reaction may be also. Insofar as the maintenance of inmates' rights depends on staff behaviour, as opposed to the practices of the administration, then it is essential that some understanding of staff fears should be shown, even if their position cannot be accepted by the administration. Perhaps the most difficult task facing the prison administration is to strike the correct sympathetic, but firm, attitude. It is, after all, the duty of the administration to obey the law of the land and to respect the United Kingdom's obligations under the European Convention on Human Rights rather than bow to the decisions of a local branch of the Prison Officers' Association. Fortunately, the National Executive of the POA has, with some caution, reserved itself 'the right . . . to deplore, fail to condone or refuse recognition of any action which, for example, (i) infringes the law' (POA, Evidence, p.175, para 1). However, it also maintains that 'Prison Officers have no legal obligation to guarantee the statutory entitlements of inmates in circumstances where these cannot be provided due . . . to industrial action (p.177, para 7).

Exactly how these matters will be resolved remains to be seen. It is to be hoped that clear and strong leadership, coupled with better industrial relations, will ensure that the rule of the law is upheld within the prison system.

2   Publicity

There can be little doubt that increased publicity has revolutionised public concern for the prison system. Despite the well documented attacks on the secrecy of the system made by Cohen and Taylor (1978) the situation is markedly different from that of, say, 1948. The Prison

Department would undoubtedly claim that it has become much more open than in the past, but this claim, while true in some respects, is less so in others. The interiors of prisons have become familiar sights on the TV screen, and journalists are writing more and better informed reports than in the past. At least one academic criminologist was even allowed to see the notorious Wakefield Control Unit, and described it at a Frank Dawtry Memorial Seminar (Hood, 1976). Possibly others could have done so too if they had asked. Members of Boards of Visitors have been encouraged to improve relationships between their establishments and the community, and have been told the Official Secrets Act does not apply to them (though they must not talk about security matters or individual inmates). Criminology and other students visit prisons and Borstals and have discussion groups with inmates. None of these would have been conceivable in 1948.

Nevertheless, the openness is distinctly qualified. Given any sort of trouble the Prison Department will resume its old defensive posture. The aftermath of the Hull riot was certainly not treated in a candid manner and the police even complained of the extent to which their investigations had been impeded. Stories differ as to how the matter was eventually brought to light, but the substantial lapse of time between the incident and its reporting to the police does not suggest that a concern for law was paramount.

Things were better done at Gartree (Martin, 1980), but the handling of the Wormwood Scrubs incident in August, 1979, was as publicly inept as it is possible to imagine. The story leaked out through prisoners being discharged, through relatives and through two prison visitors — who were promptly struck off for breach of confidence. No doubt they were in breach of undertakings given when they were accepted as prison visitors but, faced with conflicting moral obligations, who is to say where the balance of morality lay? The successive admission of larger and larger numbers of injuries — starting from a total denial — suggests at the very least a high level of administrative confusion, at worst a deliberate attempt to mislead the public.

The proclaimed openness on the part of Prison Department is also suspect in a more subtle way. It is one thing to have TV crews in a prison; they can film physical conditions, but their visit will inevitably be pre-arranged and far from spontaneous. It is another matter when the visitors are better informed and likely to stay longer; the amount of research done in English prisons must be described as limited, and only a part of that relates directly to conditions. Not all that is done is published. Even the Home Office Research Unit, which has now published some 55 reports, has devoted a minute proportion of its efforts to the study of prisons as such.

The system may be more open than it was, but it is difficult to avoid the conclusion that the interest developed by the press over the past decade or so has contributed as much to the safety of inmates as have some of the official safeguards. The influence has been indirect, but the possibility of bad publicity has come to be feared. Even at Gartree, whose staff behaved so professionally in the face of their riot in 1978, they were very conscious of potential publicity. The Chairman of the Board of Visitors, in his account noted:

> The staff, too, were supported. A number of them said quite openly to me 'We'll get such a caning from the Press', but the fact that during the most sensitive hours four independent people — each of some standing in their localities — were present made it impossible to start a fiction about beatings up, etc. (Martin, 1980).

Future prospects

This discussion can best be rounded off by returning to the list of 'areas of concern' outlined at the beginning of this chapter.

First came order and physical security. Despite all the bad publicity this is an area where the system has done relatively well. As Thomas (1972a) has commented in a survey of murders of prison staff — remarkably few in number —

> . . . it is possible to argue that, on the whole, at a personal level, relationships between staff and inmates are very much closer and more workable than some investigations would claim. There is an especial need in this respect to challenge the stereotype of the severe Victorian officer bearing heavily upon the prisoners (p.10).

Clearly assaults by prisoners on each other are liable to be under-reported, and assaults by staff on inmates even more so, but the published figures for assaults by male inmates on each other average only 4 per 100 of the population. This rate varies enormously according to the type of establishment, with very high rates for young offenders and much lower ones for adult prisoners. Combining assaults on officers and on inmates, the rates reported per 100 population were 3.4 per cent for closed prisons (males) and 4.2 per cent for locals (Home Office, 1979a, table 9.2). Unquestionably the system is at its most vulnerable in times of crisis, but even here the system is more successful than is commonly recognised. According to the Prison Department's Report for 1978 there are about 30 incidents a year involving groups of inmates — 'almost all were passive in character and were resolved without serious injury or damage to property' (Home Office, 1979, para 88).

While this should be recognised to be an official description and perhaps therefore partly playing down what took place, in fact none of these incidents developed into anything more notorious except for the Gartree riot, and even that showed that the worst consequences of disturbances can be prevented. It requires, however, an existing basis of good staff/inmate relations, cool heads and a conscientious Board of Visitors.

Despite all the criticisms, the debacle of the Hull adjudications, and the various legal actions against Prison Department, there are grounds for optimism with regard to the fairness of the system. One has only to read the comments of the Franklin Committee on Punishments in Prisons and Borstals (Home Office, 1951) to appreciate how much progress has been made in the last thirty years. There has been a definite move from seeing adjudications simply as opportunities for supporting the staff to regarding them as (to use the Lord Chief Justice's phrase) 'judicial acts'. The Home Office may be mistaken in its reliance on Boards of Visitors for adjudications, but its efforts to improve them are commendable. Justice may not always have been done in prison adjudications, but there is no doubt of the seriousness with which it is now being attempted.

In other respects, such as giving reasons for decisions about parole, the situation is less satisfactory. No doubt the impossibility of challenge to such decisions is a good bureaucratic reason for not explaining them, but it is a negation of any educational influence the decision might be used to generate. It is no good on the one hand criticising prisoners for being immature (as they often are), while on the other reinforcing that immaturity by not pointing out how the decision related to their own behaviour.

Least satisfactory of all have been the restrictions on communication with lawyers. Again, the reasons have probably been the old mixture of bureaucratic self-protection and a paternalistic attitude to the prisoner. However, the series of reverses which the Home Office has suffered at the hands of the European Commission and the Court of Human Rights may eventually alter the fundamental attitude, if necessary, by a series of piecemeal changes.

Finally, the system also has grave weaknesses in respect of the mental life of prisoners. The often fragile ties between inmates and their friends and families are rarely helped by separation and censored communication. Once again the British tradition is out of step with European standards so that our undoubted progress has still not brought us to a level consistent with the principles of Rule One. The deficiencies and their consequences are fully examined in *Losing Touch*

(Howard League, 1979), and it is in this respect that the concept of *humane* containment as interpreted by the Editors of this book has most to offer. We have come a long way from the penitentiaries described by Ignatieff (1978), where suffering was a matter of policy. The intentions of the 1980s are certainly different, but every age has its aberrations, and the limits of regimes still have to be set and maintained by the law. It cannot be done without making full use of the checks and balances discussed in this chapter.

Conclusion

This book has been about the future of the prison system. Inevitably the immediate future will be influenced to an important extent by the findings and recommendations of the May Inquiry. Committees of inquiry are creatures of government. No minister creates a committee likely to produce advice he does not wish to hear. And, in as much as committees of inquiry are appointed on the advice of senior civil servants, are serviced by and generally receive their most authoritative advice from government departments, it would be surprising were they to arrive at conclusions which did not serve departmental interests. This is not to assert that government departments are monolithic or that their interests are invariable and can be taken for granted. But it suggests that, in analysing the prisons inquiry, we must be careful to assess the work of Mr Justice May and his colleagues within this establishment context. Suffice it to say that it would be politically unsophisticated to look to an official inquiry for a radical critique of departmental policy: for such challenges we must look to individuals and groups independent of government.

What then was the nature and purpose of the May Inquiry? What might have been expected from it? Clearly it had been long awaited. The expectations aroused by the announcement of the Inquiry went far beyond a solution to the industrial relations crisis which had led to the creation of the Committee. The 1964 Royal Commission on the Penal System had been asked 'to review the work of the services and institutions dealing with offenders and the responsibility for their administration and to make recommendations' (Morgan, 1979, pp 2-3). But in the event it failed to agree on basic principles and was abandoned without producing a report. It was followed during the next decade, by a series of *ad hoc* inquiries. There were investigations into prison security and the regime for long-term prisoners (Mountbatten, 1966; ACPS, 1968); detention centres and, subsequently, all sentences for young adult offenders were reviewed (ACPS, 1968a; ACPS, 1970; ACPS, 1974); the problems of habitually drunken and mentally disordered offenders were considered (Home Office, 1971; Butler, 1975); efforts were made to find alternatives to custody and to increase the use of bail (ACPS, 1970a; Home Office, 1974a); prison adjudication procedures were scrutinised (Home Office, 1975); and finally, further consideration was given to the powers of the courts to use imprisonment (ACPS, 1978). None of these inquiries was concerned with the overall administration and organisation of prisons. The only report which had a significant bearing on these matters — the Advisory Council's *Young Adult Offender* — was curiously out of phase with current penal thought (Hood, 1974). It was riven by internal dissent and, unsurprisingly, left to wither, unimplemented, on the shelf. The 1964 Prison Rules, with only minor amendment, continued to apply. The principles and organisational framework outlined in the 1959 White Paper *Penal Practice in a Changing Society* continued to operate, despite serious questioning of their treatment emphasis, a greatly increased prison population, public expenditure cuts, and mounting prisoner and uniformed staff discontent. Indeed, so serious was the condition of the prison service generally regarded that it was the subject of an investigation undertaken by the all-party House of Commons Expenditure Committee (1977-78).

The long wait for a thoroughgoing inquiry which might prove a penal landmark comparable to the 1895 Gladstone Committee, had important consequences for the May Committee. Above all it probably led the Home Secretary to agree to terms of reference broader than he would otherwise have considered appropriate for a speedy solution to the prison officers' pay dispute. Certainly, given the breadth of the May Committee's remit, Mr Merlyn Rees' request that they report within four months seemed inappropriate. Furthermore, the non-expert character of the Committee's membership, though consistent with the task of arbitrating, like a super-vetted jury, in an industrial dispute, was scarcely suited to the more complex policy appraisal suggested by parts of the terms of reference.

Given calmer circumstances the remit might have been reasonable. An assessment of 'the adequacy availability, management and use of resources in the prison services' *should* have regard to 'the size and nature of the prison population, and the capacity of the Prison services to accommodate it'; 'the remuneration and conditions of service of prison officers' *should* be related to 'the need to recruit and retain a sufficient and suitable staff'; and 'the organisation and management of the prison services' *can* only be considered in relation to the responsibility 'for the security, control and treatment of inmates'. But what every informed commentator on the penal system knows, and what Mr Justice May and his colleagues occasionally came to recognise, is that the size and composition of the prison population is itself determined by social policy; and the responsibilities of the prison services are based on judgements as to what is desirable and feasible. There is no automatic consensus on these issues. There are no *independent* facts to which one can merely 'have regard'. As a result the items to which the Committee was to 'have regard' might as easily have been placed among those which they were required to 'examine and make recommendations upon' — or *vice versa*.

Of course, many of those who gave evidence to the May Committee were only too well aware of these complexities. As a consequence many witnesses wistfully spoke to terms of reference other than those announced. This is not an unusual phenomenon. The May Inquiry, like most inquiries, was looked to by a variety of people and interest groups for a variety of reasons. It follows that the scope and meaning of the Committee's terms of reference were always likely to prove the focus of disputes. Terms of reference are carefully constructed: they reflect ministerial objectives. It is the periphery, rather than the centre, which is the politically sensitive area of any official inquiry's work. Whereas departments are anxious that committees should restrict themselves to assumptions and issues which are politically acceptable and controllable, those wishing to challenge departmental policy tend to urge a broader review. Quite predictably most of the criticisms of the May Report hinge on the issue of whether particular questions did or did not fall within the Committee's terms of reference.

It seems reasonable to speculate that senior Home Office officials advising the Home Secretary to establish the Prisons Inquiry had the following considerations in mind. First, the Committee would act as an independent arbitrator in a pay dispute with all the legitimacy which that role typically confers. Arbitration was vital for, quite apart from the sensitivity of the dispute, the prison service is the only one for whose administration the Home Office has direct operational control. Secondly, the Inquiry would buy time. Whatever the outcome of the dispute the Department needed contingency plans. Almost a year later, just prior to the publication of the May Report, the national press carried stories, which had all the characteristics of inspired leaks, of emergency plans involving the police and army should prison officers take strike action in protest against the Committee's pay recommendations. Thirdly, there can be little doubt that senior Home Office officials saw a need to expose some of their own personnel to critical public scrutiny. The May Committee was used as a disciplinary weapon: an external body to cudgel those from whom the Home Office had previously flinched. Prison Department is justifiably accused of excessive secrecy. But paradoxically secrecy is often contrary to Departmental interests. When the Department wishes to reveal a skeleton it cannot easily do so. The May Inquiry served as a vehicle to expose the restrictive practices of prison officers. Fourthly, senior officials must have recognised that the administration of prisons was

202

Hidden agenda behind the Inquiry !.

unsatisfactory and that changes had to be made. But they had preferred solutions. Those solutions would be more acceptable if they were delivered by an independent committee. At the same time more radical solutions would be more effectively undermined by an official inquiry than by the Department itself. Finally, the Department sought reaffirmation of the broad organisational strategy to which they were committed and an endorsement of their claim for increased resources.

Given the background to the industrial relations dispute it was impossible for anyone to pretend that a pay settlement alone would end the troubles. It was generally agreed that the dispute was symptomatic of more deep-seated stresses. By stating that Mr Justice May and his colleagues should have regard to the size of the prison population and the responsibilities of the prison service, the Home Secretary demonstrated recognition of the broader context. Encouraged by that recognition, outside witnesses to the Inquiry, who looked to it for a radical challenge to both the aims and use of imprisonment, chose to ignore the fact that both questions were technically beyond the Committee's competence. They were further encouraged when Mr Merlyn Rees' suggested four month deadline came and went, and it was announced that no report would be published before the Autumn. This suggested that other matters besides the arbitration of the pay dispute were being seriously considered.

What the May Committee actually did was to effect a compromise. On the one hand it took the whole of its terms of reference seriously and refused to separate the pay dispute from broader issues. Its most important decision, made early in its deliberations, was not to issue an interim report on continuous duty credits. This was the most inflammatory part of the prison officers' claim on which they expected an early answer. On the other hand the Committee made a second crucial decision, to breach the purely legalistic interpretation of its terms of reference. One doubts whether this was arrived at in a self-conscious manner. In the event it both examined and made recommendations on issues to which, according to Merlyn Rees' instructions, it was only to have regard. Because of the nature of the wider opinions and evidence with which it was deluged by non-Departmental witnesses, the temptation to do this must have been very great. Indeed, it is certain that had it struck rigidly to its remit, the May Report would have been met by an immediate protest from the penal pressure groups.

As it was, the May Report was greeted on the whole with an astonishing silence. The media failed to find any dramatic proposals or statements on which to focus and so, following brief references to the largely irrelevant suggestion that Dartmoor be closed, and

Mr Whitelaw's immediate assurance that it would not be so, passed over it. Prison Department personnel — both governors and prison officers — indicated, to put it mildly, that they were not impressed by the Report. But initial howls of anguish soon resolved themselves into murmurs of disapproval accompanied by limited forms of industrial action. It is difficult to assess which factors produced this muted response: the justice of the May Committee's arbitration, and the Home Secretary's acceptance of its recommendations on pay, or the widespread perception, in this instance reinforced by the threatened use of army and police cells in the event of a strike, that 'no more' from Mrs Thatcher's Conservative administration meant 'no more'.

But an equally significant part of the general silence has been that from informed observers and academics and the penal pressure groups. Most commentators have felt that some of the May Committee's recommendations are welcome and their adoption should be encouraged. Informal discussions we have had with a number of groups suggests at least a luke-warm reception for the proposed changes in the organisation of Prison Department headquarters (see chapter 5), for the formation of a national inspectorate (chapters 5 and 6) and for a review of security classification procedures (chapter 3). Furthermore, without being very knowledgeable as to the details, most observers have been disposed to think that the pay claim has been dealt with justly and that it was right and proper for several points of dispute to be returned to the Department for continued negotiation.

But the overriding impression we have gained from all our discussions, with members of Boards of Visitors, prison governors, academics, penal activists, and even members of Prison Department headquarters staff, is one of gloom, of overwhelming pessimism. This more than anything else explains the minimal response to the May Committee's recommendations. The general view has been that, however important the organisational proposals might be under other circumstances, they are almost irrelevant to the real problems bearing down on the prison system. On these problems the May Committee gave virtually no lead. It almost fiddled while Rome burned.

If our speculations as to the Department's motives in setting up the May Inquiry are correct, then the Department has largely achieved its objects. There has been no strike though, at the time of writing, industrial action continues in over a score of prisons. Sufficient light has been shed on prison staff practices to promote the feeling that staff claims for increased manning levels should be met with a more incisive scrutiny. The most radical, and in some cases reactionary, organisational proposals have been headed off. Prison Department's insistence on the need for a considerably increased building programme, its preference for the present distribution of resources among establishments, and its long cherished ambition of one man one cell, have all been endorsed. Indeed, the May Committee went so far as to provide a defence for Departmental interests which even Home Office officials might find embarrassing, so lacking is it in credibility. Prisons are so vital a part of our civil defence, Mr Justice May suggested, that to judge expenditure on them in terms of what is provided for other services, or to make the prison service subject to public expenditure cuts applying elsewhere, would be irresponsible. It was almost as if all the volumes of evidence and argument, a chorus to which the Home Office voice has been added from time to time, calling for fewer and shorter sentences had not existed. An astonishing outcome, not least because the May Committee, elsewhere in its Report, expressed support for the efforts made by the Advisory Council on the Penal System (ACPS, 1978) for the reduction of sentence lengths.

This brings us to the manner in which the May Committee breached its terms of reference. Though the penal pressure groups urged the Committee to make the breach, in retrospect most would now maintain that it would have been better had it not been done. Stated baldly, the May Committee did a reasonable job in tackling several issues which the Minister and Department wished it to review. In these areas, the Committee was furnished with generally thorough evidence, well prepared by the Department. But on those questions on which the Committee chose to exercise its initiative, where it went beyond its brief, it did so without adequate backing, without any expertise of its own to guide it, and with disastrous consequences.

On the questions of prison system goals (and their implications for the distribution of resources), and the size of the future prison population, it is not simply that the May Committee confused what are in any case complex issues. Nor even that a year has been wasted. But that the likelihood of our quickly developing long-term solutions has actually been reduced as a result of the Committee's deliberations. All official committees produce a degree of what may, in departmental terms, be thought of as planning blight. Ministers, having set up an independent policy review, generally feel honour bound to await the outcome of that review before taking new initiatives. For similar reasons, most inquiry reports are followed by a gestation period during which consultation, real or pretended, takes place. Since inquiries *are* the creatures of government they cannot readily be explicitly repudiated — unless they were created by a previous administration in connection with matters over which there is a clear party divide. The danger created by the May Committee's disturbingly confused and superficial treatment of the prison population question and the aims of the prison system, is that it may now be claimed that these basic issues *have* been dealt with: that the Department should now be left to get on with the job.

The whole burden of our discussion in chapters 1 to 4 hinges on two arguments. First, that in relation to prison system goals the May Committee has inadequately challenged existing Departmental policy. In our judgement the May Committee's reformulation of Rule One in terms of 'positive custody' will do no more to produce defined and humane standards for the custody of prisoners than did the doctrine of treatment and training. It imposes no greater obligations on staff, and if anything its meaning is less clear, than the formulation it is intended to replace. We have also argued that the May Committee's failure to analyse correctly the real implications of Rule One underpins its uncritical acceptance of the existing and inequitable allocation of prisoners and resources to establishments. Both produce greater deprivation and stress, for prisoners and staff, than is necessary.

Our second argument is that, no matter what the May Committee says, the size and composition of the prison population is *always* a policy choice. To say that the government does not have a population policy — and that is how the Home Office describes its position — is plainly an exercise in passing the buck. The fact is that 'merely' reacting to the *ad hoc* decisions of sentencers, leaving sentencing powers as they are, and refusing to take executive intervention measures, is itself a prison population policy, albeit a rather poor and irrational one. There is no 'penal momentum' as the May Committee termed it. There are no trends to be complied with. Only policy choices as to whether we are to have an ever increasing prison population or whether, for reasons of economy, humanity or constructive social policy, we wish to reduce it. This issue the May Committee was either unable or unwilling to grasp. The Committee might, quite properly, have ducked it completely as outside its terms of reference. In fact, it claimed to have tackled the scope for reducing the prison population and concluded, at least in the short term, that there was none. The minimal reactions from non-Departmental groups to these sections of the May Report can only be explained by a desire not to dignify the Committee's conclusions with public debate.

Our initial response, on reading the May Report, was that a great opportunity for radical change had been missed. Simply because the review had taken place, and alternative choices and strategies brushed aside, it would be more difficult to reopen these questions afresh. Given a relatively stable system, planning blight might have occurred. However, the prison system is passing through what is probably the most volatile period in its history. Our reading of present events is that the May Report is likely to be overtaken by more potent forces for change.

The most important factor, of course, is the continued, but now quite dramatic, rise in the prison population. As we write – March 1980 – the average daily population has risen to an all time high of over 44,800. Only a month ago, when we wrote chapter 2, we recorded that the population had risen to 43,000. There are now nearly two thousand more prisoners in custody than were forecast by the Home Office for 1982. The number of female prisoners, at over 1,600, is also up to the level forecast for 1982 and still rising. We cannot help but wonder whether this is not the response of the courts, in an atmosphere of 'law and order', to the May Committee's promised land of more resources and more prisons recommended a few short months earlier. Is the prison population being made to rise in anticipation of prisons yet to be built?

In any case conditions in many prisons, where regimes have already been curtailed by continuing staff industrial action, are now quite indefensible. After a recent conference of prison governors and Boards of Visitors Chairmen, on past records not a body given to inflammatory or critical statements, there was a public call for immediate Government action to reduce the prison population (*The Guardian*, 10 and 11 March, 1980). The crisis, it is claimed, is so great that nothing short of an amnesty can relieve the acute overcrowding in local trial and remand establishments.

The legacy of past tensions is now also filtering through to the public domain. In May 1980, the High Court rejected the case of Williams, detained in the Wakefield control unit in 1974 and claiming damages from the Home Office. His case rested on the grounds that he allegedly suffered psychological injury as a consequence of his experience and that the control unit, and therefore his detention in it, was unlawful under the Prison Rules. The Williams decision came too late for its implications fully to be considered here. But the very fact that the case was brought, and the nature of the evidence admitted, is bound to affect future Prison Department policy. First, the Home Office has been forced to reveal documents, including memoranda prepared for ministers by senior civil servants, connected with the planning of control units. The secrecy with which the Home Office has typically shrouded its activities has been dealt a major blow. Secondly, the evidence has called into question whether the day-to-day operation of the Wakefield control unit was in accordance with directions formulated by headquarters. Matters relating to the accountability of institutional staff, and what kinds of watchdog bodies are appropriate, have thus been brought to the fore.

Similar issues are emerging from the incident involving the use of the MUFTI (Minimum Use of Force Tactical Intervention) squad at Wormwood Scrubs on 31 August 1979. At the NACRO Conference discussing the May Report on 30 November 1979, the Director General of the prison service, Mr Trevelyan, declared that 'we are deliberately and continuously trying to increase public understanding of the prison system, and to open that system up'. That was a most welcome expression of intent — but it was understandably lost on an audience preoccupied by the fact that Prison Department officials appeared to have lied to the media about events at the Scrubs. Initial Prison Department denials that anyone was hurt in the incident, and even that the MUFTI squads existed, were later corrected with an admission that five prisoners were slightly hurt and that there were such squads. Later still came the statement that fifty-three prisoners had been injured, that similar squads had been formed in February 1979 and had been used in several prisons. Most recently, and almost certainly not the end of this sorry saga, following an unpublished internal inquiry conducted by the Prison Department's South East Regional Director, it has been announced that the incident at Wormwood Scrubs is to be the subject of a police investigation (*The Guardian*, 29 February, 1980).

Our concern here is not to comment on whether there is or is not a justification for MUFTI squads, still less to judge events at Wormwood Scrubs. If anything, the issues are more important than those. The point about this unedifying sequence, reminiscent of that which followed the Hull riot in 1976, is that we are in no position to offer an appraisal. The formation of MUFTI squads, like the control units, was not publicly discussed, and there was no mention of them in the May Report. Regarding Wormwood Scrubs, either Prison Department headquarters did not know what had happened — this was Mr Trevelyan's explanation of the discrepancy between early and later press statements — or sought to hide what happened. Seven months after the event Prison Department has still to provide a detailed account of the way in which the Wormwood Scrubs demonstration was quelled and why. The impression which the Home Office has given of its own organisation is, at best, one of ineptitude and confusion; at worst, of dissimulation and a cynical disregard for public accountability. The real tragedy is that during a period when efforts should have been made to educate public opinion as to the problems facing the prison service, most attention has been focused on a single incident and accusations have been levelled at uniformed staff which ought to have been directed at the policies which have brought the prison system to its present state.

The responsibility for all this rests squarely with the Home Office. Already a further hardening of uniformed staff attitudes is discernible.

In the light of the Regional Director's announcement that a police investigation into the events at Wormwood Scrubs was called for, prison officers have talked of withdrawing to consider appropriate actions when instructed to break up demonstrations. A breakaway group of officers, demanding more effective (militant) trades union leadership, has formed the Prison Force Federation (*The Guardian*, 17 March, 1980) which for once has put the POA and the Home Office on the same side. The likelihood of further industrial actions seems assured. Staff willingness to accept organisational change, or to respond flexibly to overcrowding will be no less certainly reduced. Try as we might we can see no light in this tunnel except that which will be sparked in the coming crisis.

Prediction is a hazardous business. However, we think it very likely that before these words appear in print the scene will have changed considerably. In many prisons staff have already declared a willingness to refuse to take prisoners in excess of their establishment's certified normal accommodation. Our informal discussions with Prison Department officials suggests that there is a considerable pressure throughout the service for executive action to reduce the prison population. Mr Whitelaw has already stated that major changes in the prison service will be announced in April, including a modest building programme (*The Guardian*, 22 March, 1980). We expect these will be largely token measures to implement some of the May recommendations and to restore some prison building already planned but delayed. But so far it is said that the Thatcher Cabinet has set its face against any executive or legislative measures that would appear to weaken their resolve that law and order should remain a potent political force (*The Observer*, 16 March, 1980). If that indeed be the case, it cannot be long before Mr Whitelaw is forced into recommending a U-turn.

Ultimately, whatever measures might be taken to relieve population pressure — be they in the form of an amnesty or increase in the period of remission or parole — they will produce only short-term relief: and they will in no way diminish the importance of the issues discussed in this volume. If sentencing policies remain unchanged the prison population will creep upwards once again. Because of the inadequacy of the 1964 Prison Rules, standards in prison, which at present are largely dependent on the good will of staff, will be eroded once more. The inequities between conditions in local and training prisons will grow starker. And, unless the dispersal policy is abandoned, many prisoners will continue to be subject to more secure custody than their security risk warrants, and further riots and disturbances are virtually guaranteed.

There is little or no prospect, even were it considered desirable (and that, clearly, is not our view), that Prison Department will receive a substantial increase in resources. And, even if the Government were to agree to a major building programme, it could not be completed in time to release the pressure resulting from short-term population fluctuations.

So, whether or not Mr Whitelaw' hand is forced this Spring or Summer, we suggest that there is no alternative but to undertake the wide ranging review which we have urged and which the May Committee spurned. We have stated and elaborated three guiding principles for the use and organisation of imprisonment: the *minimum use of custody*, *the minimum use of security* and *the normalisation of the prison*. We do not underestimate the difficulties attaching to operationalising these principles. However, we believe that both in our evidence to the May Committee, and in chapters 1 to 4, we have laid the foundations of a practicable, humane and defensible policy. In chapter 5, Dr Thomas has indicated what is wrong with prison administration and what could be done to improve it; and in chapter 6, Professor Martin has outlined the kinds of safeguards that must be built in if standards are to be achieved and then maintained. We do not pretend that these are the only, or necessarily the best, proposals that are available — but they are much more relevant to the real problems at hand than most of the recommendations of the May Committee.

What now is needed is debate, leading to policy formation, perhaps by one of the specialised *ad hoc* committees with which the Home Secretary intends to replace the Advisory Council on the Penal System (Written answer to Mr Charles Irving, MP, 18 February, 1980), followed by action. But it had better be quick if the 1980s are not to be very much worse than the 1970s. Attica and Santa Fé could happen here.

Bibliography

Abraham, Henry J. (1972), *Freedom and the Court: Civil Rights and Liberties in the United States*, Second Edition, New York, OUP.

Abt Associates (1977), *Prison Population and Policy Choices, Volume 1: Preliminary Report to Congress*, Washington, US Department of Justice, Law Enforcement Assistance Administration.

ACPS (1968), *The Regime for Long-term Prisoners in Conditions of Maximum Security*, Report of the Advisory Council on the Penal System (Radzinowicz Report), London, HMSO.

ACPS (1968a), *Detention of Girls in a Detention Centre*, Report of the Advisory Council on the Penal System, London, HMSO.

ACPS (1970), *Detention Centres*, Report of the Advisory Council on the Penal System, London, HMSO.

ACPS (1970a), *Non-custodial and Semi-custodial Penalties*, Report of the Advisory Council on the Penal System, London, HMSO.

ACPS (1974), *Young Adult Offenders*, Report of the Advisory Council on the Penal System, London, HMSO.

ACPS (1977), *The Length of Prison Sentences*, Interim Report of the Advisory Council on the Penal System, London, HMSO.

ACPS (1978), *Sentences of Imprisonment*, Report of the Advisory Council on the Penal System, London, HMSO.

American Friends Service Committee (1971), *Struggle for Justice: A Report on Crime and Punishment in America*, New York, Hill and Wang.

Ashworth, A.J. (1979), 'Judicial independence and sentencing reform', Paper presented to Cambridge Criminology Conference, July.

Bailey, Roy (1979), 'Alternatives to imprisonment', Paper presented to NACRO Conference on the Report of the House of Commons Expenditure Committee, 15 June, London, NACRO.

Banks, C. and Fairhead, S. (1976), *The Petty Short-term Prisoner*, Chichester, Howard League for Penal Reform and Barry Rose.

Barnard, Elizabeth and Bottoms, A.E. (1979), 'Facilitating decisions not to imprison' in *The Petty Persistent Offender*, Proceedings of a NACRO Seminar, 26 June, London, NACRO.

Bottomley, A. Keith (1979), 'Sentences of Imprisonment — a valueless report?', *The Howard Journal*, 18, 85-91.

Bottoms, A.E. (1977), 'Reflections on the renaissance of dangerousness', *The Howard Journal*, 16, 70-96.

Bottoms, A.E. (1977a), 'The suspended sentence after ten years: a review and reassessment', Paper delivered to the Frank Dawtry Memorial Seminar, University of Leeds.

Brody, S.R. (1976), *The Effectiveness of Sentencing*, Home Office Research Study no.35, London, HMSO.

Butler Report (1975), *Report of the Committee on Mentally Abnormal Offenders*, Cmnd 6244, London, HMSO.

Cawson, P. (1975), *Referrals to the Units and Behaviour Prior to Referral*, DHSS Research Division unpublished mimeograph.

Clarke, D. (1978), 'Marxism, justice and the justice model', *Contemporary Crises* II, 1, 27-62.

Cohen, S. and Taylor, L. (1972), *Psychological Survival: The Experience of Long-term Imprisonment*, Harmondsworth, Penguin Books.

Cohen, S. and Taylor, L. (1978), *Prison Secrets*, London, NCCL and RAP.

Conservative Party (1977), *The Proper Use of Prisons.* A Conservative Study Group Report, London, Conservative Political Centre.

Corden, John, Kuipers, Joe and Wilson, Kate (1978), *After Prison*, Papers in Community Studies no.21, Department of Social Administration and Social Work, University of York.

Council of Europe (1950), *European Convention on Human Rights*, Strasbourg, Council of Europe.

Council of Europe (1973), *Standard Minimum Rules for the Treatment of Prisoners*, Strasbourg, European Committee on Crime Problems, Council of Europe.

Cronin, H. (1967), *The Screw Turns*, London, John Long.

Cross, Rupert (1971), *Punishment Prison and the Public*, The Hamlyn Lectures, Twenty-third Series, London, Stevens.

Crossman, R.H.S. (1977), *The Diaries of a Cabinet Minister*, vol.III, London, Hamish Hamilton and Jonathan Cape.

Edmund-Davies, H.E. (1978), *Report of the Committee of Inquiry on the Police*, Cmnd 7283, London, HMSO.

Elwyn-Jones, The Right Hon. Lord (1976), Presidential Address to the Annual General Meeting of the Magistrates' Association, reported in *The Magistrate*, 32, 12, December, 187-90.

Expenditure Committee (1978), *The Reduction of Pressure on the Prison System*, Fifteenth Report of the House of Commons Expenditure Committee, Session 1977-78, HC 662-1.

Fairhead, Suzan and Marshall, Tony F. (1979), 'Dealing with the Petty Persistent Offender' in *The Petty Persistent Offender*, Proceedings of a NACRO Seminar 26 June, London, NACRO.

Fitzgerald, Mike (1977), *Prisoners in Revolt*, Harmondsworth, Penguin Books.

Fitzgerald, Mike and Sim, Joe (1979), *British Prisons*, Oxford, Basil Blackwell.

Fowler, G. (1977), *Report of an Inquiry by the Chief Inspector of the Prison Service into the cause and circumstances of the events at H.M. Prison Hull during the period 31 August to 3 September 1976*, Session 1976-77, HC 453.

Fox, Lionel (1952), *The English Prison and Borstal Systems*, London, Routledge and Kegan Paul.

Gibbens, T.C.N., Soothill, K.L. and Pope, P.J. (1977), *Medical Remands in the Criminal Court*, Maudsley Monograph no.25, OUP.

Gladstone Report (1895), *Report from the Departmental Committee on Prisons*, C.7702.

Hawkins, K. (1972), 'Some consequences of a parole system for prison management' in West, D.J. (ed.), *The Future of Parole*, London, Duckworth.

Hobhouse, S. and Brockway, F. (1922), *English Prisons Today: Being the Report of the Prison System Enquiry Committee*, London, Longmans, Green and Company.

Home Office (1949), *The Prison Rules 1949* (S.I. no.1073), London, HMSO. See also Home Office (1964).

Home Office (1951), *Report of a Committee to Review Punishments in Prisons, Borstal Institutions, Approved Schools and Remand Homes*, Parts I and II, Prisons and Borstal Institutions, Cmd 8256, London, HMSO, Sessional Papers 1950-51, xviii.

Home Office (1959), *Penal Practice in a Changing Society*, Cmnd 645, London, HMSO.

Home Office (1964), *The Prison Rules 1964* (S.I. no.388). These are known as the Principal Rules but they have been significantly amended by subsequent Statutory Instruments, viz. 1968 – no.440, 1971 – no.2019, 1972 – no.1860, 1974 – no.713, 1976 – no.503. HMSO.

Home Office (1964a), *Prisons and Borstals 1963*, Report on the work of the Prisons Department in the year 1963, Cmnd 2381, London, HMSO.

Home Office (1969), *People in Prison*, Cmnd 4214, London, HMSO.

Home Office (1971), *Report of the Working Party on Habitual Drunken Offenders*, London, HMSO.

Home Office (1972), *Report on the work of the Prison Department 1971*, Cmnd 5037, London, HMSO.

Home Office (1973), *Report on the Work of the Prison Department 1972*, Cmnd 5375, London, HMSO.

Home Office (1974), Circular Instruction Prison Department, 35, quoted in Fitzgerald, M. and Sim, J. (1979).

Home Office (1974a), *Report of the Working Party on Bail Procedures in Magistrates' Courts*, London, HMSO.

Home Office (1975), *Report of the Working Party on Adjudication Procedures in Prisons*, London, HMSO.

Home Office (1976), *Report of the Parole Board for 1975*, London, HMSO.

Home Office (1977), *Prisons and the Prisoner*, London, HMSO.

Home Office 1977a), *A Review of Criminal Justice Policy 1976*, Home Office Working Paper, London, HMSO.

Home Office (1977b), *Procedure for the Conduct of an Adjudication by a Board of Visitors*, London, Home Office Prison Department. (Printed for private circulation, but apparently not a classified document).

Home Office (1978), *The Sentence of the Court*, Third Edition, London, HMSO.

Home Office (1978a), *Youth Custody and Supervision: A New Sentence*, Cmnd 7406, London, HMSO.

Home Office (1978b), *Report on the Work of the Prison Department, 1977*, Cmnd 7290, London, HMSO.

Home Office (1979), *Report on the Work of the Prison Department, 1978*, Cmnd 7619, London, HMSO.

Home Office (1979a), *Prison Statistics England and Wales 1978*, Cmnd 7626, London, HMSO.

Hood, Roger (1974), 'Young Adult Offenders', *British Journal of Criminology*, 14, 4, 388-95.

Hood, Roger (1976), 'Penal policy and the rights of prisoners', Paper delivered to the Frank Dawtry Memorial Seminar, University of Leeds.

Howard, John (1777), *The State of the Prisons in England and Wales*, Warrington, William Eyres.

Howard League for Penal Reform (1979), *Losing Touch: Restrictions on Prisoners' Outside Contacts*, London, Howard League for Penal Reform.

Ignatieff, M. (1978), *A Just Measure of Pain: the Penitentiary in the Industrial Revolution 1750-1850*, London, Macmillan.

Jacobs, F.G. (1975), *The European Convention on Human Rights*, Oxford, Clarendon Press.

Jellicoe, Rt. Hon. Earl (Chairman), (1975), *Boards of Visitors of Penal Institutions*, Report of a Committee of Justice, Howard League for Penal Reform and the National Association for the Care and Resettlement of Offenders, Chichester, Barry Rose.

Jones, H. and Cornes, P. (1977), *Open Prisons*, London, Routledge and Kegan Paul.

Justice (1977), *Our Fettered Ombudsman*, Report of a Committee under the Chairmanship of David Widdicombe, Q.C., London, Justice.

King, Roy D. (1972), *An Analysis of Prison Regimes*. Report to the Home Office, University of Southampton, unpublished.

King, Roy D. and Elliott, Kenneth W. (1978), *Albany: Birth of a Prison — End of an Era*, London, Routledge and Kegan Paul.

King, Roy D. and Morgan, Rodney (1976), *A Taste of Prison: Custodial Conditions for Trial and Remand Prisoners*, London, Routledge and Kegan Paul.

King, Roy D. and Morgan, Rodney (1979), *Crisis in the Prisons: the Way Out*. A Paper based on evidence submitted to the Inquiry into the United Kingdom Prison Service, Universities of Bath and Southampton.

Labour Campaign (1979), Labour Campaign for Criminal Justice Working Paper on 'Reducing the prison population', unpublished.

Lipton, D., Martinson, R. and Wilks, J. (1975), *The Effectiveness of Correctional Treatment*, New York, Praeger.

Macartney, W.F.R. (1936), *Walls Have Mouths: A Record of Ten Years' Penal Servitude*, London, Victor Gollancz.

Martell, M. and Cawson, P. (1975), *The Development of Closed Units in the Child Care Service*, DHSS Research Division Monograph.

Martin, J.P. (1974), 'Justice in Prisons', *New Society*, 28 March, 766-67.

Martin, J.P. (1980), 'Jellicoe and after: Boards of Visitors into the eighties', *Howard Journal*, 19, 2.

Martin, J.P. and Webster, D. (1971), *The Social Consequences of Conviction*, London, Heinemann Educational Books.

Mathiesen, Thomas (1965), *The Defences of the Weak: A Sociological Study of a Norwegian Correctional Institution*, London, Tavistock.

May, Mr Justice (Chairman), (1979), *Report of the Committee of Inquiry into The United Kingdom Prison Services*, Cmnd 7673, London, HMSO.

McCleery, C.H. (1978), 'The Treatment of psychopaths with Depixol', in restricted circulation *Prison Medical Journal*, cited in Timms, P. (1978), 'The current crisis — danger plus opportunity', *Community Care*, 15 November, 20-23.

Miles, I. and Irvine, J. (1979), 'Social forecasting: predicting the future and making history' in Irvine, J., Miles, I. and Evans, J., *Demystifying Social Statistics*, Pluto Press.

Millham, Spencer, Bullock, Roger and Hosie, Kenneth (1978), *Locking Up Children*, Farnborough, Saxon House.

Mitford, Jessica (1973), *Kind and Usual Punishment: The Prison Business*, New York, Alfred A. Knopf.

Morgan, Rod (1979), *Formulating Penal Policy: the Future of the Advisory Council on the Penal System*, London, NACRO.

Morgan, Rod and Smith, Brian (1979), 'Advising the Minister on crime and punishment', *Political Quarterly*, 50, 3, 326-35.

Morris, T.P., Morris, P. and Barer, Barbara (1963), *Pentonville: A Sociological Study of an English Prison*, London, Routledge and Kegan Paul.

Mountbatten Report (1966), *Report of the Inquiry into Prison Escapes and Security*, Cmnd 3175, London, HMSO.

NACRO (1980) *The May Report, Proceedings of a Conference held at Central Hall Westminster on 30 November 1979*, London, NACRO.

Nagel, W. (1977), 'On behalf of a moratorium on prison construction', *Crime and Delinquency*, 23, 154-72.

National Health Service (1969), *Report of the Committee of Inquiry into Allegations of Ill-treatment of Patients and Other Irregularities at the Ely Hospital, Cardiff*, Cmnd 3975, London, HMSO.

New Approaches to Juvenile Crime (1980), *Some Facts About Juvenile Crime*, Briefing Paper no.3, Association of Directors of Social Services etc.

New York Special Commission on Attica (1972), *Attica*, New York, Bantam Books.

Peterson, A.W. (1961), 'The prison building programme', *British Journal of Criminology*, 1, 4, 307-16.

Prime Minister (1980), *Report on Non-Departmental Public Bodies*, (The Pliatzky Report), Cmnd 7797, London, HMSO.

Prison Commission (1932), *Principles of the Borstal System*, printed for private circulation and generally attributed to Alexander Paterson.

PROP (1979), *Wormwood Scrubs: Special Report*, Preservation of the Rights of Prisoners, 21, Atwood Road, London, W6.

Radzinowicz, L. and Hood, R. (1978), 'A dangerous direction for sentencing reform', *Criminal Law Review*, 713-24.

Rees, M. (1976), Speech to NACRO European Conference, London, 13 December.

Royal Commission on Legal Services (Chairman Sir Henry Benson), (1979), *Report*, Cmnd 7648, London, HMSO.

Ruck, S.K. (ed.) (1951), *Paterson on Prisons*, London, Muller.

Scottish Council on Crime (1975), *Crime and the Prevention of Crime*, Edinburgh, HMSO.

Sparks, R.F. (1971), *Local Prisons: The Crisis in the English Penal System*, London, Heinemann.

Streatfeild, Mr Justice (Chairman) (1961), *Report of the Interdepartmental Committee on the Business of the Criminal Courts*, Cmnd 1289, London, HMSO.

Sykes, Gresham, M. (1958), *The Society of Captives: A Study of a Maximum Security Prison*, Princeton University Press.

Thomas J.E. (1972), *The English Prison Officer since 1850: A Study in Conflict*, London, Routledge and Kegan Paul.

Thomas, J.E. (1972a), 'Killed on duty: an analysis of murders of British prison staff', *Prison Service Journal*, July, 9-10.

Thomas, J.E. (1975), 'Policy and administration in penal establishments' in Blom-Cooper, L. (ed.) *Progress in Penal Reform*, Oxford, Clarendon Press.

Thomas, J.E. (1975a), 'Special units in prisons' in Jones, K. (ed.) *Year Book of Social Policy*, London, Routledge and Kegan Paul.

Thomas, J.E. (1978), 'A good man for gaoler? Crisis, discontent and prison staff' in Freeman, J. (ed.) *Prisons Past and Future*, London, Heinemann.

Train, C.J. (1977), 'The development of criminal policy planning in the Home Office', *Public Administration*, 55, 373-84.

Tulkens, Hans (1979), *Some Developments in penal policy and practice in Holland*, London, NACRO.

United States Commission (1973), *Corrections*, a Report of the United States National Advisory Commission on Criminal Justice Standards and Goals, Washington, US Department of Justice.

Vera Institute of Justice (1977), *Further Work in Criminal Justice Reform*, New York, Vera Institute of Justice.

Von Hirsch, A. (1976), *Doing Justice: The Choice of Punishments*, Report of the Committee for the Study of Incarceration, New York, Hill and Wang.

War Office (1949), *Report of the Army and Air Force Courts-Martial Committee 1946* (Chairman Mr Justice Lewis), Cmnd 7608, London, HMSO.

Watson, J. (1969), *Which is the Justice?* London, Allen and Unwin.

Webb, S. and B. (1922) *English Prisons under Local Government*, London, Longmans, Green.

Wilkins, Geoff (1979), *Making them Pay*, London, NACRO.

Wilson, J.Q. (1975), *Thinking about Crime*, New York, Basic Books.

Wynn Parry Report (1958), *Report of the Committee on Remunerations and Conditions of Service of Certain Grades in the Prison Services*, Cmd 544, London, HMSO.

Zander, M. (1975), *A Bill of Rights?* Chichester, Barry Rose and the British Institute of Human Rights.

Zellick, G. (1974), 'Lawyers and prisoners' rights', *LAG Bulletin*, August, 186-7.

Zellick, G. (1979), 'Prison discipline and the courts', *New Law Journal*, 29 March, 308-9.

Evidence submitted to the May Committee

BAPG (Evidence), British Association of Prison Governors.

Cadbury Trust (Evidence), Barrow and Geraldine S. Cadbury Trust.

Central Departments (Evidence), see Volume III of Home Office Evidence.

FDCS (Evidence), Association of First Division Civil Servants (Home Office Branch).

Haldane Society (Evidence), Haldane Society of Socialist Lawyers.

Home Office (Evidence), *Inquiry into the United Kingdom Prison Services*, vols I and II. Evidence by the Home Office, the Scottish Home and Health Department and the Northern Ireland Office; vol.III. Evidence by H.M. Treasury, the Civil Service Department and the Central Policy Review Staff, HMSO.

Howard League (Evidence), Howard League for Penal Reform.

Justices' Clerks (Evidence), Justices' Clerks Society.

King (Evidence), *Dangerous Prisoners: Dispersal or Concentration*. See King and Morgan, 1979.

NACRO (Evidence), National Association for the Care and Resettlement of Offenders.

NAPO (Evidence), National Association of Probation Officers.

NCCL (Evidence), National Council of Civil Liberties.

POA (Evidence), Prison Officers' Association.

PROP (Evidence), National Prisoners' Movement (Preservation of the Rights of Prisoners).

SCPS (Evidence), Society of Civil and Public Servants, Prison and Borstal Governors (England and Wales) Branch.

Society of Friends (Evidence), Society of Friends.

Index

accommodation: building condition, 103-7, 107-14; certified normal, 114-21; in detention centres, 52

administration: and Board of Visitors, 175-6, 180-2; Council of Europe's Standard Minimum Rules for, 173-4; and the courts, 176-7, 186-93; and European Convention on Human Rights, 167-73; history of, 1-8; and humane containment, 31; internal reviews, 174-5, 177-80; legal basis of, 165-7; and maintenance of standards, 159-99; Parliamentary Commissioner for Administration, 176, 182-6; Prison Rules and Standing Orders, 165-7; and prisoner's rights, 159

Acklington, 110

Advisory Council on the Penal System: abolition of, 64, 210; and criminal law legislation, 56; and long-term prisoners, 72; and security, 3, 3-4; and sentence length, 58-9, 66; and young offenders, 124, 126, 127

Albany: control unit, 5-6; CNA, 116; cost of upgrading, 78; as dispersal prison, 74; fires at, 75; as maximum security prison, 83, 96, 124; prosecution of offences at, 193; publication, 91, 161; riots at, 5, 7, 74, 80; under-use of, 79

Alvington (Vectis), 72, 73, 78

Amory, Lord, 3

Aylesbury, 123

BAPG (British Association of Prison Governors): on Boards of Visitors, 180; on building programme, 100-1; and control of size of prison population, 42, 173; and dispersal of dangerous prisoners, 76-7; and inspection of prisons, 178; and treatment and training, 26-7

bail: power of courts to refuse, 46, 65; versus remand, 54

Bail Act, 1976: effects of, 54; and needless remand, 46, 49; and population forecasts, 50; shortcomings of, 57

bail hostels, 54

Barlinnie Special Unit, 77, 160

Bath, 107

Bedford, 107, 111, 152

Blundeston, 20, 124

Boards of Visitors: adjudication of serious offences by, 187, 190-3; and maintenance of standards, 175-6, 180-2, 197; May Committee on, 180-2; and the Ombudsman, 182; and publicity for prison regime, 196; and riots, 181, 197, 198; role of, 157, 175-6, 181, 197, 198

Borstal: founding of, 2; increased use of, 62, 106; overcrowding in, 46; and pre-sentence

219

custody, 58, 61; and resources, 121

Brecon, 107

Bristol, 111, 112

Brixton: CNA, 115, 118; women at, 129

building programme: BAPG on, 100-1; and dispersal prisons, 75, 78; finance for, 112; and Frankland, 78; Home Office on, 107-14; May Committee on, 51, 58, 103-7, 209; moratorium on, 132-3; and normalisation of prisons, 107-14, 132-3; and overcrowding, 21; POA on, 100; Mr Whitelaw and, 209

buildings: categorisation and condition, 103-7, 107-14; and certified normal accommodation, 114-21

CNA (certified normal accommodation), 114-21, see also buildings

Cadbury Trust (research project), 44, 46

Callaghan, James, 73

Cambridge, 107

Camp Hill, 120

Canterbury 107, 111

Cardiff, 152

Carr, Robert, 74, 75

casework: and regionalisation, 141-2

cell sharing, 114-21

censorship, 172, 183-4, 198

centralisation (of the prison system), 135-9, 147

Chelmsford: CNA, 119; as local prison, 123; special wing, 71, 94

Chester, 107

Children and Young Persons Act, 1969, 62, 127

civil liberty: and sentence length, 69; see also NCCL, European Convention on Human Rights

classification of prisoners, see security classification

Code of Discipline, 156

Coldingley, 124

Committee of Inquiry into the United Kingdom Prison Services, see May Committee

community: facilities for prisoners in, 61, 63, 64, 66, 67; finance for facilities in, 64; gap between prison and, 37-8, 130-1; integration of prison facilities with, 130-1

community service, 66

concentration of high security risk prisoners: administrative difficulties of reorganisation of, 92; Home Office on, 86; May Committee on, 98; Mountbatten on, 3, 88-9

conscientious objectors, 2

construction: design, 1; see also building programme

continuous duty credits, vii, 7, 9

control problems (and subversive prisoners): control versus security, 78-84; Home Office on, 84-94; legality of dealing with, 207; staff for, 86

control units: BAPG on, 77; legality of, 5-6, 207; POA on, 76; and security, 74-5; and use of excessive power, 163; and Williams' case, 207

Cookham Wood, 124

Council of Europe: Standard Minimum Rules for the Treatment of Prisoners, 36, 164, 173-4

courts: and prison standards, 176-7, 186-93;

Crime Policy Planning Unit, 64
crime rate: and detention centres, 52-3; and prison population, 52-3
Criminal Law Act, 1977, 62

DHSS: health service and psychiatric prisoners, 53, 63-4, 77; and detoxification centres, 53-4
'dangerous' prisoners: definition of, 80; evidence to May Committee, 76-84; history of containing, 70-6; security of prison versus control of prisoners, 68-70
Dartmoor: closure, 104, 112-3, 125; mutiny at, 188; retention of, 107; staff industrial action at, 152
death penalty: abolition of and increase in prison population, 71, 79
debt (default of fine or maintenance): as non-imprisonable offence, 65; punishment for, 46
democracy and due process, 33
Derby, 107
detention centres: increase in use of, 62; size of population in, 50, 52; resources for, 121
detoxification centres, 53, 57
Dispersal Prison Steering Group, 91
dispersal system: and classification of prisoners, 81-2; and 'control units', 75; control problems in, 78-84; conversion of existing prisons, 74; costs of, 86; and high security risk prisoners, 86-7, 160; Home Office on, 84-94; and Mountbatten report, 80; Radzinowicz on, 72-3, 79;

review of, 74, 75; security problems of, 78-84; and tension from 'control units', 75
diversion of prisoners, 61; see also redirection
Dover, 107, 110
drugs: marijuana as non-imprisonable offence, 65; prisoner's fear of use of, 164; use of to control prisoners, 160
drunken offenders: decriminalising of, 65; May Committee on, 53; Society of Friends on, 45
du Cane, Sir Edmund, 2, 136, 164
due process model: 31-3, 35, 65, 69
Durham: special wing, 71, 94; women at, 129

English Prisons Today, 1922, 2
Erlestoke, 110, 127
European Convention on Human Rights: British prisoners resorting to, 33; and cell sharing as viewed by May Committee, 116; and censorship, 198; impact of, 167-73; and justice in prisons, 189; and standard of life for prisoners, 164; UK government condemned by, 159
European Court of Human Rights: British prisoners resorting to, 33, 142; forcing change in UK Prison Rules, 31; workings of, 172
Everthorpe, 111
Exchequer, see Treasury

Featherstone, 119, 120, 123
Federal Bureau of Prisons, USA, 91
female prisoners: and normali-

sation of prisons, 127-9
finance: and building costs, 78, 112; and detoxification centres, 53; implications of penal policy change for, 61-2; May Committee on, 58; and sentence length, 66; and staff for dispersal prisons, 86;
fine default: as non-imprisonable offence, 65; punishment for, 46
forecasts (on prison population): extrapolation versus scenario, 47-50, 57; use of scenario, 62-3
Fox, Sir Lionel: and conditions for staff and prisoners, 137; and Prison Rules, 165; purpose of imprisonment, 11-12; and treatment and training, 2-3, 13
Frankland: accommodation, 78; as dispersal prison, 75; as maximum security prison, 83, 96, 124; purpose of, 90
Franklin Committee on Punishments in Prisons and Borstals, 198
Full Sutton, 75, 78

Gartree: Board of Visitors, 181; control unit, 5-6; as dispersal prison, 74; prosecution of offences at, 187, 193; public image of, 196, 197, 198; riots at, 80, 180; under-use of, 79
Gladstone, Herbert, 2
Gladstone Committee, 1895, 13, 144
Gloucester, 107, 110, 111
governors: and industrial action by staff, 148, 152; power of, 154-5;
Grendon, 119, 124

Haldane Society of Socialist Lawyers: and control of size of prison population, 44, 45-6
Hamlyn Lectures, 8
Haverigg, 112, 123
Hereford, 107
Highpoint, 123, 124
high security risk: classification of prisoners, 68, 86-7, 91; and dispersal prisons, 160; Home Office on, 88-90; POA on, 82-3
Hollesley Bay Borstal hostel scheme, 47
Holloway: rebuilding of, 106-7, 128
home leave, 46-7
Home Office: on building programme, 107-14; confusion of security and control problems, 84-94; Crime Policy Planning Unit of, 64; on dispersal system, 84-94; forecasts on prison population, 47-50, 57, 60, 61, 62; normalisation of prisons, 107-21; and penal policy, 63-4; powers of, vii; and Prison Force Federation, 209; on security, 84-94
Home Office Research Unit, 3
House of Commons Select Committee on Home Affairs, 64
Howard League: and contact between prisoner and family, 198-9; and control of size of prison population, 46-7; and dispersal of dangerous prisoners, 77; and use of courts to deal with discipline offences, 187; use of resources, 101, and security, 77
human rights: and British Prisons, 31, 33; and European Conven-

tion on Human Rights, 167-73; and prisoners, 36

'Humane containment': and administration of prison, 164; BAPG on, 26-7; development of, 19-23; flaws in, 24; Howard League on, 198-9; in local prisons, 24, 26, 27; and normalisation of prisons, 121-2; and positive custody, 24-5, 28-9; in practice, 30-40; and purpose of imprisonment, 12; and security, 22, 23; in training prisons, 24

Hull: Board of Visitors, 180-1; CNA, 119; as dispersal prison, 74; internal review at, 175, 177; as local prison, 123; and MUFTI, 6; POA and, 76; prosecution of offences at, 187, 193; and public image, 196; and regionalisation, 141; reprisals by staff at, 75; riots at, 5, 75, 80, 180-1

IRA prisoners, 85, 92-4
Ilford, 107
industrial action of prison officers, vii, 6, 136, 148
industrial relations, 136, 144-58
industrial training, 15
injury statistics: of prisoners and staff, 162-3, 197
inspection of prisons, 144, 174-5, 177-80
Inspector General, 139
Institute of Criminology, 3
internal reviews, 174-5, 177-80
Ipswich, 107

Jebb, Sir Joshua, 1, 164
Jellicoe Committee: and operation of Prison Rules, 166; and role of Board of Visitors, 175, 180, 181-2, 190-1, 193

Jenkins, Roy, 71
justice model, 31-3, 35, 65, 69
Justices' Clerks Society, 60
juvenile custody, 126-7

Kirkdale, 107
Kirkham, 118
Knechtl case, 184-5
Knutsford, 107

Lancaster, 111, 112, 123
Leeds, 107
Legal Advice to Prisoners, 185, 191-2
legislation: to reduce prison population, 55, 66
Leicester: phasing out of, 107, 111; special wing at, 71, 93, 94
'less eligibility' principle, 164-5
Leyhill, 124
life sentence prisoners: increase in, 71, 79
Liverpool, 120
local prisons: allocation of prisoners to, 14, 24; and humane containment, 24, 26, 27; and lack of training prisons, 68; and localisation, 122-4; overcrowding in, 22, 24, 116, 117; purpose of, 19-20, 22, 26; under-occupation of, 117, 118-9
localisation, 122-4, 127
Long Lartin: as dispersal prison, 75; disturbances at, 80; as maximum security prison, 83, 96, 124; under-use of, 79
long term prisoners: classification of, 82
Low Newton, see Frankland

MUFTI (Minimum Use of Force Tactical Intervention) Squads:

and Board of Visitors, 181; and control problems, 160; introduction of, 6; legality of, 208; use of in Wormwood Scrubs, 1980, 76, 208

Maidstone, 123

maintenance default: as non-imprisonable offence, 65; punishment for, 46

management problems, 134-58: inspection problems and inspection of prisons, 144, 174-5, 177-80; lack of leadership, 137-9

Management Review, 139

Manchester, 120

maximum custody period, 54, 58, 59, 126

maximum security prisons: category of prisoners requiring, 88-90, 91; costs of, 78-9; criticism of, 82; disadvantages of, 70; growth in accommodation of, 78, 79; history of, 70; Home Office on, 85-6, 88, 89; riots in, vii, 74

May Committee (committee of Inquiry into the United Kingdom Prison Services): and Board of Visitors, 180-2; and building programme, 58, 103-4; on control of size of prison population, 41-7, 50-5, 60-7; and courts and prison administration, 186-93; on dangerous prisoners, 76-84; on dispersal prisons, 94-7; humane containment versus treating and training, 24-30; and inspection and internal review, 177-80; and justice model, 32; on normalisation of prisons, 102-107; and POA's control over

members, 146; and Parliamentary Commissioner for Administration, 182-6; projected alternative action for, 55-67, 177-93; purpose of, vii-ix; reaction to Report of, 203-5; on redirection of offenders, 56-7, 58, 60; and staff conditions, 145; and Standard Minimum Rules for the Treatment of Prisoners, 173; terms of reference of, 8-10, 201-2, 205-6; on terrorist prisoners, 94; on use of resources, 102-7, 145

Maze, 160

mentally disturbed prisoners: causing riots, 76, 77; nursing care and, 131; redirection of, 53, 56, 58, 65, 76

minimum use of custody, 34, 41-67

minimum use of security, 36-7, 68-97

Mountbatten, Lord: criticism of report of, 82; and dangerous prisoners, 71-2, 76, 78, 88-9; and dispersal system, 80; and lack of leadership, 138-9; and management of prisons, 134, 138-9, 139-40; versus Radzinowicz, 73; Report of, 21, 71-2; on security, 3-4, 19, 22, 37, 71-2, 77-8, 78, 88-9; on security classifications, 160; on terrorists, 92

NACRO (National Association for the Care and Resettlement of Offenders): on control of size of prison population, 43, 46; and dispersal of dangerous prisoners, 77; and resources,

prison officer, 18; and staff conditions, 145; and subversive prisoners, 6-7, 81

PROP (National Prisoner's Movement): on Boards of Visitors, 181; on control of size of prison population, 44-5; demonstrations organised by, 5; on dispersal of dangerous prisoners, 77-8; on Mountbatten proposals, 77-8; and reaction of POA, 6; on rights of prisoners, vii

Parkhurst: as dispersal prison, 74; receptions at, 120; reprisals by staff at, 75; retained, 107; riots at, 5, 74, 80, 188; special wing at, 71, 93, 94; under-use of, 79

Parliamentary Commissioner for Administration (Ombudsman), 176, 178, 181, 182-6

parole: cost of, 59; eligibility for, 58, 61; release criteria for, 58, 61

Paterson, Alexander, 2, 3, 6, 16, 35

penal pressure groups, 51-2, 55, 57, 101, see also Haldane Society, Howard League, NCCL, Society of Friends

Pentonville: CNA, 116; design, 1, 104; POA conference at, 7

Peterson, Sir Arthur, 3, 70, 72, 73

petitions, 175, 177-8

political prisoners, 160

politics: in limiting prison population, 44-6, 55

population (Prison): and building programme, 45, 58; control of size of, 41-67; government role in size of, 55; Haldane Society on size of, 44, 45-6; Home Office forecasts of, 47-50, 57;

Howard League on size of, 46-7; and humane containment, 22; increase in, vii, 3, 11, 21; legislation to control size of, 55, 56; in local prisons, 68; management view of, 41-3; May Committee on size of, 50-5, 55-67; NACRO on size of, 43, 46; NCCL on size of, 44; normative view of, 43-4; and parole, 58; policy for, 60-7; political view of, 44-6; pre-sentence custody and, 58, 68; proportion of offenders committed, 66; and remission length, 52, 58; and redirection of specified offences, 45, 53, 56, 57, 58, 60, 61, 65; and security, 207; and sentence duration, 66; Society of Friends on size of, 45; statistics of, 207

'positive custody': definition, 28-9; and humane containment, 28; and justice, 35; May Committee on, 12, 24-5, 27-30; and treatment and training, 16, 52, 206

pre-release employment scheme, 47

Preston, 123

Prison Commission, 2, 3, 136, 137-8

Prison Force Federation, 209

Prison Medical Service, 58

Prison Officers' Magazine, 6, 137, 146

prisoners' friend, 191-2

Prison Rules, 165-7, 189

probation service, 59

protests: by prisoners, 5-6; see also riots

psychiatric care, 53, 56, 58, 77

psychologists, 15

psychotherapists, 15

publicity: role of in prison regime, 195-7

Pucklechurch, 128

Radzinowicz Committee: confusion of security and control problems, 80-1; and dispersal prisons, 78; findings of, 72-3; on maximum security, 79; and terrorists, 92

Ranby, 124

Reading, 119, 123

recidivism: petty, 61, 66; and treatment and training, 13-14, 16, 17, 19, 24

redirection (of certain groups of offenders): drunks, 45, 53, 56, 65; fine defaulters, 65; forecasts of, 61; and May Committee, 56-7, 58, 60; mentally disordered, 53, 56, 58, 65, 76; remands, 65

Rees, Merlyn, 76

regime: 'for Longterm Prisoners in Conditions of Maximum Security', 4, 72-3; and normalisation, 129-32

regionalisation, 139-44, 147, 157

rehabilitation ideal: decline of, 68; and justice model, 69

release policy, 50

Remand Centres, 127

remand prisoners: versus bail prisoners, 54; conditions for, 125-6; financial implications of, 62; increase in, 49; maximum custodial time for, 54, 58, 59, 126; redirection of, 65

remission, 52, 58, 61

Report of the Inquiry into Prison Escapes and Security, 1966, 3; *see also* Mountbatten, Lord

Report of the Working Party on Adjudication Procedure in Prison, 191

resources: and building moratorium, 132-3; and female prisons, 128; and normalisation of prisons, 98-133; and security, 52, 68, 121; shortage of, 51, 99

riots: and Board of Visitors, 180-1; at Hull, 75; and MUFTI squads, 76; and prison conditions, vii, 5; supervision of and European Convention on Human Rights, 168-9

Risley, 152

Rochester, 109, 110

Royal Commission on Legal Services 1979, 188-9

Royal Commission on the Penal System 1964, 3, 8

sanitation standards, 116-7

security: according to need, 68-70, 71; classification levels of, 37, 77, 81-2, 95-7, 160; and control problems, 78-84; and dangerous prisoners, 68-70; history of, 70-6; Home Office on, 84-94; Howard League on, 77; and humane containment, 22, 23; May Committee on, 8, 10, 94-7; Mountbatten on, 3-4, 19, 22, 37, 71-2, 77-8, 88-9; NACRO on, 77; and normalisation, 37; under Paterson, 3; and resources, 52, 68, 121; and sentence length, 159-60; staff for, 86; and treatment and training, 18, 20, 20-1

security classification (of prisoners): criteria for, 88, 95-6; levels, 37, 77; Home Office on, 86, 87, 95; May Committee on, 98; reclassification, 81-2; and subversion, 83-4; and sub-

227

versive prisoners, 91-2; uniformity of approach, 143; *see also* concentration of high risk prisoners

segregation units, 84, 160; *see also* control units

sentence length: according to crime, 35, 45-6, 61; and availability of prison accommodation, 132-3; bifurcation in policy, 68-70; and civil liberty, 69; and dangerous prisoners, 68-70; and due process model, 32-3, 64-6, 69; and effectiveness, 16, 34; guidelines for, 66, 133; Haldane Society on, 45-6; in Holland, 53; Home Office forecasts, 48-9; NACRO on, 45; NCCL on, 44; PROP on, 44; policy on, 43, 44, 56, 61, 64-5, 66; and prison population size, 52, 55, 63, 64-6; and resources, 132-3; in Scandinavia, 53; and security, 159-60

sexual segregation, 128-9

Shepton Mallet, 123

Shrewsbury, 107, 111

social damage of imprisonment, 164

Society of Civil and Public Servants: ambitions of executive grades of, 149-50; governors branch, 42

Society of Friends: on control of size of prison population, 45

Southampton, 107

'special wings', 71, 93-4, 160

specialisation of prisons, 121, 124-5, 127-9

staff: anxieties of, 161-5; behaviour of, 148-9; for category A prisoners, 95; conditions, 130, 145, 165; cost of, 99; for dispersal prisons, 95; increase in, 86; morale of, 194-5; and Prison Commission, 137-8; and prisoners' rights, 144, 145-6, 150-1, 156, 165, 194-5; reprisals by at Hull, 75; role of, 18, 27, 35, 136, 147; and security, 18, 72, 86; source of, 146; and treatment and training, 17-18

staffing levels, 102-3

Stafford, 123

Standard Minimum Rules for the Treatment of Prisoners (Council of Europe), 36, 164, 173-4

Streatfeild Committee on the Business of the Criminal Courts, 189-90

strike of prison staff, 152-3

suffragettes, 2

supervision: additional safeguards, 194-7; improvements to, 177-93; and maintenance of standards, 174-7

suspended sentences, 62

Swansea, 107, 111

Swinfen Hall, 127

tariff, 63; *see also* sentence length

Taunton, 107

terrorists, 71, 85, 92-4

theft, petty: as non-imprisonable offence, 65

totalitarian states: and due process, 33

train robbers, 71

training prisons: aims of, 14, 22, 23; and allocation of prisoners, 24, 68; and humane containment, 24; and May Committee, 24-30; lack of, 68; and localisation, 122-4; and resources, 121; under-use of, 119

Treasury: and control of use of prisons, 90-1; role of in determining penal policy, 63-4

treatment and training: aims of, 12, 13-19, 21, 23; and allocation of prisoners, 24; BAPG on, 26-7; and justice, 35; and local prisons, 22; and May Committee 24-30; and normalisation, 129-32; and positive custody, 52, 206; and reform/rehabilitation, 35-6; resources for, 52; security and, 18, 20-1; in training prisons, 26

trial prisoners: conditions for, 125-6

UN Rules, 116
under-occupation, 117, 118-9
Usk, 111

Vectis, 71-2
Verne, 119
vocational training, 15
voluntary endeavour: in treatment of drunken offenders, 53-4

Wakefield: condition of, 110; control unit in, 75, 153, 196, 207; as dispersal prison, 74; disturbances at, 80; as local prison, 123; and maximum security, 78; POA on control unit in, 153

Welfare officers, 15
Whitelaw, William, 76, 106, 209
Williams' case, 207
Winchester, 107, 109-10, 111
Woking, 107
Wormwood Scrubs: Board of Visitors, 181; control unit in, 75; as dispersal prison, 74; internal review at, 175, 179-80, 181, 209; MUFTI in, 76, 181, 208; and maximum security, 78; police investigation at, 209; public image of, 196; riots at, 80, 180

young offenders, 124, 126-7